THE
MIDDLE EAST
MAZE | *Israel and Her Neighbors*

THE MIDDLE EAST MAZE

MAZE | Israel and Her Neighbors

DAVID A. RAUSCH

MOODY PRESS

CHICAGO

© 1991 by
THE MOODY BIBLE INSTITUTE
OF CHICAGO

ISBN: 0-8024-5191-8

1 2 3 4 5 6 Printing/VP/Year 95 94 93 92 91

Printed in the United States of America

To My Mother,
Marion June Palette Rausch

Contents

INTRODUCTION

I t was in early January 1991, just days before the United States and its allies launched the air campaign against Saddam Hussein's Iraq. An evangelical college professor and his Arab Christian student appeared on a morning television program in a major city to "try to strike a note of rationality before the U.S. makes a major blunder," to "give an accurate appraisal of events in Kuwait," and to "dispel the horror stories and misinformation the Western press is disseminating." Looking the television hosts straight in the eyes, the student insisted that Kuwaitis were not being hurt by the Iraqis and that the United States had moved forces near the border of Kuwait under false pretenses. The professor added that he had no doubt that his student's information was accurate because the student had family in Kuwait. The professor added that war was simply wrong. The television hosts were moved with sympathy.

Now, of course, we know that at that very hour Kuwaiti women were being raped by Iraqi soldiers as they had been for months in one of the most horrible pogroms that Arabs had committed against Arab civilians in many years. By April 1991 Kuwaiti doctors were preparing for a wave of illegitimate children to be born, and a cry had gone forth for psychiatrists to help the traumatized Kuwaiti population. Several women had committed suicide, one burning herself to death rather than face humiliation in a Muslim culture that usually blames the rape victim for "enticing" her attacker. Other women lapsed into deep depression, some unable to talk or perform even menial functions. Emotionally drained, these Kuwaiti women sought death because Muslim men preferred to marry virgins. The rape victims were consigned to life as outcasts.

Kuwaiti children also suffered. Both boys and girls were molested by Saddam Hussein's soldiers while the world debated for months the actions to be taken against Iraq. Like the Nazi atrocities against children during the Holocaust, Iraqi soldiers tortured and maimed their victims. For example, Iraqi soldiers stuck electric cattle prods into the ears of a six-year-old girl, making her deaf for life. Razor blades, knives, and the dreaded electric probes wielded by sadistic soldiers scarred the bodies of young and old during the Iraqi invasion. For those who lived, the psychological scars are almost too much to bear.

Thousands of Kuwaitis were abducted and executed while their land was ravaged by their Iraqi oppressors. After Saddam Hussein lost Kuwait, he turned his vengeance against the Kurdish people, who rebelled against him in northern Iraq. The peoples of the world viewed on television news programs atrocities against Kurdish victims even as they were alerted to the full extent of the Iraqi massacre of Kuwaitis. Reminded that Saddam Hussein had killed thousands of Kurds with chemical weapons in 1988, the world now watched as he used helicopter gun ships to spray the Kurdish population with chemicals as well as bullets.

WHO DO YOU BELIEVE?

How could that evangelical professor, and others, be taken in by such propaganda as that which was dispensed prior to the Persian Gulf War? Why would a Christian Arab student pass on false information? It turned out that the student was actually one of 400,000 Palestinian Arabs who had been welcomed as workers by the Kuwaitis (one of the few Arab countries actually to let Palestinian Arabs dwell en masse). Most Palestinian Arabs in the Middle East had welcomed Saddam Hussein as a liberator of the Palestinian people and a defender of their cause. It mattered little to them that the Iraqi leader began mentioning their cause as part of his rationale for attacking Kuwait only after all other explanations appeared to fall on deaf Arab ears.

Yasser Arafat and his Palestine Liberation Organization (PLO) were duly impressed and immediately declared on the side of the Iraqi leader. As Iraqi Scud missiles hit Israel and Saudi Arabia, Palestinian Arabs in Jordan, the West Bank, and the Gaza cheered, many sitting on their roofs to gain a better view of the impending destruction of their enemies. Some Palestinian Arabs, along with the Iraqi soldiers, helped to loot and torture the Kuwaiti population.

For those Palestinian Arabs who did not participate in such actions, the behavior of their brethren seemed destined to spoil their economic opportunites in Kuwait for decades. In 1948 some of their predecessors had lost their homes in Palestine because of such Arab actions. Now forty-three years later, the Palestinians appeared to lose once again. Those who cried out against Yasser Arafat and Saddam Hussein were murdered by other Palestinians. And yet the murmuring persists. Many others, however, continue to blame the United States and Israel for the war against Saddam Hussein.

Was the Christian Arab student deceived by his Palestinian relatives in Kuwait as to the condition of the country under the Iraqis? Only the Lord knows for sure. Certainly his being pawned off as a "Kuwaiti" was misleading. For a while, even the program hosts were sold on the accuracy of the account. It is personal testimonies such as these that make the Middle East maze illusive and difficult. Everyone who has a stake in the Middle East has a first-hand account or pet story to sway the emotions of friends and colleagues. These are passed on to audiences around the world. Historical information that might broaden one's view is bypassed for the quick fix of modern propaganda. Inaccurate information and incorrect perceptions soon capture scholar and novice alike.

WHO SUPPLIED SADDAM?

Like his hero Adolf Hitler, Saddam Hussein wished that he had had an ultimate weapon during the Gulf War. Ironically, he might have had one if it were not for the Israelis in 1981. Israel had watched the rise of Saddam Hussein and his penchant to obtain nuclear weapons. Iraqi leaders had often asserted that one day they would "wipe Israel off the map." As the summer of 1981 approached, Iraq's nuclear reactor, which could have produced plutonium for an atomic bomb, neared completion.

The French had provided Saddam Hussein with 93 percent enriched weapons-grade uranium. Tons of other purchased substances and the size of the reactor underscored the fact that Saddam Hussein was either enamored with having one of the greatest research facilities in the world or was solely interested in having an atomic bomb. The Israelis believed that he would soon have the bomb and that he would terrorize the Middle East as he had terrorized his own people. On June

7, 1981, Israeli warplanes demolished Iraq's nuclear plant by dropping 2,200-pound bombs at low level on it.

Today the world sighs with relief that Saddam Hussein does not yet have his nuclear weapons. Being threatened with his chemical weapons had caused enough grief as the decade of the 1990s began. A decade earlier, however, the response of the international community was quite different. The United Nations Security Council unanimously passed a resolution that strongly condemned Israel for the air attack that destroyed the Iraqi reactor. It was one of the harshest rebukes against Israel in which the United States had ever participated.

The U.S. delegate to the United Nations in 1981, Jeane J. Kirkpatrick, was authorized to accuse Israel of "damaging the confidence that is essential for the peace process to go forward" in the Middle East. Kirkpatrick equated the Israeli raid on Saddam Hussein's nuclear reactor with the brutal Soviet intervention in Afghanistan and the violent Libyan occupation of Chad. Her speech, cleared by both the Reagan White House and the State Department, added that "nothing has happened that in any way alters the strength of our commitment or the warmth of our feelings [toward Israel] . . . an important and valued ally." Today, Kirkpatrick is a strong supporter of the state of Israel and at times lectures on the difficulties a democracy such as Israel faces in the midst of the sprawling Arab world.

In its defense, Israel cited a passage in an official Iraqi journal, which declared: "The Iranian people should not fear the Iraqi nuclear reactor, which is not intended to be used against Iran but against the Zionist enemy." A number of nuclear experts also confirmed that Iraq was well on its way to nuclear capability and that it appeared that Saddam Hussein's main interest was a destructive weapon. Roger Richter, an American nuclear inspector at the International Atomic Energy Agency, told the Senate Foreign Relations Committee as well as the U.S. State Department that he believed "that the Iraqi nuclear program was organized for the purpose of developing a capability to produce nuclear weapons over the next several years."

Instead of learning from this warning, the United States and her allies continued during the 1980s to supply Iraq with billions of dollars in aid and modern weaponry. France supplied $12 billion in military hardware from 1981 to 1988. Iraq was able to buy the most sophisticated missile-development technology from firms in the U.S., Britain, Italy, and West Germany, while upgrading many facets of its military technology. The Reagan and Bush administrations approved millions of dollars of credit to Saddam Hussein's government as he was struggling with Iran's Ayatollah Khomeini.

Even when banking irregularities were found in assistance to Iraq in the latter part of the 1980s and sting operations uncovered Iraq's attempt to obtain nuclear triggering devices as well as a giant artillery gun, the Bush administration still approved a $500 million credit line for Iraq in 1990. Coupled with the billions of dollars of assistance from Arab countries, including Saudi Arabia and Kuwait, Saddam Hussein was able to build a massive and threatening military capability.

After the Gulf War, it was found that Saddam Hussein had stashed billions of dollars around the world, skimming $10 billion in oil profits and other billions in bribes from international corporations. He cheated the Iraqi people even as he mouthed platitudes of sacrifice and decency in his escalating conflict with "the Great Satan." While he convinced Palestinian Arabs and even King Hussein of Jordan that his chief concern was providing peace for the Middle East and liberating the oppressed from Israel and the "wealthy oil Sheikhs," at the same time he was using his oil profits for war and hiding his excessive wealth from the needy. Such is the insidious and perfidious network of passages of the Middle East maze.

WHO WANTS PEACE?

Slow to react against their Muslim Arab brother, most Arab leaders came to realize that Saddam Hussein had lied to them. In the aftermath of the Gulf War, the Bush administration and many leaders of the world believed the time was ripe for a comprehensive peace in the Middle East. U.S. Secretary of State James Baker said that he sensed "a greater willingness than before to pursue the peace process" and began shuttle diplomacy that covered Israel and her neighbors. Even in the midst of an Arab and Western allied victory, in the midst of U.S. prestige from the war and heightened foreign expectations for U.S. leadership in the Middle East peace talks, a comprehensive peace continued to be elusive and transitory. Quoting from the book of Psalms, Baker said that he would suggest that the psalmist's advice be taken: "Seek ye peace and pursue it." Baker soon found that although some Arab leaders appeared to be willing at least to begin an exploratory process of peace with Israel, specifics were nonexistent. Lots of talk, very little progress.

From an Israeli helicopter Secretary Baker viewed the slim boundaries of the Jewish state. He saw what a strategic buffer zone the kidney-shaped West Bank was to Israel and how the Golan Heights peered down on the Sea of Galilee. He also met with Palestinian intellectuals who had received permission from the PLO to hear his proposals. Suspicious that the United States was attempting to create a new Palestinian leadership, nearly all Palestinian intellectuals clung to Yasser Arafat and the PLO. "We have our problems with the PLO, as you know," Baker told newsmen, affirming the break in the newly found American dialogue with Arafat. "We used to have a dialogue with the PLO—that dialogue is terminated." Later, Baker clarified to Palestinian intellectuals that he meant "suspended" rather than "terminated."

The Americans and the Israelis now agreed again that there was no place for the PLO in negotiations. Saudi Arabia withdrew huge monetary support from the PLO in April 1991 because Arafat and his followers had supported Saddam Hussein. Baker reaffirmed, however, that the Palestinians had legitimate rights and that the United States could negotiate with PLO sympathizers. Unfortunately, the legacy of Palestinian violence continued. While Baker was in the Middle East, six heavily armed Palestinian guerrillas came across the Jordan-Israel border and lay in ambush for an Israeli patrol. A number of Palestinian Arabs purposely ran down Israeli soldiers with their cars, and a Palestinian from a Gaza Strip refugee camp stabbed and killed four Israeli women in Jerusalem. The latter said he wanted to send "a message" to Secretary Baker.

PLO spokesman Bassam Abu Sharif, Arafat's chief political adviser and a member of the Palestinian National Council for more than twenty years, told the news media that Arafat was president and chairman of the PLO and that the PLO was the representative of the Palestinian people. He stated that anyone who believed a settlement could be arranged in the Middle East without the participation of the PLO was sadly mistaken. His words were a veiled threat. PLO publicists attempted to portray Arafat's embrace of Saddam Hussein as a distortion of Arafat's views on the Gulf War. They cranked out mountains of position papers and hours of interviews that stated that Arafat was working for a political solution. The United States, they emphasized, had blocked that effort for peace by going to war.

Quickly the PLO tried to switch attention from the atrocities of Saddam Hussein to a diatribe against Israel. The PLO ploy went like this: Israel is involved in a clear case of occupation. The real issue is whether or not the United States is going to use two different standards. Saddam Hussein did nothing more than the Israelis have been doing. The credibility of the United States was "in serious danger" in the eyes of the "general Arab world and in Palestine." The United States had not been firm with Israel, and the Americans had better shape up if they wanted to have a role in the Middle East. The PLO is still committed to peace, seriously waiting for the U.S. to be as firm with Israel as she was with Saddam Hussein. Because the Bush administration was violent in how it handled Saddam Hussein, it must use the same "uniform standards" against Israel.

PLO-funded intellectuals insisted that no matter what the Palestinians did, the "rightness of their cause" should override any actions they had taken or alliances that they had made. No emphasis was put upon Saddam Hussein's atrocities—all Palestinian efforts were turned to a diatribe against Israel. The United States was maligned constantly for having its own agenda and being consumed with its own interests—that is why the Bush administration attacked Saddam Hussein. Noting that "all" Palestinian people had supported Saddam Hussein and that the Jordanian people as well as many other Arabs had also supported Iraq, the PLO propagandists maintained that Arafat had taken the higher moral ground by attempting to find a "political solution to the Gulf crisis."

When James Baker returned from his first shuttle diplomacy mission after the war, columnist George Will asked the secretary of state a blunt question: "For many, many years we've been hearing it whispered to us that there's new thinking in the Middle East and new trust of us. Saudi Arabia owes its protection to the United States. Kuwait owes its existence to the United States. Has the United States gone so far as to ask them such a minimalist request as 'Will you please recognize Israel's right to exist and end the state of belligerency?'"

Secretary of State Baker replied that in the past the question had been asked routinely and that such a proposal had been "routinely rejected." Although there seemed to be some hope for new cooperation after the Gulf War, Baker had to admit that "it [a positive answer to Will's question] hasn't been accepted now." Baker was aiming for "reciprocal confidence measures" between Israel and her Arab neighbors. He explained: "These are extraordinarily difficult and intractable problems that we now have to deal with, and which we have been dealing with for many years." He also admitted that although he had had seven hours of discussion with Hafez Assad, Syria was "still in a state of war with Israel."

THE PURPOSE OF THIS BOOK

As diplomats still deal with the question of Israel's existence as a sovereign state among her Arab neighbors, one perceives the complexity of the Middle East maze. This book will give the reader the historical background necessary to put these deep feelings into context and to provide the reader with the milieu of the modern Middle East. Chapter 1 provides a historical overview from the Ottoman period to the emergence of Israel as a modern state in 1948. Chapter 2 discusses the history of Israel and the Arab world from 1948 onward. Chapter 3 explores the volatile area of Christian perceptions of the Middle East conflict and theological views concerning current (and future) events.

Chapters 4 to 8 give the background of the nations of the Arab world and their current leadership. Yasser Arafat and the Palestine Liberation Organization are also discussed in this section. Chapter 9, "Israel and the 1991 Persian Gulf War," summarizes the conclusions of our study and the complexities that face Israel at this critical juncture of history. A plethora of English-language source material that is available to the reader is furnished in the bibliography, and the detailed index may be used as a valuable cross-reference. Every effort has been made to assure that this book will not only provide an interesting synopsis of the Middle East maze but will also serve the owner as a cherished reference volume.

One of the most important lessons the reader can learn at the outset is that wonderful words, even religious and biblical words, can be twisted into a rationale for the brutal destruction of men, women, and children. One must be ever aware that the deep passions of the people involved with this region often lead to self-deception and the dissemination of inaccurate information. Furthermore, when a leader genuinely utters words leading toward peace or decrying injustice, other Middle Eastern leaders are able to ignore such decisions and appeal to a greater peoplehood.

This tendency is clearly illustrated in the PLO's refusal to condemn Saddam Hussein's atrocities. Although few expected the PLO to decry the Scud missile attacks against Israel, many were alarmed that brutal attacks against an Arab nation (Kuwait) could be treated so cavalierly by fellow Arabs. On ABC News's "Nightline" (March 12, 1991), host Ted Koppel questioned PLO representative Bassam Abu Sharif when he smoothly averred that "all the Arab nation had stood against the Gulf War." Koppel insisted that this was not true, because many

Arab nations joined the West in fighting Saddam Hussein. "I'm talking about *nation*, Ted, I'm not talking about *government*," Sharif calmly replied. "Hundreds of thousands demonstrated . . . we've never supported invasion," he went on to assert. In the rhetoric of the Middle East, the actions of the majority of Arab governments against a blatant defiance of international law suddenly meant nothing in the eyes of the PLO and its Palestinian and Arab supporters. The "accurate" view was held by a surreal "Arab nation."

In the first two chapters of historical overview we shall discuss this elusive concept of "Arab nation," as well as another important term that permeates the Middle East maze—*Palestine*. May your journey into this strange and fascinating world be sobering as well as enlightening.

1

MIDDLE EAST HISTORY:
THE OTTOMAN EMPIRE
THROUGH WORLD WAR II

There is no other country in the world of equal territory," an official of the United States government reported from Jerusalem in 1881, "of which so much has been written, and of which so little is really known, as Palestine." More than a century later his statement continues to be relevant.

On February 15, 1991, Radio Baghdad teased the world with Iraqi leader Saddam Hussein's promise to withdraw from Kuwait. It was soon learned, however, that one of Saddam Hussein's conditions was that "Palestine" be liberated. Few stopped to question what he meant by "Palestine."

Likewise, in 1964 the Palestine Liberation Organization (PLO) was formed. What was considered Palestine in its name? What was to be liberated? Certainly not the West Bank and Gaza, which the world always mentions today. Those territories were under Arab rule and Arab control in 1964 (along with East Jerusalem). The West Bank and East Jerusalem were under the control of King Hussein of Jordan. The Gaza Strip was ruled by Gamal Abdel Nasser of Egypt. Not until Is-rael's capture of those territories three years later during the Arab-initiated Six-Day War would the West Bank, Gaza, and East Jerusalem be out of Arab hands. The question remained: What was the PLO formed to "liberate"?

As Yasser Arafat led the PLO negotiations with world leaders in the 1980s to set up a state for the Palestinian people in the West Bank and Gaza, he referred frequently to "Palestine." But little was known by laypersons of the 1968 charter of the PLO's National Congress, formulated in Cairo and stating in part:

1. Palestine is the homeland of the Arab Palestinian people; it is an indivisible part of the Arab homeland, and the Palestinian people are an integral part of the Arab nation.
2. Palestine, with the boundaries it had during the British Mandate, is an indivisible territorial unit. . . .
6. The Jews who had normally resided in Palestine until the beginning of the Zionist invasion will be considered Palestinians. . . .

As one can see, Jews who came after "the Zionist invasion" would not be allowed to reside in a PLO Palestine. More questions arise. When was the "Zionist invasion"? What did Yasser Arafat consider to be Palestine in 1968? In 1974 (when he insisted on a "democratic, secular Palestinian state")? In 1988? In 1991 (when he declared total support for the goals and aspirations of Saddam Hussein in the Persian Gulf War)?

Furthermore, what did former Egyptian president Anwar Sadat refer to when he addressed the People's Assembly in Cairo on October 16, 1973, asserting that "the Zionist state usurped Palestine" in 1948? Is this the same Palestine that Arab rights organizations, Arab apologists, Arab scholars, and Arab leaders refer to as Palestine today? Why are Arab statements regarding Palestine left vague in English for consumption by the Western world but are more explicit in Arabic for consumption in the Arab world?

A historical overview cannot solve the problems of the Middle East, but it certainly can help us to put them into perspective and avoid the pitfalls of misleading rhetoric and false assumptions. History also can help us to put Saddam Hussein into perspective and, more important, aid us in recognizing and thwarting the Saddam Husseins of the future. Our study of the past, the current countries and leaders in the Middle East, case studies, and recent events should give us the tools to assess more intelligently the current and future situations in this volatile area of the world—the world of the Bible, the world of the sword.

THE OTTOMAN EMPIRE AND PALESTINE

It is important to realize that each of the modern nations involved in the Middle East conflict today became independent in the twentieth century. Recent boundaries were formed and national governments organized in the Arab world and Israel as the automobile and the airplane became commonplace in the Western world. The Middle East is one of the most volatile and coveted regions in the modern world, but the Middle East has always been the center of conflict. As a center for trade and commerce, it historically has spawned vicious rivalries, even among related groups.

In its broadest definition, the Middle East encompasses all the countries that border the southern and eastern coasts of the Mediterranean Sea, from Morocco to Turkey, the Red Sea, the Gulf of Aqaba, and the Persian Gulf. As we focus on those nations that are neighbors to Israel and those that vie for the "holy lands" of the Middle East, we must keep in mind the larger picture. Historically, the Ottoman Empire's control of Palestine in the 1800s and early 1900s set the stage for many modern events in the region.

The Ottoman Empire, a group of conquering Turks that during the time of Martin Luther had attacked Europe in the west and sent military expeditions into Persia in the east, considered Palestine a part of its province of Syria. Although the term *Palestine* was used in some languages to depict the Holy Land on both sides of the Jordan River, it was not even an administrative unit under the Ottoman regime and connoted no official designation. The Ottomans soon divided the territory once called Palestine by the Romans into four districts, or *sanjaks*, namely, Gaza, Jerusalem, Nablus, and Safed. These were further divided into regions. The Sanjak of Jerusalem, for example, was divided into the regions of Jerusalem and Hebron. All of these sanjaks were in the province of Damascus, which included more sanjaks. Under the golden period of Ottoman rule (1517-1574), each of the four sanjaks enjoyed a semblance of stability under this highly organized administration.

Although the Ottomans under great rulers like Suleiman the Magnificent (1520-1566) had subdued much of the Middle East, the overextended empire languished under corrupt regimes and weak administration in following centuries. The early 1800s witnessed a period of decline in the greater Syria area of which Palestine was a part. Palestine's total population was under 250,000 during the first three decades of the nineteenth century, and only a small portion of the land was utilized for agriculture. Local chieftains fought each other for supremacy in the mountainous rural areas, while Bedouin tribes roamed the deserts to the east and south. Security was minimal, bandits traveled throughout the region, and entire villages were destroyed by warfare or were abandoned. Napoleon succeeded in conquering Egypt in 1798 and moved up through Palestine (which he was unable to hold). With French support, the pasha of Egypt, Muhammad Ali, dominated Palestine from 1832 to 1840. This Muslim ruler planned to create an Arab empire that would include "greater Syria," Iraq, and the holy cities in Arabia (the Ottoman sultan had promised him as much for his support in suppressing a revolt of the Greeks). The sultan reneged on the promise, however, and the Ottomans regained control of Palestine and surrounding areas.

In these early centuries, most of the Jewish population resided in Jerusalem, Hebron, Safed, or Tiberias and was so oppressed by Turkish officials and so heavily taxed that it was said the people "had to pay for the very air they breathed." To make matters worse, a powerful earthquake devastated the area in 1837, killing thousands. Charitable funds called *halukkah* had to be collected by Jewish organizations in Europe for the poverty-stricken and starving Jews of Palestine. In spite of these conditions, Jews from Europe emigrated to Palestine, and the population of the area began to increase. In fact, after 1840 both Jewish and Arab immigration increased. Representatives of Christian churches from Europe and America as well as Muslims and Christians from Syria, Lebanon, Egypt, North Africa, and Turkey all came to Palestine as well. Conflicts arose between the Jewish community and the Christian missionaries, who were forbidden to evangelize Muslims by Ottoman law but concentrated on potential Jewish converts.

When Muhammad Ali of Egypt led his armies in a coup against the Ottoman sultan, there was some discussion in Great Britain, Western Europe, and Russia of allowing the Jewish community in Palestine an autonomous territory or state to act as a buffer between Egypt and the Ottoman Turks. Massacres had broken out against Jews in Syria, as well as in other towns and villages, and the European powers were concerned. Even Russia spoke out about the Damascus Affair of 1840 during which Christian and Muslim Arab mobs ravaged the Jewish community. (It is ironic that Russian Jews would need to emigrate to Palestine from Russia during the 1800s because of the pogroms that were inflicted upon them.) In 1839 the great Jewish leader Sir Moses Montefiore began negotiating with Muhammad Ali concerning Jewish settlement in the Holy Land, but the pasha of Egypt's demise stifled the effort.

Nevertheless, by 1895 only 10 percent of Palestine was cultivated. Absentee landlords purchased hundreds of thousands of acres from the financially strapped Ottomans and settled Jewish and Arab tenant farmers on some of the land. Sursuk, a Greek entrepreneur from Beirut, owned more than sixty thousand Palestinian acres. By the end of the First World War, 144 wealthy landowners owned approximately seven hundred fifty thousand acres in Palestine. Concurrently, Jews owned and had reclaimed from marsh areas and deserts more than one hundred thousand acres. Urban areas also expanded. In fact, the urban population increased at a greater rate than the rural population. Cities accounted for only 18 percent of the total population in Palestine in 1800 but had increased to 27 percent in 1882 and to 38 percent in 1907. In 1909 a group of Jaffa Jews founded Tel Aviv, destined to become the country's largest city. An Arab nationalist movement began to form in response to other nationalist movements around the world and in response to the growing Zionist movement.

Although the word *Zion* was an early synonym for Jerusalem and in pre-modern times was linked to a Jewish return from exile to the Land of Promise, the actual term *Zionism* was not used until the 1890s. The Russian persecutions of the latter 1800s brought thousands of Jewish settlers to the Holy Land, and groups such as *Hoveve Zion* (Lovers of Zion) were organized to raise money for colonization. Zionism grew to prominence when Theodor Herzl (1860-1904), a correspondent in Paris, founded a modern Zionism based on political and economic theory. In February 1896 Herzl published a small booklet entitled *Der Judenstaat* (English title: *The Jewish State: An Attempt at a Modern Solution of the Jewish Question*).

Theodor Herzl's main thesis was that anti-Semitism was inevitable as long as the majority of Jewish people lived outside their own homeland. He expounded political, economic, and technical efforts that he believed were necessary to create a functioning Jewish state. He called the First Zionist Congress to meet in Basel, Switzerland, in August 1897. More than two hundred delegates from all over the world attended. The platform drawn up at this congress guided the Zionist movement for the next fifty years. The Basel program read:

> Zionism seeks to create for the Jewish people a home in Palestine secured by public law. The Congress contemplates the following means to attainment of this end.
>
> 1. The promotion by appropriate means of the settlement in Palestine of Jewish agriculturalists, artisans and manufacturers.

2. The organization and binding together of the whole of Jewry by means of appropriate institutions, both local and international, in accordance with the laws of each country.

3. The strengthening and fostering of Jewish national sentiment and national consciousness.

4. Preparatory steps toward obtaining the consent of governments where necessary, in order to reach the goal of Zionism.

Herzl was named president of the newly formed World Zionist Organization.

In the realm of Arab nationalism, another Paris journalist, Negib Azouri, a Christian Arab and former official of the Ottoman Empire, published a program in his book *Le Reveil de la Nation Arabe* (1905) that called for "an Arab empire stretching from the Tigris and the Euphrates to the Suez Isthmus, and from the Mediterranean to the Arabian Sea." He warned Arabs about "the effort of the Jews to reconstitute on a very large scale the ancient kingdom of Israel," and he insisted that Arab and Jewish nationalism represented "two contradictory principles." Azouri rejected the idea of bringing Egypt into this Arab empire "because the Egyptians do not belong to the Arab race" and are of the "African Berber family." Negib Azoury's advocacy of the breakup of the Ottoman Empire fit in well with the Young Ottoman movement (or "Young Turks"), an intellectual reform movement that had been building during the late nineteenth century among exiles without, and underground revolutionaries within, the sultan's corrupt regime.

When the Young Turks revolted against the sultan in 1908 they also warned that world Jewry was developing self-government in Palestine and that this was contrary to Arab goals. Arabs in Palestine took the charge to heart and immediately formed an anti-Zionist movement. Anti-Jewish societies and demonstrations occurred in following years. Arabs protested to the sultan that Jews were purchasing land in Palestine and asked him to eliminate such sales. To make matters worse, the Zionists were afraid (when asked) to join the Arabs in a joint effort against the Ottomans in 1913. Without Arab assurance of support for Zionist aims, the Zionists were wary of provoking the Ottomans with a revolt in the name of Arab nationalism. The Arab Congress that met in Paris in June 1913 said that it could not support Zionist aims because of "tactical reasons." During the First World War, however, both Jews and Arabs would fight against the Ottomans. An opportunity for cooperation between their respective nationalist movements had been lost. In retrospect, one wonders if such "contradictory" (in Azouri's word) national movements could have ended in a spirit of cooperation when it came to Palestine.

THE FIRST WORLD WAR

In 1914 most of the world was plunged into war. When the Ottoman Empire became the ally of the Germans and Austrians in the First World War, the British sought and gained the support of both Arabs and Jews in the Middle East. Through the McMahon Letter of October 24, 1915, the British promised to support the founding of an Arab state in the Middle East. This state was to include areas of present-day Syria (east of Damascus), Iraq, and Saudi Arabia. Through the Balfour Declaration of November 2, 1917, the British promised the Jews a national home in Palestine after the war. Interpretation and misinterpretation of these promises would set the stage for later developments and struggles between Arabs, Jews, and the Western powers.

Sir Henry McMahon (1862-1949) was British High Commissioner in Cairo. To gain Arab support for the British war effort, McMahon negotiated with Hussein Ibn Ali of Arabia, the Hashemite protector of Mecca and Medina. A series of letters flowed back and forth, but the most important correspondence was the summary letter of October 24, 1915. In that letter, the British promised to support the Arab leader's hope of instituting an Arab caliphate in the Middle East and his desire to become the undisputed leader of the Arab world. Palestine was not mentioned in the letter, and the territory of Lebanon was excluded.

When Arab leaders later claimed in the 1930s that the British high commissioner had promised an Arab state in Palestine, Sir Henry McMahon was still living. He categorically disputed such an Arab claim and affirmed that only territory east of Damascus, British-administered areas of Iraq, and the guarantees for the Muslim holy places were listed as intended. McMahon's October 24 letter also protected both British and French interests in the area, going so far as to note in the third point that "when the situation admits, Great Britain will give to the Arabs her advice and will assist them to establish what may appear to be the most suitable forms of government in those various territories." Point four declared: "On the other hand, it is understood that the Arabs have decided to seek the advice and guidance of Great Britain only, and that such European advisers and officials as may be required for the formation of a sound form of administration will be British."

The British informed the French at every stage in this negotiation with the Hashemite dynasty of Hussein. In the Sykes-Picot Agreement of 1916 the two countries decided on their general division of the Middle East into British and French "mandates" after the Ottomans were defeated. They planned to make the Ottoman Turks pay for their support of the Germans (just as they made the Germans pay dearly for their role in the war). Originally control over Palestine was to be shared by the great powers, but as tens of thousands of General Edmund Allenby's British troops prepared for a massive onslaught against the Turks in the Holy Land, the British made clear that Palestine was a strategic buffer to the protection of the Suez Canal in Egypt. Sir Mark Sykes (1873-1919), who was the British formulator of the Sykes-Picot Agreement, stated that from a purely British point of view "a prosperous Jewish population in Palestine, owing its inception and its opportunity of development to British policy, might be an invaluable asset as a defense of the Suez Canal against attack from the north and as a station on the future air routes to the East." The British had decided that after the war Palestine would be part of Great Britain's "zone of influence."

It is therefore significant that the Balfour Declaration was issued in November 1917. Arthur James Balfour (1848-1930), a former British prime minister, had been a strong proponent of the restoration of the Jews to Palestine. His appointment as foreign secretary by Prime Minister David Lloyd George at the end of 1916 made him much more influential. Negotiations with the British for a Jewish homeland in Palestine had been going on for years, and Balfour right from the beginning threw his whole weight on the side of the Zionists. Chaim Weizmann (1874-1952), a distinguished British scientist, helped his Jewish brethren as well by discovering a process that would yield acetone, a solvent desperately needed for munitions production during the war. He asked only that negotiations continue toward a Jewish homeland in Palestine, and he became quite a negotiator himself, meeting personally with Faisal of the Hashemite dynasty and obtaining written pledges from him to support the Zionist cause.

Ironically, some of the most formidable opponents to a Jewish state were assimilated British Jews. In fact, in an earlier draft of the declaration, Lloyd George and Balfour used the phrase "that Palestine should be reconstituted as the National Home" of the Jews. Edwin Montagu, the one Jew in David Lloyd George's government, argued against the phrase. The official letter communicated to Lord Roth-schild, of the famous family of Jewish financiers and member of the British Parliament from 1899-1910, by Arthur J. Balfour read as follows:

Foreign Office
November 2nd, 1917

Dear Lord Rothschild,

I have much pleasure in conveying to you, on behalf of His Majes-ty's Government, the following declaration of sympathy with Jewish Zionist aspirations which has been submitted to, and approved by, the Cabinet.

"His Majesty's Government view with favour the establishment in Palestine of a national home for the Jewish people, and will use their best endeavours to facilitate the achievement of this object, it being clearly understood that nothing shall be done which may prej-udice the civil and religious rights of existing non-Jewish communi-ties in Palestine, or the rights and political status enjoyed by Jews in any other country."

I should be grateful if you would bring this declaration to the knowl-edge of the Zionist Federation.

American president Woodrow Wilson's decision to accept the Bal-four Declaration was a necessary step to the British issuance of it. To-ward the end of his life, the devout Presbyterian president mused: "To think that I, a son of the manse, should be able to help restore the Holy Land to its people." In the next chapter, Christian attitudes will be dis-cussed; but suffice it to say that the religious faith of politicians and diplomats had quite an effect on the Declaration's being issued. In the Congress, a large majority of Senators and Representatives favored the Balfour Declaration, many of them asserting that justice was finally be-ing obtained for the Jewish people, a people that had suffered so long at the hands of the Christian nations. Some legislators called for an imme-diate resolution by Congress in favor of Jewish statehood. These legis-lators were representative of the American public as a whole. Most Americans in 1917 seemed of a mind to grant the Jewish people a na-tional homeland and welcomed the Balfour Declaration.

In spite of the opposition of Secretary of State Robert Lansing and the constant negative input of others in the U.S. State Department, including the Near Eastern Division and consular representatives in Palestine, two members of President Wilson's administration greeted the idea of a Jewish state with enthusiasm: Newton D. Baker, Secretary of War, and Josephus Daniels, Secretary of the Navy. Throughout the twentieth century, the State Department would attempt to scuttle the development of a Jewish state in Palestine and would issue negative statements and evaluations of the state of Israel once it was established.

At the formal conclusion of World War I in 1919 neither Arabs nor Jews had an independent state in the Middle East. Even Egypt with its Suez Canal was under the control of Great Britain. The Hashemite dynasty in Arabia had been negotiating with the major Western powers to obtain regional hegemony. Many of the Jewish nationalist leaders had a Western orientation and were afraid to risk alienating Great Britain for the fleeting Arab promise to work together. Negotiators for the fledgling Arab nationalist movement were individuals who did not realize the antipathy that Arabs in Palestine and Syria held for the Jewish people and toward a Jewish state. Only hindsight affords the luxury of viewing the storm clouds between Arabs and Jews that were forming on the horizon. The French and the British did carve out zones of influence in the Middle East after the war. The French Mandate encompassed the Syria-Lebanon area. The British Mandate encompassed the Palestine area on both sides of the Jordan River and the Iraq area.

THE ERA OF THE GRAND MUFTI

An important segment of the world Jewish community lived in Muslim countries in the nineteenth and twentieth centuries. These communities stretched from Morocco in western North Africa to Afghanistan in the east. These Jews developed their own traditions within the larger framework of the particular country, combining an observant Judaism with cultural customs. Some of these Jewish communities went as far back as the ancient period. The Ottoman Empire had brought a semblance of unity to. this area of the world, and the persecution of Jews was local and sporadic. As the European nations colonized the Muslim territories, the Jewish community benefited from the protection and Western style of diplomacy. At times, Jews in the Western world represented the concerns of their African brethren. The Jews of the Middle East were often concentrated in more urban areas and were generally more educated than the surrounding peoples.

This link with the West and affinity toward Europe caused more friction between the Jews and their Arab neighbors. As General Allenby's army was poised to take Palestine, Ottoman officials began confiscating Jewish farms and terrorizing Jewish communities. Killing Jews indiscriminately, the Ottoman Turks also systematically starved the Jewish people. As a result, the Jewish Palestinian population of 85,000 before the war dwindled to less than 55,000. Nearly 10,000 of these Jews died of starvation and illness in less than a year. They were surrounded by 560,000 Arabs in Palestine, many of whom had immigrated from other territories to capitalize on new work opportunities and some who had taken advantage of the Jews' weakened condition to loot and pillage. Nevertheless, the Jewish community continued to help the British win the war.

By 1948, more than 900,000 Jews lived in Muslim countries—countries that had become independent during the twentieth century and had broken (or were in the process of breaking) the shackles of European domination. Today, in spite of birth rates and increase of population, no more than 90,000 Jews remain in Muslim countries. During the Nazi era, as the Arab world aligned itself with Adolf Hitler, Jews were horribly persecuted by Muslim and Christian Arabs alike. When it appeared that a Jewish state would be formed in Palestine, Arab communities exiled and murdered their Jewish neighbors and stole their property. By the time the Arab Palestinian refugee problem developed, a Jewish refugee problem from Arab countries was in full swing. This would complicate a world in transition after the Second World War.

Thus, the period between the world wars created problems between Arabs and Jews that appear to defy solution today. As the First World War ground to a halt, it seemed that perhaps Arabs and Jews could live in harmony in the Middle East and that both a Jewish state and Arab states could prosper. Moderate Arabs and Jews appeared in good rapport when the Ottomans were defeated. Hussein of the Hashemite dynasty in the Arabian kingdom of Hejaz had sent his oldest son, Abdullah, to ask for British protection from the Ottoman overlords at the beginning of World War I. His second son, Faisal, led an Arab revolt and army against the Ottomans in cooperation with British officers such as T. E. Lawrence ("Lawrence of Arabia"). Faisal wanted to be king of Syria, an area the McMahon letter had specifically mentioned as the reward for Arab support for the British.

During the 1919 Paris Peace Conference that formally ended World War I, Faisal signed an agreement with Chaim Weizmann, now leader of the Zionist movement, that began by emphasizing "the racial kinship and ancient bonds existing between the Arabs and the Jewish people." It also pointed out the economic development that could result from the cooperation between both groups. Article 4 stated:

> All necessary measures shall be taken to encourage and stimulate immigration of Jews into Palestine on a large scale, and as quickly as possible to settle Jewish immigrants upon the land through closer settlement and intensive cultivation of the soil. In taking such measures the Arab peasant and tenant farmers shall be protected in their rights, and shall be assisted in forwarding their economic development.

As head of the Arab delegation to the peace conference, Faisal agreed in this document, dated January 3, 1919, that "any matters of dispute which may arise between the contracting parties shall be referred to the British government for arbitration." Faisal added, however, in an addendum that the British promises of territory to the Arabs must be honored if this agreement were to be carried out.

In a March 3, 1919, letter to American Felix Frankfurter, Faisal insisted that "Arabs and Jews are cousins in race, having suffered similar oppressions at the hands of powers stronger than themselves, and by a happy coincidence have been able to take the first step towards the attainment of their national ideals together." The Arab leader continued:

> We Arabs, especially the educated among us, look with the deepest sympathy on the Zionist movement. Our deputation here in Paris is fully acquainted with the proposals submitted yesterday by the Zionist Organization to the Peace Conference, and we regard them as moderate and proper. We will do our best, in so far as we are concerned, to help them through: we will wish the Jews a most hearty welcome home. . . .
>
> People less informed and less responsible than our leaders and yours, ignoring the need for cooperation of the Arabs and Zionists, have been trying to exploit the local difficulties that must necessarily arise in Palestine in the early stages of our movements. Some of them have, I am afraid, misrepresented your aims to the Arab peasantry, and our aims to the Jewish peasantry, with the result that interested parties have been able to make capital out of what they call our differences.
>
> I wish to give you my firm conviction that these differences are not on questions of principle, but on matters of detail such as must inevitably occur in every contact of neighbouring peoples, and as are easily adjusted by mutual goodwill. Indeed nearly all of them will disappear with fuller knowledge.

Faisal had set himself up as king of Syria in 1918, and he hoped to capitalize on his gains and the new Arab state that he led. He soon was surprised to find that Arabs in Palestine were vehemently opposed to Jewish presence in and immigration to Palestine. They were willing to kill any Arab leader who made peace with the Jews. To further complicate matters, the French kicked Faisal out of Syria when the territory came under their mandate. Faisal had hoped the Zionists would lend diplomatic support against the French, but the British insisted the Jewish leaders not get involved. Faisal was crushed. He soon asked both Chaim Weizmann and Felix Frankfurter not to quote or publicize his former agreements and letters. The Zionists respected his wishes, and those documents were kept secret for a number of years.

Threats against Jews began appearing in the Arab press in Palestine, and unrest in Palestinian Arab villages increased. The General Syrian Congress meeting in Damascus (July 2, 1919) issued one of the first direct statements opposing Jewish migration to Palestine and declared that Palestine was "the southern part of Syria." Their memorandum to the King-Crane Commission insisted:

> We oppose the pretensions of the Zionists to create a Jewish commonwealth in the southern part of Syria, known as Palestine, and oppose Zionist migration to any part of our country; for we do not acknowledge their title but consider them a grave peril to our people from the national, economical, and political points of view.

Arabs killed Jews during riots in 1920 in Palestine and, even in Jerusalem, Arab police joined in demonstrations against Jews, which led to bloodshed and death.

In March 1920 the Syrian National Congress repudiated the prospects of French control and once again offered Faisal the throne of Syria. Faisal began talking of a "greater Syria" that included Palestine, and Syrian Arabs became one of the harshest group of critics of Jewish immigration and the establishment of a Jewish state. In December 1920 an Arab convention held in Haifa demanded an Arab government in Palestine and from this point on unequivocally opposed any Jewish national home in the area. Arabs would terrorize Jews in the emerging Arab countries and in Palestine for the next three decades.

During the summer of 1920, Faisal's older brother, Abdullah, began marching from Arabia toward Syria to restore Faisal to the throne. The British convinced him to stay in the land beyond the Jordan River, which was dubbed Transjordan. They actually created another Arab country (that later would become Jordan) from the Palestine mandate, a shift of policy that surprised and thrilled the Arabian leader. "Allah granted me success in creating the Government of Transjordan," Abdullah would write, "by having it separated from the Balfour Declaration which had included it since the Sykes-Picot Agreement assigned it to the British zone of influence." Although the British insisted they were the ultimate authority in the region, Abdullah became the leader of Transjordan. To further pacify the Hashemite dynasty, Great Britain also made Faisal the leader of Iraq.

On June 30, 1922, a joint resolution that supported the Balfour Declaration and "favoring the establishment in Palestine of a national home for the Jewish people" was unanimously adopted by the U.S. Congress. It was signed by Woodrow Wilson's Republican successor, Warren G. Harding, on September 21, 1922. In Great Britain, however, the British realized they had opened a Pandora's box, and they soon began to reinterpret their promises in the Balfour Declaration. Because of the growing Arab nationalist movement and its increasing opposition to Jewish restoration to the Holy Land, the British colonial secretary, Winston Churchill, in June 1922 issued the Churchill White Paper. It did not totally repudiate the Balfour Declation but emphasized that the former declaration did not refer to "Palestine as a whole" becoming a Jewish national home, but instead that "such a Home should be founded in Palestine." Jewish Zionist leaders reluctantly had to support the British policy statement because of the assurance that at least some part of Palestine would be turned into a Jewish national home. Therefore, Jews were aghast when, following Arab riots in 1929, the British began to limit Jewish immigration.

This policy of appeasement was no more effective than it would later be with the rising German dictator Adolf Hitler. In fact, this British policy led them to make one of the greatest blunders at the beginning of their mandate in the Middle East. At Arab instigation, the British appointed the right-wing Palestinian Arab nationalist Hajj Amin al-Husseini to be mufti (official expounder of Muslim law) of Jerusalem in 1921 and chairman of the Supreme Muslim Council in 1922. Viewed as the greatest Arab nationalist leader until Gamal Abdel Nasser, the Grand Mufti would be responsible for further riots and would wreak havoc among moderate Arabs as well as among the Palestinian Jewish community.

The Husseini clan consisted of wealthy Arab landowners in southern Palestine. Constantly struggling with the other influential Muslim family in Palestinian politics and economics, the Nashashibis, the Husseinis had thirteen of their relatives elected mayor of Jerusalem between 1864 and 1920. The British had to dismiss one of them, Musa Kazem al-Husseini, for instigating riots against Jews and Britons in 1920. Hundreds were wounded, and several were killed during that uprising.

Amin al-Husseini was born in Jerusalem in 1893, and his early education was provided in Ottoman government schools there. He traveled to Cairo for his university education (al-Azhar University) and served as an Ottoman officer during the First World War. After the war he returned to Jerusalem to oppose the British there as an Arab nationalist leader. He was sentenced in absentia to ten years in prison for his direct instigation of the anti-Jewish riots in Jerusalem in April 1920. He received a reprieve from this sentence in 1921 and was appointed Grand Mufti of Jerusalem the same year. The British believed this move would achieve balance between the rival families and would ingratiate themselves with Amin.

His appointment as chairman of the Supreme Muslim Council in 1922 allowed him free reign over the financial, educational, and religious institutions of the Muslim community, and he used the opportunity to spread hatred of the Jews and to foster anti-British conspiracy. He was directly responsible for anti-Jewish riots in Palestine in 1929 and 1936, and he coordinated terrorist activities in the 1920s and 1930s. The British finally dismissed this Grand Mufti in October 1937, after he had spent nearly two decades in coordinated dissemination of his poison. By this time, he had begun terrorizing moderate Arab leaders and a broad spectrum of political opponents. In fact, his henchmen tried to assassinate King Abdullah in Transjordan in the 1930s. Some believe it was one of the Mufti's followers who finally was able to kill the Hashemite ruler in East Jerusalem in 1951 (see chapter 4).

The Nazis began to increase their activity in the Middle East during 1937. German officials were issued instructions to oppose the formation of a Jewish state in Palestine. The Nazi rationale was that such a state could not take all of the Jews they wanted to get rid of throughout the world and would only become another power base for "international Jewry" and its machinations. Arab newspapers and periodicals began using Nazi anti-Semitic slogans freely and openly praised Adolf Hitler as a strong leader who knew how to handle "the subversive activities of Judaism." During the 1937 Islamic celebration of Muhammad's birthday, Arab demonstrators in Palestine carried placards with pictures of Adolf Hitler and Benito Mussolini. Some had German and Italian flags in their hands.

Ironically, during the 1970s and 1980s Adolf Hitler's *Mein Kampf* and the spurious *Protocols of the Elders of Zion* (an "account" of a supposed Jewish conspiracy to take over the world) were on the bedstands and coffee tables of cultured Arab homes (even in Kuwait). These sympathetic attitudes toward Adolf Hitler and the Nazis, men seen as strong leaders who "showed the Jews," underscore the support Saddam Hussein found for his anti-Jewish and anti-Western views (not only among Palestinian Arabs but across the spectrum of Arabs throughout the Middle East). These views among Arabs are not new, inasmuch as they were first promulgated by Hajj Amin al-Husseini, the Grand Mufti of Jerusalem.

Hiding in the Mosque of Omar in October 1937 and then secretly fleeing British retribution in Palestine, Amin al-Husseini was forced into exile in Beirut, Lebanon, and Damascus, Syria. From these locations he continued to consolidate his power in Arab Palestine. His terrorist units attacked Jewish settlements and murdered Jewish civilians. His more than ten thousand guerrillas paralyzed civil authority in the Holy Land and forced the British to ship two additional infantry battalions to the area. Several thousand people lost their lives, including Arab leaders who would not totally submit to his demands. When he could not murder the Arab opposition, he had their wives and children murdered. In 1940 Amin al-Husseini moved to Iraq, attempting in 1941 to overthrow the Iraqi government in a pro-German coup. When that failed, he escaped once again, this time to Italy and Nazi Germany.

Totally omitted from many books on the Middle East conflict, this former Grand Mufti is an important link between the Nazi Holocaust and the resulting events that led to the founding of the state of Israel. An admirer of Adolf Hitler and his treatment of the Jews in Germany, Amin al-Husseini strengthened his ties with the Führer. Supporting the Nazi cause in the Middle East during the Second World War, he traveled to Nazi Germany, lectured to SS officers, and defended the Nazi program of extermination of the Jews. He even toured the extermination camps with Heinrich Himmler. Hitler had a personal meeting with the Arab nationalist leader and gave him half a million dollars to fight the

Allies and the Jews. The Nazi leader also promised the aid of Adolf Eichmann after the war to "solve the Jewish problem in the Middle East." In fact, with Amin's encouragement every major Arab nation in the Middle East declared on the side of Nazi Germany during World War II. After the war Amin al-Husseini escaped French imprisonment as a war criminal and settled in Cairo. That became his home base as he traveled to Beirut, Damascus, and other areas of the Middle East, directing terrorist operations against Jews in Palestine. He was instrumental in drumming up support for the 1948 attack by the Arab armies against the fledgling state of Israel.

The British policy of appeasement toward the radical Arabs bears a resemblance to the policy they pursued with Adolf Hitler. In both cases the consequences for the Jewish people were disastrous and led to conflict. The British, in neglecting to honor their own Balfour Declaration, attempted to limit Jewish immigration into Palestine. Arab oil supplies and "peace" in the Middle East were important factors, even as they are today. The British realized that the Jews did not represent a powerful force in world politics, but were in fact an unpopular minority. They were dispensable. By 1931 there were 175,000 Jews in Palestine amid a total population of more than 1 million. By 1947 the Arab population was 1.2 million (more than doubled by immigration and birthrate from the 1917 figure). The British were restricting Jews while simultaneously the persecution of the Nazi regime was growing stronger. In 1939 the British tried to suspend all Jewish immigration into and land purchase in Palestine. Jewish underground organizations were appalled. Great Britain was attempting to seal off the only safety route the European refugees had.

As the war progressed, the Jewish victims of the Nazis understandably believed that the British were consigning them to death. Although thousands were able to immigrate illegally into Palestine, many more were stopped as the British, to appease the Arabs, enforced the new immigration restrictions. The tragedy of the Struma, an old cattle boat carrying 769 passengers (the cream of middle-class Romanian Jewry), is a case in point. In December 1941 the British ordered port authorities in Istanbul to stop the boat en route to Palestine. Pleas went out to save the more than 70 children on board. In February 1942 the Turkish authorities dragged the ship out of the harbor (over the protest of the Bulgarian captain, who refused to let his crew depart with it). Whether by mine, torpedo, or faulty conditions on the boat, it sank—killing all but one of the passengers.

Thus, the Second World War set the stage for a confrontation of the varied forces of Middle East politics. Arabs viewed the Nazis as liberators from British imperialism and joined the forces of Adolf Hitler to defeat the Allies. Jews supported the Allies wholeheartedly but balked on British immigration policy. They fought to subvert a British pro-Arab policy of appeasement. In 1944 the French ended their mandate in Syria and Lebanon, both of which became independent. More independent states were added to the list of twentieth-century Arab enclaves, which included Saudi Arabia and Iraq (both were granted independence in 1932).

The British found the Middle East too volatile to control and relinquished their mandate to the United Nations in February 1947. They had given Egypt independence in 1922 and in 1946 had allowed Transjordan to become another independent Arab state (called the Hashemite Kingdom of Jordan in 1950). The British were in continual conflict with Jewish guerrillas, who were incensed over the mass murder of 6 million Jews in Nazi Europe and the terrorism inflicted on Palestinian Jews by Arabs. The unfairness of the situation nearly overwhelmed the Jewish community. The Arabs had been given many independent states that consumed large tracts of land, whereas the Jews still awaited their national home. Even the United States opposed what it viewed as a "pro-Arab" British policy, and many in the newly formed United Nations believed a compromise must be formulated in fairness to the Jewish people.

In 1947 the United Nations Special Committee on Palestine recommended the partition of the remaining Palestine area to solve the Arab/Jewish conflict. Zionist leaders were not happy with the division but reluctantly accepted it as a compromise. Moderate Arabs were not allowed the luxury of compromise. Even with ironclad Jewish guarantees to keep within their own slim borders and to support the neighboring Arab state economically, Azzam Pasha, secretary general of the newly formed Arab League of Nations, told negotiators that if he or any Arab leader returned to Damascus or Cairo with a peace treaty, the person would be murdered by other Arabs within hours. During the resolution debate in the United Nations, the Arab League (under partial instigation from Amin al-Husseini) threatened war.

Nevertheless, the United Nations on November 29, 1947, voted in favor of the partition plan, which it believed fairly divided the remaining area of Palestine along Jewish owned/Arab owned territorial lines. Even the Soviet Union gave its approval. But, regrettably, within a week more than one hundred Jews were killed by Arab guerilla attacks and terrorist explosions in Palestine. In January 1948 the first detachments of the Arab Liberation Army entered Palestine from Syria and Transjordan. In fear, the United Nations Security Council did not put the partition resolution into effect, but neither did it rescind the order.

The state of Israel was formally established on May 14, 1948. Five Arab armies (Egypt, Syria, Transjordan, Lebanon, and Iraq) with the support of other Arab nations (including Saudi Arabia) immediately invaded Israel. The British had left these Arabs with arms and supplies, and the warriors of Allah felt quite confident of victory. With words reminiscent of their Nazi allies in World War II, they claimed they would finish the task that Adolf Hitler had begun—they claimed their Arab armies would exterminate the Jews and push them into the sea.

2

THE RISE OF THE JEWISH STATE:
MAJOR DEVELOPMENTS SINCE WORLD WAR II

One must understand the modern history of the Middle East to comprehend that each of the countries involved gained its independence during the twentieth century. The state of Israel is one of these countries. Although commentators debate the politics involved in the formation of Israel (or, for that matter, of any of the modern Arab states), one thing is clear: the modern state of Israel exists today and has existed since 1948. It must be accepted as an entity in the modern Middle East. Even though some Arab leaders have had to come to grips with this fact, many others as well as a number of Christians cannot bring themselves to accept Israel's existence. Even during the 1991 Persian Gulf War, pro-Iraqi Arabs insisted that the Christian Crusaders had had states in Palestine and Syria for a much longer period than modern Israel's existence and that the Arabs finally defeated the Christian invaders. This logic and rhetoric leads to vicious conflict that defies rational solutions. Outside of the numerous debates and endless negotiations, however, Israel is an enduring reality.

THE 1948 WAR OF INDEPENDENCE

The United Nations' boundary lines for the new state of Israel created a sliver of territory surrounded by a vast Arab-controlled expanse. One area north of Tel Aviv was only nine miles across from the Mediterranean Sea to the border of the proposed Arab portion of Palestine. Arabs refused to accept even this concession to the Jewish people.

Even the Hashemite king Abdullah, a man often considered to be moderate and who had just gained the independent Arab state of Transjordan, appointed himself commander-in-chief of the armed forces of the Arab Legion. He appears to have wanted the territory of the proposed Arab state in Palestine for himself. In fact, he met with Jewish representatives three days before the state of Israel was formally established. (These representatives included Golda Meir, who had disguised herself as a peasant woman to elude Arab forces already in Palestine.) Abdullah tried to convince the Jews not to declare statehood and to give negotiations a further chance. When they refused, King Abdullah said he had to go against his earlier promise to the Jews and instead join the other Arab leaders in a massive assault against the new Jewish state. Abdullah yearned to control Jerusalem, and he could not afford to let other Arabs control it. His Hashemite family had lost Mecca and Medina to the Saudi dynasty in 1925, and he wanted the prestige of controlling the third-holiest spot in Islam. He was also promised by the Arab League a war chest containing millions of dollars.

The Syrians had their own agenda—to make at least part of Palestine a portion of Greater Syria. They seemed to have no interest in being commanded by Abdullah. The Egyptians planned to expand their buffer zone in the south. The radical followers of the Grand Mufti simplistically insisted that every Jew be driven from Palestine. Thus the varied agendas of the Arab nations gave them no central military leadership during the 1948 war. Unbelievably, they also had little knowledge of the terrain of Palestine that they planned to invade. For example, the Syrian and Iraqi commanders did not have one single military map of Palestine and were forced to use tourist maps and children's school maps. The commanders had little insight that they would have to move their forces 4,000 feet uphill in crossing the Jordan Valley.

The Arabs planned that the Syrian and Lebanese forces would invade from the north and northeast. They planned to capture Safed, Tiberias, and Nazareth and to set up command posts in those areas. Two Egyptian brigades were to take the south through the Negev and Gaza, but they had no communication links with the northern forces. The Iraqi army was to come across the Jordan River from north Transjordan while the three Arab Legion brigades moved through the West Bank of the Jordan River. As the battle progressed, a good portion of the Arab forces lacked the heart to fight. Some Iraqi soldiers (like their modern counterparts) were just peasants conscripted to fight a battle for which they had little understanding. During the 1948 skirmishes, Israeli soldiers found some Iraqi gunners chained to their weapons.

The Jews, in contrast, had a dedicated military force and a resourceful command structure. What they lacked were numbers and armaments, but they kept these facts secret. If the Arab forces had known how poorly armed the Israelis were at the beginning of the war, they would have pressed forward instead of holding their ground or retreating to better field advantage. For example, a resourceful Israeli field commander, Lieutenant Colonel Moshe Dayan, used two old nineteenth-century howitzers to blow up the first Syrian tank to enter Galilee. Although the Syrians had more than forty other tanks and more than one hundred fifty armored vehicles, they were fooled into believing that the Israelis had formidable weaponry. In reality, the Israelis had no other heavy weapons. The Syrians retreated and continued to hold portions of eastern Galilee. Because they feared the Jews would trap them, other Arab forces with overwhelming numerical advantage did not counterattack when they had the chance. The Iraqis could have cut the newborn Jewish state in half by waging another counterattack, but they seemed to lack the fortitude for more battle.

Egyptian commanders treated their soldiers like slaves. Although their troops were poorly trained, they believed the sheer numerical advantage in the south would scare the new Jewish state into submission. Indeed, a force of 10,000 Egyptians marched to within sixteen miles of Tel Aviv. The fall of that important city probably would have meant the end of the war for Israel. Israel's commander of operations, Yigael Yadin, took a risk, encircled the Egyptian troops, and attacked them from the rear. The Egyptian force became confused and panicked. While they were regrouping, Yadin called a press conference and declared that the Egyptian supply lines had been cut and that "overwhelming concentrations" of Jewish troops had them surrounded. This news reached Cairo through the international news media, and officials there radioed their generals to regroup and hold their ground. The major counterattack by Israeli forces that was implied never took place. A June 11, 1948, United Nations' truce allowed for a short cessation of hostilities. Israeli forces took the opportunity to refortify and regroup. To underscore the hostility some British officials held for the new Jewish state, the British representative to the U.N., Sir Alexander Cadogan, voted several times against a truce resolution and called the new state "the Jewish authorities in Palestine." He refused to use the word *Israel*.

In fact, some British commanders led Abdullah's Arab Legion forces in the battle for Jerusalem. Their heavy artillery was too much for the fledgling Jewish defenders, and the Jewish quarter of the Old City surrendered to Abdullah's forces on May 28, 1948. Jews had struggled to live in the Holy City from the ancient period to the present. Now they had lost their revered Western Wall—the Wailing Wall. The "moderate" King Abdullah had lobbed more than ten thousand shells into the city, destroying more than two thousand homes and killing twelve hundred civilians. The Israelis brought in reinforcements to hold on to West Jerusalem.

Both sides used the truce to their advantage. By July, Arabs had increased their troop strength to 45,000. France and Czechoslovakia sold weapons to the Israelis, and Jewish organizations around the world clandestinely provided money for shiploads of armaments to their endangered brethren. Although the war continued, Arab morale was primarily broken by the presence of an armed Jewish state and the tenacious attitude of Jewish soldiers and civilians. Every Jewish citizen participated in the war effort. Their backs were against the wall, and they fought like cornered wildcats. The last Jewish campaign was against the Egyptian forces from December 22, 1948, to January 8, 1949. The Israelis pushed ten miles into Egyptian territory. Negotiations for an armistice were begun through the auspices of the United Nations.

The Rhodes Armistice Agreement was signed in April 1949. Only the Iraqis did not sign an agreement directly with the Jewish state. Iraqi officials asked that the Jordanian delegation be permitted to negotiate for them. That allowed Iraq to take an uncompromising, belligerent stance toward Israel. Israel's other Arab neighbors treated the armistice as an interlude in warfare. They stalled on a permanent peace agreement. Egypt went so far as to interpret the armistice's statement against war from Arab or Israeli territory ("No warlike act or act of hostility shall be conducted from territory controlled by one of the Parties to this Agreement against the other Party") as legally condoning guerrilla activity. That would lead to other anti-Jewish activity from Gamal Abdel Nasser's Egyptian government that culminated in the 1956 Suez crisis (the Sinai Campaign, "Operation Kadesh") and the 1967 Six-Day War.

THE PALESTINIAN REFUGEES

It was during the 1948 war and its aftermath that both a Palestinian Arab and a Palestinian Jewish refugee problem began. In every Arab country, Jews were persecuted, stripped of their possessions and bank accounts, tortured, even murdered. They were encouraged to leave their countries penniless. The Arab nations not only refused but also would not monetarily compensate the Jews expelled from the Arab nations for their loss of property and homes. More than 684,000 of the Jews went to the fledgling, strife-torn state of Israel from 1948 to 1951, while another 150,000 went to Western nations. Another 71,000 European Jewish refugees from the Nazi Holocaust entered Palestine from 1945 to 1948. Sadly, a high percentage of those Holocaust survivors lost their lives during the 1948 War of Independence. Four thousand Jewish soldiers and 2,000 Jewish civilians were killed during this war for Jewish statehood, almost 1 percent of the population of the Jewish state in 1948.

These severe hardships occurred even though Israel had been recognized by many nations of the United Nations and been immediately recognized by the governments of the United States and the Soviet Union. Soviet delegate to the United Nations Andrei Gromyko told the Security Council on May 29, 1948: "This is not the first time that the Arab states, which organized the invasion of Palestine, have ignored a decision of the Security Council or of the General Assembly." He and other delegates insisted that a firmer approach should be taken toward Arab belligerence. The Arabs would lose even more territory because of their intransigence as the 1949 Rhodes Armistice lines allocated 21 percent more territory to Israel if it would pull back its armies. Israel would keep the western sector of Jerusalem, while Jordan occupied the eastern part.

Unfortunately, Palestinian Arabs would be the big losers. They had been told by the Arab high command on many occasions to leave their homes in Palestine during the 1948 war. "A cannon cannot differentiate between a Jew and an Arab," the Arab high command insisted in broadcasts and leaflets. "Leave the country for two weeks and you will come back victorious." Although some Jewish leaders begged their Palestinian Arab neighbors to stay in the new Jewish state, hundreds of thousands of Palestinian Arabs left the sliver of territory allocated by the United Nations to the Jews and moved to the territory allocated to the Arabs in Palestine and to the borders of Lebanon, Iraq, Syria, and

Jordan. Approximately 600,000 were uprooted throughout the total area of Arab and Jewish Palestine.

Although it is common today for Arabs to insist that "Jewish terrorism" drove out the aforementioned refugees, this claim appears in most cases to be a propaganda afterthought. Initially, the Palestinian Arabs who were relegated to U.N. refugee camps bordering Israel were bitter at their Arab brethren for luring them from their homes and failing to "push the Jews into the sea." In contrast, the Palestinian Arabs who chose to stay in Israel during the 1948 war were not only welcomed as citizens of the new Jewish state but also were able to obtain considerable wealth. This was especially true of the Haifa Arabs, whom Golda Meir had begged to stay. By contrast and to make matters worse, while Europeans and the peoples of India and Pakistan were resettling millions of their refugees to new homelands, almost all the twenty Arab nations refused to permit Palestinian Arabs to become citizens of their nations. The Arab nations wanted those unfortunate refugees to remain as a political ploy in the Arabs' ultimate operation to destroy Israel. In some ways this ploy worked, for young Palestinian Arabs today know nothing of this history. They simply blame Israel for all their problems.

In contrast, Israel had a massive resettlement job. Tens of thousands of Arabs were allowed to return to their families, but the large majority of the Palestinian Arabs who left remained in U.N. camps. Israel had to help pay for those camps. To complicate matters, many Jews expelled from Arab countries had nowhere to go. Their only hope was that Israel could settle them on a sliver of land that many believed could not support millions of Jews. Nevertheless, the Law of Return was passed by the Knesset (Israeli parliament) on July 5, 1950, declaring that every Jew had a right to settle in Israel. For more than a million Jews in the Soviet Union today, this promise (which is basic to the Jewish state) is their only escape from Russian anti-Semitism. The homes of Palestinian Arab refugees that were saved through the early years of hopeless negotiations were now taken by Jewish refugees. In the 1950s almost 90 percent of the population of Israel was Jewish.

Even today, Palestinian Arabs do not fare well among their Arab brethren. When homelands were given away in Iraq or jobs were provided in Libya and Saudi Arabia in the 1970s, advertisements in Arabic newspapers stated: "Palestinians need not apply." Kuwait used 400,000 Palestinians to run the bureaucracy of their country before

1990. Because Palestinian Arabs supported Saddam Hussein of Iraq in the Gulf War, however, those positions may not be available again. Although there are a good number of wealthy Palestinian Arabs in the Middle East today (and around the world), even these men and women longingly look toward Israel as their homeland. They will not give up the belief that this Holy Land will some day be theirs. The Palestinian Arabs continue to be used by terrorist organizations and Arab nations, who have their own agendas. Aside from all the confusing rhetoric of peace and negotiation, this factor militates against a resolution of the conflict between Jews and Arabs (and Arabs against Arabs) in the Middle East.

THE 1956 SUEZ CRISIS

Following the 1949 armistice arranged by the United Nations, there was a wave of Arab radicalism. This massive outpouring reacted against the old regimes in Arab countries that were held responsible for the Arab defeat in 1948-1949. During the 1950s key countries such as Egypt, Syria, and Iraq changed leadership. King Abdullah in Jordan was assassinated for being "too moderate" toward Israel, and his grandson Hussein was later crowned king. King Hussein of Jordan is the only Middle East ruler to remain in power from the 1950s to this day (see chapter 4). Between 1949 and the Suez/Sinai campaign in 1956, Arabs launched into Israel hundreds of terrorist missions that resulted in more than 1,300 Jewish casualties.

As will be seen in chapter 4, Gamal Abdel Nasser of Egypt assumed the active leadership of the Arab world in the 1950s. Nasser gained such a following that it appeared Jordan and Lebanon would fall to his forces. He signed a mutual defense treaty with Syria in 1955 that linked Syria and Egypt in the United Arab Republic from 1958 to 1961. In 1956 Egypt signed a five-year military alliance with Saudi Arabia and Yemen. Although Israel had offered friendship to the new Egyptian regime after the officers' coup in July 1952, Nasser and his cronies stalled on any peaceful settlement. The Egyptian government increasingly initiated hostile acts against the Jewish state. Ex-Nazis were invited to participate in Nasser's government, and, ironically, Nasser at the same time became closer to the Soviet Union. In December 1954 Egypt's minister of national guidance, Salah Selim, declared that even if Israel took back all of the Palestinian refugees and gave up Jerusalem, Egypt would never make peace.

Indeed, Egypt began sending terrorist squads through Gaza and into Israel. Approximately fifty terrorist incidents occurred within two months of Selim's statement, and Israel felt forced to send a retaliatory raid into Gaza on February 28, 1955, to stop Egyptian atrocities. Nasser turned to the Russians for enough armaments to (in his words) "destroy Israel." The Arabs gained a six-to-one military armament advantage from the package deal the Soviet Union worked out between Czechoslovakia and Egypt, and even President Dwight Eisenhower remarked to French Prime Minister Guy Mollet that fewer than 2 million Jews stood little chance against 40 million Arabs. On October 31, 1955, Israel appealed to the Soviet Union not to foster a new war in the Middle East by arming the Arab states. The cries of the Jewish state fell on deaf ears within a determined Soviet leadership.

The Western powers, however, soon became alarmed at the shift in the balance of power in the Middle East, the Russian involvement, and the radical Arab nationalism that grew stronger each day. Egypt had blocked Israeli ships from using the Suez Canal, and the French and British knew that Nasser could use this ploy on any nation. Indeed, the Egyptian president "nationalized" the Suez Canal on July 27, 1956, and imposed martial law there. Nasser also began to fortify the Straits of Tiran in an effort to cut off Israel's access to the Red Sea. The Egyptian leader also brought the Syrians and Jordanians into joint military command. When the British tried to threaten Nasser with talk of their Arab Legion commanders in Jordan, he was able to gloat that King Hussein had just exiled all of the British commanders from Jordan. Nasser bragged that Egypt was the last hope of the Arab world to "regain their stolen land" and to "destroy" the Jewish state.

As the French and British mobilized their forces against Egypt and compared Nasser to Adolf Hitler, Israel was being harrassed by the "Hitler on the Nile." Nasser had stepped up his attacks on civilians, killing more Israeli women and children to fulfill his promise to "be strong in order to regain the rights of the Palestinians by force." To the delight of and with backing from the Anglo-French forces (and to the chagrin of the United States and the Soviet Union), Israel launched Operation Kadesh even as Nasser built up his forces for the "final" Arab conflict with Israel.

This campaign lasted only eight days (October 29-November 5, 1956), as Israeli forces moved across the Sinai in a multipronged attack. They outflanked Egyptian divisions and gained air superiority. In fact, the Israeli armor prevented the Egyptians from making a systematic retreat (although Nasser's forces fought desperately to do so). The British and French compelled Israeli forces to stop ten miles from the Suez Canal. The Israel Defense Forces (IDF) lost 171 men and had several hundred wounded. The Egyptians had several thousand dead and wounded. Six thousand Egyptians were taken prisoner with all of their armaments.

Israel finally had a buffer zone between herself and Nasser's Egypt. The IDF had captured the Gaza and much of the Sinai. Arab terrorism would be much more difficult to insititute. However, in the U.N. Security Council the United States and the Soviet Union joined forces to coerce an Israeli withdrawal. Israel only evacuated the territory, however, with the assurance that troops of the United Nations Emergency Force (UNEF) would be posted on the Egyptian side of the border to protect Israel against terrorist attack. The UNEF was also posted at Sharm el-Sheik to guarantee Israel's right to send ships through the Straits of Tiran.

Israel trusted the United Nations once again and gave back conquered territory in the hope of promised peace. Learning the lessons of Arab perfidy in the 1948-49 armistice negotiations that were supposed to result in a lasting peace, however, the Israeli government stated unequivocally that any Egyptian deviation from the U.N. arrangements would result in war. The U.N. assured Israel that such changes would not occur. Characteristically, by May 1967 Gamal Abdel Nasser felt strong enough to prepare to attack Israel again. He dismissed the UNEF troops and blocked Israeli shipping. In doing so, he brought upon the Egyptian people and the Arab world a fateful day. The resulting Six-Day War would revamp the political, economic, and social patterns of the Middle East, while further complicating the Palestinian refugee problem.

THE 1967 SIX-DAY WAR

Israel was prepared for the worst in the spring of 1967. While Nasser was involved in escapades throughout the Arab world (most notably in the civil war in Yemen—see chapter 8), he had continued to fan the flames of Arab hatred of Israel. He declared of Israel in 1962 his people's "determination to liquidate one of the most dangerous enclaves opposing the struggle of our peoples." He was joined by politicians, teachers, and journalists throughout the Arab world. In 1964 Arab leaders decided at their summit conferences to disrupt Israel's water supply by diverting the headwaters of the Jordan River. The same year the Palestine Liberation Organization (PLO) was established to eradicate the Jewish state from an Arab Middle East.

Israel celebrated her nineteenth Independence Day on May 15, 1967. In compliance with the 1949 armistice agreement with Jordan, aircraft and artillery were excluded from the parades. Just four days after that observance, Nasser asked the United Nations' forces to withdraw from the region. They quickly abandoned a decade of peacekeeping on Israel's southern frontier. On May 22, Nasser closed the Strait of Tiran to Israeli ships, and both the United States and Israel issued strong protests against the Egyptian provocation. On May 27, the Israeli government made one more attempt to avert war through negotiations and diplomacy, but the Arab armies were building up all around the Jewish state. On May 30, King Hussein of Jordan placed his forces under Nasser's command, and Saudi Arabia and Iraq sent forces to join the Egyptians in Jordan to the west of Israel. Algeria and Kuwait sent troops to fight alongside the Egyptians on Israel's southern border. The Syrians massed on the Golan Heights to the north. On June 3, Radio Cairo quoted an order by the commander of the Egyptian forces in the Sinai, General Murtaji, proclaiming their impending and unified Arab attack as "the Holy War through which you will restore the rights of the Arabs which have been stolen in Palestine and reconquer the plundered soil of Palestine." On June 4, Iraq put its forces under the general command of the Egyptians.

On the morning of June 5, Israel once again begged King Hussein of Jordan not to join in the attack. He was assured that Israel had no desire to fight him and that if he remained peaceful he would not be attacked. The "moderate" Jordanian monarch, however, saw the opportunity for a pan-Arab victory. Almost immediately his forces began firing across their 1949 armistice lines with Israel, indiscriminately shelling the Jewish quarter of Jerusalem.

That very morning, June 5, 1967, Israel launched a surprise attack against her Arab challengers. Within three hours the Israeli air force had destroyed 452 Arab planes, 391 of them still parked or taxiing on the airfields of Egypt, Jordan, Syria, and Iraq. In brilliant tank maneuvers, Israeli commanders pierced through the "indomitable" Egyptian coalition forces on the Negev border and in the Sinai. By the third day of fighting, Israeli forces had encircled the Egyptian forces and had blocked all avenues of escape. By the evening of June 8, the Israelis had reached the Suez Canal and were moving south along the eastern shore of the Gulf of Suez. They destroyed more than 400 Egyptian tanks, killed more than 10,000 Egyptian soldiers, and took 12,000 prisoners of war in the Sinai. Gamal Abdel Nasser had lost the Gaza and the Sinai once again.

To the north and west, Israel's garrison on Mount Scopus held on in a valiant effort until relief forces arrived on June 6. By that time all of the territory around Jerusalem had been taken from the Jordanian forces, and by June 7 Israel was in control of Bethlehem, Jericho, Nablus, and Ramallah. A paratroop unit broke through Jordanian forces in East Jerusalem. Fierce hand-to-hand combat ensued, because the Israelis did not want to damage the holy places. By evening the Old City was in Israeli hands, as well as all of the West Bank. Israeli Prime Minister Levi Eshkol assured the appropriate religious communities that their holy places would remain under the control of their religious orders, and the Wailing Wall was once again open to Jewish visits. Defense Minister Moshe Dayan declared from the Old City: "We have unified Jerusalem, the divided capital of Israel. We have returned to the holiest of our holy places never to depart from it again." The nineteen-year-old barriers of wire and mines that separated East and West Jerusalem were removed, and the population of the Holy City (195,000 Jews, 54,000 Muslims, and 12,000 Arab Christians) now was free to travel the entire urban area.

Through greed, miscalculation, and hatred, King Hussein had lost his grandfather Abdullah's prized Jordanian conquests. East Jerusalem and the West Bank, which had been claimed by Jordan in the 1949 armistice, were now occupied by the Israelis. After this latest war, King Hussein would visit the capitals of the world, posing as a minister of peace in the Middle East. As so often has occurred in the four decades of his rule, many world leaders and many Israelis believed that his influence might promote a lasting peace. Never able completely to quell his hatred, greed, and opportunistic ways, however, King Hussein was by December 1968 calling upon Egypt, Saudi Arabia, Iran, Kuwait, and Lebanon to unify in a fight against Israel "to liberate Arab lands."

During the first three days of the war, the Syrians had shelled the Israeli forces and civilians in Galilee mercilessly and without discrimination. With the Egyptians taken care of, the Israeli air force began to pound the Syrian artillery positions. At the same time Israeli infantry and armor attacked. By June 10, the sixth day, Israeli forces were on their way to Damascus. Terrified and demoralized, Egypt, Jordan, Iraq, Lebanon, and Syria quickly accepted the cease-fire resolutions passed by the United Nations Security Council during the war. Israel accepted a cease-fire as well. Syria signed a cease-fire agreement with Israel on June 11 (although the Syrians would remain the most intransigent against the idea of a peace treaty with Israel). Most of the world believed that David had once again defeated Goliath. When the Soviet Union sponsored a proposal in the Security Council on June 14 to condemn Israel, the proposal was immediately rejected. The General Assembly also turned down three subsequent condemnations.

In what became known as the Six-Day War, Israel lost 777 soldiers and had 2,586 wounded. The Arabs, however, lost approximately 15,000 men. The Israelis had decimated the Arab air forces and had destroyed hundreds of Arab tanks. At Israel's nineteenth anniversary the month before, Israelis could not go to the Wailing Wall, had Syrian guns pointed at them in Galilee from the Golan Heights, were in danger of losing access to the Red Sea, and could not use planes and heavy artillery in a military parade. Now Israel controlled the Golan Heights, held all of Jerusalem, had captured the West Bank, had driven Egypt from the Gaza Strip, and totally occupied the Sinai Peninsula. Incredibly, Israel held nearly 26,500 square miles of territory that was previously under Arab control.

The Israelis were certain that now they could trade land for lasting peace. Certainly, they rationalized, they had captured areas for which the Arab nations would have to negotiate. Although a few areas (such as Jerusalem) were nonnegotiable, all other areas were open for discussion. Israeli citizens rushed to view the sites and towns throughout the West Bank, Gaza, and Sinai because they were certain that Israel would not hold them for long and that Arab leaders would be "telephoning" for a lasting peace. On June 12, Israel announced that she would not withdraw to the 1949 armistice boundaries as she had done in 1956 and declared that the Arab states should pursue direct negotiations with the Jewish state. On July 19, Israel told the General Assembly of the United Nations that the Arab states must recognize Israel's "statehood, sovereignty and international rights" before peace talks could begin. Formal acceptance of Israel's right to exist and a peace treaty were high on the Israeli agenda.

On November 22, 1967, the U.N. Security Council unanimously adopted the British-sponsored Resolution 242 that guaranteed "the sovereignty, territorial integrity and political independence" of every state in the Middle East. In both this resolution and the following Resolution 338 (adopted October 22, 1973, during the Yom Kippur War),

Israel was asked to withdraw from occupied territories only after Arab hostility had abated and Israel's Arab neighbors had recognized the existence and integrity of the Jewish state. It is important to note that in both cases a number of resolutions had been defeated that called for Israel's withdrawal first. Today, Arab leaders quote both resolutions while conveniently forgetting or reinterpreting their history.

Indeed, the Arabs would not negotiate to recognize Israel's existence. They blamed their defeat in the Six-Day War on the poor leadership of certain military commanders and because of a conspiracy against them by Western powers. The Arabs adopted the view that they would return to fight the "Zionist enemy" another day. As the Arab heads of state met at Khartoum August 29–September 1, 1967, Gamal Abdel Nasser guided them to declare the three "no" points: no peace with Israel; no negotiations with Israel; no recognition of Israel. The other point of the Khartoum Declaration again used the Palestinian people as pawns and called for "maintenance of the rights of the Palestinian people in their nation." The territory for the Palestinian nation was presumably Israel. The results of the Khartoum meeting were the first hints to the Israeli government that the Jewish state was not about to receive the hoped-for "telephone call of peace" from the Arab nations. When Anwar Sadat would initiate such a call in the latter 1970s, he was promptly shunned by other Arab states and soon was assassinated (see chapter 4).

In Israel's newly acquired "territories," Arab terrorist organizations (often using U.N. funds designated for humanitarian causes, as well as funds from other Arab states) stepped up their opposition to the Israeli government. Many times the PLO and other groups would kill their own people who sought to negotiate with the Israelis. Hundreds of Arabs were murdered by other Arabs because they were thought to be "collaborators." Fittingly, it was a relative of the Grand Mufti of Jerusalem who led the Fatah terrorist branch of the PLO in these attacks: Yasser Arafat. He had dropped the al-Husseini from his name to obscure his connection with his notorious fascist relative. Arafat also pretended to be a native Palestinian. Terrorism, like neo-Naziism, would take on a new face and a new tactical approach in the 1970s and 1980s. In this post-war, restructured Arab world, however, old agendas (though obscured) would remain the same.

The devastating loss to Israel in the Six-Day War underscored to the conglomerate of Arab states that their passion, arms, unity, and numbers were insufficient to overcome the military capabilities of the

Israelis. There was much soul searching in the Arab world, and disappointment gave way to outrage among the general Arab population. As will be seen in chapters 4-8, the shock of defeat shattered existing governments, Arab blocs, and coalitions, generally altering the face of the Arab world. Tensions began to flare all the more between Arab leaders. The general public of most Arab nations believed it was a time for change in the old regimes. There is little doubt that the results of the Six-Day War violently toppled or bloodlessly changed a number of regimes.

For example, Egypt's Nasser offered his resignation shortly after the war. Although it was rejected, he never recovered from his defeat at the hands of the Israelis and died a shattered man in 1970 at the age of fifty-two. Anwar Sadat became president of Egypt, and Hosni Mubarak, the current president, was Sadat's vice-president. King Hussein of Jordan remained in power but had to avoid a series of assassination attempts. He violently put down a Palestinian revolt in September 1970. Iraq underwent a military coup on July 17, 1968, that brought Ahmed Hassan al-Bakr and the Ba'ath Party to power. His vice-president was Saddam Hussein. The Ba'ath Party has held a stranglehold on the nation of Iraq ever since.

Another faction of the Ba'ath Party also took control of Syria. The current leader of Syria, Hafez al-Assad, seized power on March 13, 1971. Libya's King Idris was overthrown by the current leader, Muammar al-Qaddafi, and his Revolutionary Command Council on September 1, 1969. Qaddafi had himself appointed premier and defense minister of Libya on January 16, 1970. The changes also touched Saudi Arabia when on March 25, 1975, King Faisal was shot to death by his nephew. Prince Fahd of the Saudi dynasty became king. Furthermore, by this time, Lebanon was entering the throes of a bloody Christian-Muslim confrontation that would eventually destroy the country.

Israel, too, was not exempt from political change following the 1967 war. Golda Meir, the woman who had raised funds for arms in 1948 and had tried to convince King Hussein's grandfather Abdullah not to enter the war, became the first female prime minister in the modern Middle East on March 7, 1969. She would face the catastrophe of the 1973 Yom Kippur War, a debacle that would eventually bring down her Labor government, eradicate the premise of Israel's invincibility, and encourage further radical Arab propaganda and terrorism.

Continued superpower involvement in the region and the rise of a new brand of petroleum politics would further restructure the Arab world and the fabric of the Middle East in the 1970s.

SUPERPOWER INVOLVEMENT AND THE POLITICS OF OIL

On June 10, 1967, the Soviet Union severed diplomatic relations with Israel. The Soviets promised to help the Arab nations if Israel refused to withdraw from conquered territory. On June 19 at the United Nations, Soviet Premier Alexei Kosygin called once again for condemnation of Israel and (unbelievably) asked that Israel be forced to pay Egypt, Jordan, and Syria for damage to their armies and lands during the Six-Day War. He and the Arab representatives insisted that Israel go back to its pre-1949 boundaries.

Soviet involvement in the Middle East after World War II had been as pragmatic toward an ultimate Communist conquest of the world as it had been in other areas around the globe. As we have seen, the Soviet Union actually supported Israel in the United Nations in the late 1940s. The Soviets appear to have wanted British influence in the Middle East to wane and to have wanted to be a part of subsequent agreements. By the 1950s, Soviet leaders sounded indecisive toward the Middle East and began to use more neutral language in regard to Israel.

Soon, however, the Soviets began to forge an alliance with Nasser's regime. In alliance with Egypt they opposed the Baghdad Pact, a mutual defense treaty signed by Britain, Iraq, Pakistan, Turkey, and Iran. Iraq signed the treaty on February 24, 1955, over Egypt's protests, while the Soviet Union warned Iran that the Shah's intention to join was incompatible with peace in the Middle East. Iran ignored the Soviet protest and joined on November 3, 1955.

Soviet premier Nikita Khrushchev upset the balance of power in the Middle East by arranging huge armament sales to Egypt in the mid-1950s. Israel requested a comparable arms deal from the United States on October 11, 1955. In an apparent effort to stall American involvement, the Soviets made it appear for a time that they might also be willing to sell arms to Israel. The deception held off the United States (Secretary of State John Foster Dulles suggesting on February 6, 1956, that Israel look for security in the United Nations), but France seemed to sense the impending danger and later provided arms for Israel. Although not excluding the possibility that American arms might some day be forthcoming, Dulles explained that the United States refused to arm Israel because she did not want an American-Soviet confrontation in the Middle East. Khrushchev, however, had chosen sides, and would confront the U.S. on a number of fronts (including the Middle East).

From this time forward, the ties between the Soviet Union and the Arab states were strengthened by a constant flow of Soviet arms to Arab regimes and a constant pro-Arab stance by the Soviets in the United Nations. As the Cold War escalated with the West, the Soviet Union had chosen the Arab coalition as one of her protégés. Soon, any anti-Israel proposal in the United Nations was supported uncritically by the Soviet Union. By the early 1960s, Khrushchev's regime was an established major player in Middle East politics.

The Soviet involvement in the Middle East forced the United States to become involved as well. The United States worked behind the scenes during the 1956 Suez Crisis and its aftermath. By the end of 1956, Secretary of State Dulles was talking about the United States's "major responsibility" to prevent Soviet expansionism in the Middle East, which policy became more formally spelled out in the so-called Eisenhower Doctrine. The ambassador from Syria promptly informed Dulles that the Arab states would not welcome such American "protection" against the Soviets. However, on January 21, 1957, the four Muslim nations of the Baghdad Pact endorsed the Eisenhower Doctrine, and King Saud of Saudi Arabia soon lent his approval as well. On March 22, 1957, the United States announced that it would join the military committee of the Baghdad Pact and by summer had extended $10 million in military aid to Jordan in response to King Hussein's rift with Syria and Egypt. The superpowers were destined to clash over the Middle East as they clashed over other areas of the world during the 1950s.

The 1967 Six-Day War was the turning point for the Soviet Union's involvement in Middle Eastern affairs. As the United States evolved into a prominent player in negotiations and dialogue in the Middle East, the Soviet Union made strategic miscalculations and systematically removed herself from many areas of the diplomatic arena. The Soviets had encouraged intensified PLO attacks against Israel, had fostered anti-Israel and anti-Jewish hatred, had supported Nasser in his inflammatory rhetoric, had provided huge arms buildups in Egypt and other Arab states, and had stifled the U.N.'s diplomatic attempts to de-escalate the pre-1967 madness. When Egypt and her allies attacked the Jewish state, the Soviets did not come to the aid of the Arabs and were unable to regroup on the diplomatic scene.

Every consequence of the 1967 war was grim for the Soviet leadership, and for twenty years after it can be said without qualification that the Soviets' only option was to play the spoiler, a purely negative role in the Middle East. Their only option was to keep supplying arms, and they were at the mercy of those Arab states who decided to remove Soviet advisers from their countries. The Soviets found that Arabs were not inclined to convert en masse to Marxist-Leninism. More important, by impulsively breaking diplomatic relations with Israel, the Soviets removed themselves from the international game plan with regard to the Middle East. That was the Communists' biggest mistake in 1967. The Arabs were thoroughly disillusioned with their superpower patron.

In contrast, the United States continued contact, directly or indirectly, with all parties involved in the Middle East. The Soviets only now are beginning to regroup. Recent Soviet moves to allow its Jewish population to emigrate to Israel, to try to lead Arab states toward a peaceful solution, to begin reestablishing formal relations with Israel, and to attempt to negotiate a truce before the ground phase of the 1991 Persian Gulf War erupted underscore the Soviet Union's desperate attempt to reenter the Middle Eastern diplomatic arena. Yet the Soviets provided no troops in the Gulf War and are dependent on President George Bush's statements that the Soviet Union "may well play a positive role" in the fabric of Middle East politics. As we shall discuss in chapter 8, the Gulf War victory enhanced the United States' involvement and presence in what appears to be a new restructuring of the Middle East.

In 1951 the Arab League established a system that attempted to boycott Israel and threaten the Jewish state's economic development. A "blacklist" of companies that dealt with Israel was kept, and those companies were to be shunned when Arab contracts were assigned. In some cases Western companies that dared to deal with blacklisted companies were boycotted as well. Commercial ventures that included potential Zionists or Zionist sympathizers were to be avoided in the Arab marketing scheme. Iraq, Syria, Kuwait, and Saudi Arabia formed their own boycott offices and maintained their official blacklists on the national level. Western companies were soon informed that they were not welcome to trade with the Arab states of the Middle East if they appeared on any official blacklist, shipped goods of Israeli origin, had a manufacturing plant or branch office in Israel, or used technical information patented in Israel.

Scant attention was paid to such boycotts in the West until the Arab oil producers initiated an oil embargo aimed at hurting Western nations who had dealings with Israel. In the wake of the 1973 Yom Kippur War, the Saudis led a coalition of oil states in an attempt to use oil as a weapon. In October of 1973, Arab governments cut oil production and embargoed oil to the United States. Immediately, the price of oil quadrupled. Soon industrial countries sank into recession, developing countries (without oil reserves) staggered in debt, and oil-rich countries were flooded with billions of dollars. For example, Saudi Arabia controlled a vital oil reserve and by 1977 had accumulated $150 billion in available assets. Such a massive transfer of wealth shifted economic power to once-nomadic desert princes. The Arab world had finally achieved a goal it had envisioned for more than two decades.

In the 1950s the Arab states came to realize the importance of maintaining the market price of oil. Western petroleum companies controlled Arab oil fields and at times had reduced the price of crude oil without consulting the Middle Eastern producers. In September 1960 the world's five largest oil exporting nations (Iraq, Kuwait, Saudi Arabia, Iran, and Venezuela) established the Organization of Petroleum Exporting Countries (OPEC). They were determined to keep falling oil prices from bottoming out and further reducing their revenues. OPEC's plan was to control production in an effort to stabilize price levels and oil income. By 1974 OPEC also included Algeria, Ecuador, Indonesia, Libya, Nigeria, Qatar, and the United Arab Emirates.

During the 1967 Six-Day War, Arab OPEC members attempted to use oil as a political weapon. Within the first two days of fighting, every major Arab oil producer (except Algeria) completely shut down production. The international oil market, however, turned to other producers for relief, including the United States, Venezuela, and Indonesia. The Arabs soon began to break ranks, and individual Arab oil-producing nations hurried to regain their share of the market. Saudi Arabia, in fact, held the key to a successful boycott, because the Saudi dynasty was the top Middle East oil producer. Saudi Arabia contained one-fourth of the non-Communist world's oil reserves. However, the Saudis only reluctantly joined the 1967 boycott at Nasser's urging, and they never seemed to enforce their part of the embargo strictly.

Even the Saudis realized, however, that an embargo could be an effective tool in the future if international oil consumption increased and if Arab producers stuck together. Early in 1968, Saudi Arabia, Kuwait, and Libya formed another group called OAPEC (Organization of Arab Petroleum Exporting Countries). By 1974, OAPEC also included Algeria, Bahrain, Egypt, Iraq, Qatar, Syria, and the United Arab Emirates.

The 1973 Yom Kippur War

The ominous events of 1973 brought an effective oil embargo to fruition. Sadat had become president of Egypt upon the death of his old friend Nasser. The new president began a process of "de-Nasserization" within Egypt, from the economy to political organization and control. On the international scene, he decisively stalled what on the surface appeared to be negotiations for peace by shrewdly refusing to negotiate with the Israelis until they withdrew to the pre-1967 war boundaries. Secretly, Sadat was coordinating a surprise attack against Israel with his Syrian counterpart, Hafez Assad.

On Yom Kippur (October 6, 1973), the holiest day of the Jewish calendar, Egypt and Syria carried out a surprise attack on the unsuspecting state of Israel. Five hundred Israeli defenders along the Suez Canal were attacked by 80,000 Egyptians. On the Golan Heights, 1,400 Syrian tanks assaulted 180 Israeli tanks. During the first two days, Israel suffered heavy casualties as she fought valiantly to mobilize her reservists while simultaneously conducting a defense of the country. Egypt and Syria were delighted with their initial "victory," and nine other Arab states rushed to join the battle. The Soviet Union blocked any U.N. attempt at a cease-fire and refortified the Arab forces with armaments and supplies from the air and the sea.

Jordan's King Hussein sent two of his best armored brigades to Syria. Saudi Arabia and Kuwait financially underwrote the huge cost while also sending thousands of troops to fight the Israelis. Kuwait lent her British-made Lightning jets to Egypt. Libya's Muammar Qaddafi turned over forty French-made Mirage III fighters and 100 tanks. Iraqi MiG fighter jets as well as tank and infantry divisions fought on the Golan Heights, while a squadron of Iraqi Hunter jets were utilized by Egypt. Arabs predicted the extermination of the Jewish state and the "liberation" of Palestine.

Such predictions of Arab victory, however, were premature. The Israeli counterattack drove deep into Syrian and Egyptian positions. The United States belatedly began airlifting supplies to Israel. Because of the growing success of Israel's counteroffensive, the Soviet Union now rushed to the United Nations Security Council to pass a cease-fire proposal. On October 22, 1973, the Security Council passed Resolution 338, calling upon all parties to cease firing and begin implementing in all its parts the 1967 post–Six-Day War Resolution 242. The U.N. also planned for new negotiations that would lead to a just and durable peace in the Middle East.

On November 11, a cease-fire agreement was signed between Egypt and Israel, and on December 21 the Geneva Peace Conference opened with delegates from Egypt, Israel, and Jordan. Syria boycotted the conference and only after three months of artillery duels agreed to a "disengagement" on the Golan Heights on May 29, 1974. The loss of lives in the Yom Kippur War was heavy on both sides. Israel lost 2,552, while an estimated 15,000 Egyptians and 3,500 Syrians were killed. The Arabs claimed victory because of their success in the first two days of the war and because they were able to kill so many Israelis.

As the tide of the Yom Kippur War turned against the Arabs, King Faisal of Saudi Arabia decided that oil must be used as a weapon. He no longer had to fear the dominance of a Nasser, and he despised the Israelis. He had more revenues than he had in 1967 and believed he and other Arab oil producers could cut back on production without crippling their economies. On October 17, 1973, OAPEC members met in Kuwait and agreed to cut oil production by 5 percent a month until Israel withdrew from the territories occupied since 1967 and agreed to respect the rights of the Palestinian refugees. On October 18, Saudi Arabia delivered an ultimatum to the United States to stop supplying Israel with arms and to "modify" its pro-Israel foreign policy. Immediately, the Saudis cut back oil production 10 percent.

President Richard Nixon requested $2.2 billion in emergency security assistance for Israel on October 28, 1973. True to their word, the next day the Saudis suspended all oil exports to the United States. Kuwait, Bahrain, Dubai, and Qatar of the Persian Gulf joined the embargo, completing an economic noose around the American energy system. Within five months, the Arab oil embargo had cost the United States approximately half a million jobs and a gross national budget loss of perhaps $20 billion. From January 1, 1973, to January 1, 1974, the price of Persian crude oil skyrocketed from $2.59 a barrel to $11.65.

By 1982, it had risen to $33.47 a barrel. Although the United States had declared she would never buckle under to such Arab tactics, the oil embargo was the driving force behind Secretary of State Henry Kissinger's immediate "shuttle diplomacy" and, later, President Jimmy Carter's intense negotiation efforts that led to the 1979 Egypt-Israel peace treaty called the Camp David Accords. The United States was compelled to try to find peace among (as well as relief from) the forces of the Middle East.

Any apparent friend of Israel or of the Jewish people was pressured by the Arab oil weapon. The Dutch were embargoed because they had offered aid in transporting Soviet Jews to Israel. Because the Dutch city of Rotterdam was the main port for oil tankers supplying Western Europe, the repercussions of this Arab anger were deeply felt and highly effective. Oil shipments to Canada were cut off, because the Arabs believed some oil might reach the United States through Canadian borders. Britain was put on probation, and France and Spain were exempted because of pro-Arab statements and anti-Israel political sentiment.

Even nations exempted from the embargo were limited in the fourth quarter of 1973 to their buying levels from earlier quarters in the year. Because the fourth quarter is a heavier buying period, the nations of the world were economically pinched. Japan was forced to announce that it was reconsidering its policies toward Israel. For such support from both East and West, the Arabs rewarded nations with an exemption from the further 5 percent cut in December 1973. In the United States, bumper stickers began appearing that declared: "WE NEED OIL—NOT ISRAEL."

Aside from the hundreds of millions of dollars in funds his terrorist organization received from the Saudis, Kuwaitis, and other oil producers, Yasser Arafat and the Palestine Liberation Organization were able to achieve a spectacular victory through the embargo. With the oil weapon at their throats or in their hands, the members of the United Nations General Assembly voted to disregard provisions of the U.N. charter that excluded the representative of a nongovernmental organization from addressing the international body. On November 13, 1974, the descendant of the Grand Mufti of Jerusalem, Yasser Arafat, was escorted to the rostrum of the General Assembly. With a revolver clearly visible in his belt, Arafat told the assembled delegates that he demanded a state for "all of Palestine" and that he could not accept the existence of a Jewish state.

The "plight of the Arab refugees" rhetoric from the 1950s and 1960s now turned to "the legitimate rights of the Palestinians" rhetoric of the 1970s. The U.N. dutifully condemned Zionism as racism in 1975. By the mid-1980s, with a limited moratorium on the oil weapon and with a glut of oil on world markets, the crafty Yasser Arafat would change his strategy to convince the world that he now "recognized" Israel's existence. In the early 1990s, the opportunistic PLO leader would change once again, this time linking his star to the "Butcher of Baghdad," Saddam Hussein.

In 1977, Saddam Hussein of Iraq had his book *Unser Kampf* (*Our Struggle*) published in German. Even the title sent chills through the few who read it because it was strikingly close to Adolf Hitler's *Mein Kampf* (*My Struggle*). In *Our Struggle*, Saddam Hussein defined three goals: (1) to wage war against the West and the "Zionist enemy" in an effort to unite all Arabs; (2) to use the oil weapon to split the ties binding the U.S., Western Europe, and Japan; and (3) to expel the Jews and create a Palestinian state in the place of Israel.

Today, there is more conflict than unity between individual Arab nations. Although most Arabs think and speak of an "Arab Nation" that is greater than themselves, tribal and national loyalty provides a constant tension in the family of Arab states. Even animosity toward the state of Israel cannot serve as the eternal glue to cement them into an Islamic brotherhood. Ironically, if the Jewish state ceased to exist tomorrow, there would be as much fighting and bickering in the Middle East as ever—perhaps even more. Complications arise among Muslims when allegiance to a particular Islamic belief system conflicts with allegiance to another Muslim belief system. Arab Christians are decimated and weakened in the larger Islamic context of the Middle East, yet they constantly strive to please their Muslim brethren. Further aggravating this milieu are the personal agendas and greed of individual leaders in the Arab world. The Saddam Husseins and potential Saddam Husseins of the Middle East coldly calculate their power base and opportunistically lead millions to the brink of catastrophe. Such factors defy Western logic, confounding definitive analyses of the patterns of the Middle East, heightening tensions in a volatile area, and snarling efforts at peace. It is, in fact, doubtful whether any political statement beginning with the words "The Arabs" can have any degree of precision today.

And yet the Arab world stretches before us as an awesome and dynamic specter. Its twenty-one independent, vibrant, sovereign states cover more than 4 million square miles. These Arab states have a population of more than 125 million. Israel is thus dwarfed in population and size by her surrounding Arab neighbors. The historic backgound to current events in the Middle East helps to give one a sense of the strategic importance of this area to the future of the world. A knowledge of the individual twentieth-century history and development of the Middle Eastern nations helps one sort through the rhetoric and the propaganda. Broken promises and crushed treaties abound. Perfidy permeates every turn.

Ironically, Christians and their attitudes toward Jews and Arabs have had a hand in affecting Western perceptions of the heavily Muslim Middle East and its crises. We turn in the next chapter to specifically American Christian attitudes toward Israel and her neighbors—attitudes whose repercussions have resounded throughout the world.

3

CHRISTIAN ATTITUDES TOWARD ISRAEL AND THE MIDDLE EAST

When I meet a Jew," Dwight Lyman Moody (1837-1899) often preached, "I can't help having a profound respect for them, for they are God's people." The most popular and effective evangelist of the late 1800s, D. L. Moody insisted during his meetings that the Jewish people would go back to Palestine one day and be restored to their former kingdom.

When he finally traveled to Ottoman Palestine in 1892, Moody deplored the poverty of the land and the ruins that overwhelmed the once great biblical kingdom. But he also emphasized that according to the prophetic passages of the Bible, the land would be restored even as the Jewish people would be restored. His visit to the Holy Land remained a vivid, living memory in his private conversations as well as in his public discourses.

Dwight L. Moody's emphasis on the prophetic passages of the Bible and the soon "second coming of Christ" was indicative of the growing influence of the premillennial view of the future among conservative evangelicals. This view would become the backbone of the Fundamentalist-Evangelical movement and the heart of the evangelical Christian Zionist movement. And, ironically, it ran counter to the major theological views of the early nineteenth century.

THE CENTURY OF EVANGELICALISM

Although the nineteenth century is considered the century of modern evangelicalism (Episcopalians, Presbyterians, Methodists, Baptists, and Lutherans all called themselves "evangelicals"), a postmillennial view of the future dominated mainline Christian theology. Postmillennialism stated that through the auspices of Protestantism the world would be "Christianized," would become progressively better with Christians initiating the Millennium, a thousand-year era of peace and prosperity. Then, after a final conflict between the forces of good and the forces of evil, the second coming of Jesus Christ would occur (*after* the Millennium; i.e., *post*millennial). At the second coming there would be a general resurrection followed immediately by the final judgment.

The growing premillennialist movement, in contrast, insisted that the world would not be "Christianized" by human means and that only the second coming of Jesus Christ would initiate the Millennium (*before* the Millennium; i.e., *pre*millennial). The world, according to the prophetic passages of the Bible, would actually get worse and worse and a great tribulation would occur prior to the Millennium. The premillennialists did not believe this view was pessimistic but rather was realistic according to the predictions of the Bible.

One of those predictions was that the Jewish people would again return to the Holy Land. Contrary to popular opinion, this prophetic viewpoint combated anti-Semitism and sought to reinstate the biblical promises that God had made to the Jewish people through Abraham— biblical promises that postmillennial Christendom had determined were null and void.

D. L. Moody was surrounded with premillennial Bible and prophecy teachers. The First International Prophetic Conference was held in the Church of the Holy Trinity in New York City, October 30–November 1, 1878. The inspiration for this conference was an earlier 1878 conference that had been held in Mildmay Park, England. The call for the latter conference was signed by 122 bishops, professors, ministers, and "brethren." Some of those who signed would become leaders of the early fundamentalist movement.

The object of this international forum was to stress the premillennial advent of Jesus Christ and to gather those of like mind in discussions on related topics. Bishop William R. Nicholson of the Reformed Episcopal Church in Philadelphia explained to those assembled that he found himself "in the midst of an embarrassment of riches" when it came to proving the restoration of the Jewish people to Palestine. He emphasized that "the regathering of Israel," spoken of in passages such as Ezekiel 36:22-26, "can possibly refer only to the literal Israel, and to

their restoration to Palestine. . . . It is yet in the future." Other prominent speakers concurred.

The Second International Prophetic Conference was held in Far-
well Hall in Chicago, November 16-21, 1886, with many notable ministers and theologians attending (as well as thousands of laypersons).
D. L. Moody was unable to be present because of other engagements,
but he sent written expression of support for the purpose of the conference. Again, leaders such as Nathaniel West, William J. Erdman, Ernst
F. Stroeter, J. S. Kennedy, and Henry M. Parsons made strong statements against anti-Semitism and insisted that the Jewish people would
be restored to their rightful land. Erdman criticized the "conceit" of
Christians who claim that Israel has "as a nation no future of special
blessing and pre-eminence." He noted that even John Calvin erred in
this interpretation and that it was high time that such error was brought
to light.

Such quotations supporting the restoration of the Jewish people to
Palestine and positive attitudes toward Jews are abundant in the history
of the Moody Bible Institute (MBI) of Chicago (quotations abound from
The Institute Tie, The Christian Worker's Magazine, and from the current era of *Moody Monthly* [now *Moody* magazine]). Moody colleagues
were active in the prophecy conference movement.

For example, James M. Gray, former dean and president of MBI,
gave major addresses at a number of the international prophetic conferences, including his address to the Fourth International Prophetic Conference in Boston in 1901. There he explained "the fact that the Jews
will have returned to Jerusalem as yet in an unconverted state with
reference to the Messiah" before the Great Tribulation occurs. The
same year the Moody Correspondence School was initiated at MBI,
and R. A. Torrey, the first superintendent of the Institute, stressed the
same points in one of its first courses on Bible doctrine.

In fact, the Fifth International Prophetic Conference was held at
the Moody Bible Institute just before the outbreak of the First World
War, February 24-27, 1914, and included such stalwarts as Gray, Arno C.
Gaebelein, C. I. Scofield, and William B. Riley. Even Robert McWatty
Russell, president of Westminster College and moderator of the General Assembly of the United Presbyterian Church, was there. In his
address, Russell explained why there was no need for jealousy toward
the Jewish people because of their future restoration and reign.

Christian Zionism

Moody Bible Institute also published Methodist layman William E. Blackstone's classic, *Jesus Is Coming*. Blackstone's study of biblical prophecy led him to a succinct interest in the problems of the Jewish people, and he founded the Chicago Hebrew Mission (he had also been one of those involved in the founding of Moody Bible Institute).

William E. Blackstone (1841-1935) had important political involvement with the restoration attempt. That involvement antedated the political Zionist movement and in 1918 elicited from Elisha M. Friedman, secretary of the University Zionist Society of New York, the following statement: "A well known Christian layman, William E. Blackstone, antedated Theodor Herzl by five years in his advocacy of the re-establishment of a Jewish state."

Indeed, the immigration of Jews to Ottoman Palestine and the rise of Theodor Herzl's political Zionist movement arose at a time when a resurgent emphasis on the second coming of Jesus Christ and premillennial eschatology was gaining a foothold among American Christians (as well as Christians in the British Isles and other areas of the world). After traveling to Europe, Egypt, and Palestine in 1888, Blackstone organized in Chicago in 1890 one of the first conferences between Christians and Jews. The Jews of Russia were being persecuted, and William Blackstone felt that mere resolutions of sympathy were inadequate.

He originated the Blackstone Petition of 1891. It urged the president of the United States, Benjamin Harrison, to influence European governments "to secure the holding, at an early date, of an international conference to consider the condition of the Israelites and their claims to Palestine as their ancient home, and to promote in all other just and proper ways the alleviation of their suffering condition." The petition's opening sentence is bold, asking the question, "What shall be done for the Russian Jews?" It answers: "Why not give Palestine back to them again? According to God's distribution of nations, it is their home, an inalienable possession, from which they were expelled by force. . . . Let us now restore them to the land of which they were so cruelly despoiled by our Roman ancestors."

The petition was signed by 413 outstanding Christian and Jewish leaders in the United States. The signers included Chief Justice Melville W. Fuller of the U.S. Supreme Court; Thomas B. Reed, speaker of the House of Representatives; Ohio Congressman William McKinley, who would later become president; as well as industrialists and bankers, including Cyrus H. McCormick, J. P. Morgan, and John D. Rockefeller.

Blackstone became one of the most knowledgeable experts on mission work and foreign missions (even becoming a missionary to China for a few years upon the death of his wife in 1908). He returned from China to become a trustee of the Milton Stewart Trust Fund, which distributed $6 million for general evangelistic work around the world. Blackstone continued his petition efforts with President Woodrow Wilson and addressed Zionist conferences (including a Zionist mass meeting in Los Angeles, January 27, 1918). In 1916 Blackstone convinced President Wilson's own church governing body, the Presbyterian General Assembly, to endorse Zionist aspirations for a Jewish state in Palestine.

In England during the First World War, Arthur James Balfour (1848-1930), a former prime minister, had been a strong proponent of the restoration of the Jewish people to Palestine. A fervent Christian, Balfour was appointed foreign secretary by Prime Minister David Lloyd George at the end of 1916. From this position he was much more influential as a Christian Zionist. As Christians and Jews lined up on both sides of the proposed British declaration that Palestine would be the national home of the Jewish people, Balfour was able to assure Lloyd George's cabinet that Zionism not only had "the support of a majority of Jews in Russia and America" but that the Christian president of the United States, Woodrow Wilson, "was extremely favourable to the movement."

Born on December 28, 1856, in Staunton, Virginia, Thomas Woodrow Wilson came from primarily Scottish and Presbyterian ancestry. His outlook was conditioned and sustained by his Protestant Christian faith to a greater extent than all but a few other presidents in American history. His maternal grandfather, Thomas Woodrow, for whom he was named, was a Presbyterian minister, as was his uncle, James Woodrow. Woodrow Wilson's father, Joseph R. Wilson, was held in such high regard in Southern denominational circles that the Southern Presbyterian Church was conceived and organized in meetings held in his home and church in Augusta, Georgia. Thus, it was the Georgia Presbyterian manse that molded Woodrow Wilson's mindset during his youth.

Woodrow Wilson had been president of the United States for six years when William E. Blackstone approached him in 1918 with a new memorial on behalf of Jewish restoration to Palestine. Although far from being an eschatologically minded fundamentalist during World War I, President Wilson had undergone some changes of heart concerning the Jewish people and a homeland for them in Palestine. Rabbi Stephen S. Wise had supported Wilson's successful candidacy to become governor of New Jersey. He also worked tirelessly for Wilson's candidacy for the presidency. He was joined by Louis Dembitz Brandeis, a brilliant Boston lawyer who would later be appointed to the Supreme Court. Both of these Jewish friends of Woodrow Wilson were knowledgeable Zionists.

These men were joined by another of Wilson's Jewish appointees, Felix Frankfurter, Harvard Law School professor and legal officer for Wilson's President's Mediation Commission (and a later Supreme Court appointee). They impressed upon the devout Presbyterian president the importance of the Balfour Declaration and the Jewish restoration to Palestine. On May 6, 1917, Brandeis dictated a memorandum in which he noted: "The President assured me that he was entirely sympathetic to the aims of the Zionist movement. . . . Further, the President expressed himself in agreement with the policy, under England's protectorate, for a Jewish homeland."

As we have seen, President Woodrow Wilson's decision to accept the Balfour Declaration was a necessary step to the British issuance of it and a culmination of the efforts of both Jewish and Christian Zionists. President Wilson believed he needed some positive input, because the State Department, some of his cabinet members, and even his most trusted advisers (such as Colonel Edward House) tried to scuttle the issue of such a declaration.

When Colonel House took it upon himself to inform the British on September 10, 1917, that Wilson felt "the time is not opportune" to issue the declaration, Wilson wrote to House (October 13, 1917): "My dear House: I find in my pocket the memorandum you gave me about the Zionist movement. I am afraid I did not say to you that I concurred in the formula suggested from the other side. I do, and would be obliged if you would let them know it." The Balfour Declaration was issued within three weeks.

Pressures soon mounted from Christian missionaries, educators, and archaeologists who worked among the Arabs. American Christians even wrote some of the Arab statements against the proposed Jewish state, while coaching the Arab leaders in anti-Zionist rhetoric. Those Christians used every tactic to change Wilson's mind.

Woodrow Wilson, however, held firm in his support for a Jewish homeland in Palestine and marveled that God had enabled him to be a part in the process. "To think that I, a son of the manse, should be able to help restore the Holy Land to its people," Woodrow Wilson mused near the end of his life. He died on Sunday morning, February 3, 1924. Two decades later, the Jewish people still did not have the homeland in Palestine that the Balfour Declaration had promised and Woodrow Wilson had envisioned.

CHRISTIAN OPPOSITION TO ZIONISM

Even as nearly twenty independent Arab states were on the drawing boards of the European nations, Christian leaders in the West (as well as Christian Arabs in the East) were successful in delaying the founding of the one Jewish state in the Middle East. Many of those Christians outside the premillennial fold did not agree with Christian Zionism, even exhibiting anti-Semitic behavior in their fervency. One reason for their position was that during the nineteenth century Christians in general failed to see any significant part the Jewish people would play in God's plan. They failed to understand why the growing premillennial movement placed any importance on the Jewish people's future restoration to Palestine.

Ernest Sandeen has noted in his classic *The Roots of Fundamentalism* (1970) that a nineteenth-century reviewer for the *Christian Observer* (the voice of the evangelical party in the Church of England) "seemed very much like Alice in Wonderland—stumbling around in an unfamiliar landscape, rather astounded at what he was finding and often quite cross" at the concept of the restoration of the Jews to Palestine.

During the same period, the *Princeton Review* attempted to warn Presbyterian ministers not to be swayed by the doctrine, and the Dutch Reformed *Christian Intelligencer* observed that few Dutch Reformed ministers could accept this view of the Scriptures. *Catholic World* stressed that rather than the Jewish people being restored, they would eventually accept the true faith (Roman Catholicism) and only then could "the captivity of Judah and the captivity of Jerusalem" be ended.

Unfortunately for William E. Blackstone and the persecuted Russian Jews, his 1891 Memorial reached the U.S. State Department while Selah Merrill (1837-1909) was American consul in Jerusalem. An army chaplain for the Union forces during the Civil War, an ordained Congregationalist minister, a doctor of theology, and an appointed archaeologist of the American Palestine Exploration Society, Merrill had no sympathy for Christian eschatological dreams that encompassed Jewish hopes of restoration to Palestine.

Palestine was not ready for the Jews, Merrill declared in his diplomatic reports, and the Jews were not ready for Palestine. The Blackstone Memorial disgusted him, and when queried by the State Department as to its feasibility, Selah Merrill answered that "Turkey was not in the habit of giving away whole provinces for the asking." He also questioned the Jews' ability to govern themselves. "To pour into this impoverished country tens of thousands of Jews would be an unspeakable calamity both for the country and for the Jews themselves," Merrill maintained, scorning the Russian Jews who, he believed, were "unfitted in many important respects" to become part of the proposed Jewish entity.

A thirty-eight-year veteran of the State Department (from 1886-1924), Alvey A. Adee, assistant secretary of state and head of the professional diplomatic service, concurred: "For thirty years and I know not how much longer, Turkey has writhed under the dread of a restoration of the Judean monarchy. Every few months we are asked to negotiate for the cessation of Palestine to the Jewish 'nation.' The whole project is chimerical." The Blackstone Memorial of 1891, a petition to which President Benjamin Harrison in March had promised to give "careful consideration," was scuttled by the end of the year.

In the early decades of the twentieth century, liberal theologians attacked premillennialism along with inerrancy of the Bible. In a 1912 issue of *The American Journal of Theology*, Clarence A. Beckwith, a theology professor at Chicago Theological Seminary, attacked James M. Gray's theology, suggesting that *The Fundamentals* (the twelve-volume series on the essentials of orthodox Christianity published between 1910 and 1915) be "relegated at once to the wastebasket."

By 1918, Shailer Mathews and Shirley Jackson Case of the University of Chicago Divinity School had begun total warfare on the premillennialists. Case viewed the restoration of the Jewish people to Palestine as a picture painted by "afflicted Israelites."

In his book *The Millennial Hope* (1918), he accused premillennialists of being "pessimists" and called premillennial theology "fairy stories." "To be more specific," Case intoned, "it is sheer nonsense to talk dolefully about the gradual deterioration of society to a student of history familiar with the actual course of human development from prehistoric times down to the present. This course of history exhibits one long process of evolving struggle by which humanity as a whole rises constantly higher in the scale of civilization and attainment." Case concluded his book by stating: "The pessimistic philosophy of life which underlies premillennial teaching is especially to be deplored at the present time."

In Mathews's periodical *Biblical World,* Case accused premillennialists of being secret German agents and closet socialists, a diatribe that led a future graduate of the University of Chicago to write that "the Fundamentalists, apparently, never cornered the market on invective." During the same period, *The Christian Century* warned against taking premillennial "propaganda" seriously and had misgivings about the British policy of encouraging "aggressive Jews to claim the country as a 'homeland' for their people." This, of course, was a reference to the Balfour Declaration of 1917.

Even conservative Christian friends of premillennialists, friends who fought side by side with them in the battle to uphold the inerrancy of the Bible, questioned premillennial theology. Theodore Graebner, conservative Lutheran scholar and Concordia Seminary professor, criticized James M. Gray's series of prophetic articles in the *Christian Herald* in 1917, calling premillennialism and support for the Jewish restoration to Palestine "a religious disease." He emphasized that it was a "pity" that "men who are known as Fundamentalists and as firm believers in the verbal inspiration of the Bible" had identified themselves with premillennialism.

That Graebner's message changed little from his book *Prophecy and the War* (1918) to his book *War in the Light of Prophecy* (1941) underscores the conservative opposition against premillennialism during both world wars. "'Crack-brained' is what one is tempted to call their way of reasoning on the war and its relation to the 'days of prophecy,'" the Lutheran theologian declared in his second book. By the end of World War I, most theologians either became premillennialist or amillennialist (no Millennium) because it was apparent that the world was not on its way to postmillennialism's conjectured utopia. Graebner insisted that "we Lutherans are largely amillennialists." Many conservative Reformed theologians were just as critical toward premillennialism and its support of the restoration of the Jewish people to Palestine.

The outbreak of World War I had, however, turned the whole world's attention to prophecy. Fundamentalists-evangelicals were quite upset at the number of supposed "experts" who had jumped on the lecture circuit and, to make money, had published superficial books on prophecy and the war. Yet, although they were horrified at the phenomenon of world war, those conservative theologians understood that world events were confirming their premillennial view and biblical interpretation. They felt vindicated by the headlines that appeared in the daily newspapers.

Moody Bible Institute's *The Christian Worker's Magazine* noted: "WHO ARE THE PESSIMISTS NOW? Premillennialists are charged with pessimism. They resent the charge and contend that they are only taking at face value the Scriptures. . . . But they also look for the harvest, which is the end of the age. . . . Premillennialists have never said such despairing things as are being said today in view of the raging world conflict." A large quote from H. G. Wells in an issue of *The New York Times* of that day illustrated the "doom message" that was also appearing in the secular press.

Tongue in cheek, *The Christian Workers' Magazine* concluded: "Is it not a propitious time to examine the grounds for the unshaken optimism of the premillennialist?" With this issue, the magazine began a special department and segment entitled "Prophecy and the Lord's Return." Arno C. Gaebelein's periodical *Our Hope*, established in 1894, had a "Current Events in Light of the Bible" section since its inception. Evangelical Christians therefore had opportunity to read of current events in the Middle East and around the world while comparing the relevance of prophetic passages in their Bibles.

CHRISTIANS AND ISRAEL

In spite of intense opposition by some Christians to a Jewish state in Palestine, others continued a political and information campaign between the world wars in an effort to force Britain to keep her promise to the Jewish people. With the rise of Naziism, the plight of the Jewish refugees, and the horrors of the Holocaust, those efforts became lifesaving endeavors.

CARL HERMANN VOSS

A young liberal minister, Carl Hermann Voss, was thrust into a pro-Zionist endeavor at the age of thirty-two. Courted by the eminent Congregationalist Zionist Henry A. Atkinson for a position with the Carnegie-endowed Church Peace Union, Carl Voss was asked to assume temporary authority over the newly formed Christian Council on Palestine.

Voss immediately immersed himself in Middle Eastern history and tackled the current conflicts between Arabs and Jews. Contrary to the direction of many liberal Protestant professors, missionaries, ministers, and denominational executives, Voss soon became a committed Christian Zionist, demanding justice for the Jewish people and calling for a Jewish national homeland in Palestine.

He was aided by a January 21, 1943, resolution adopted by the Board of Trustees of the Church Peace Union. This resolution protested the attempt of Adolf Hitler's government to exterminate all the Jews of Europe and insisted "that the United Nations give their immediate thought and attention to the possibilities of Palestine as a present place of refuge for some of the Jews now living in deadly peril."

Carl Hermann Voss was suddenly thrust into a whirlwind of activities on behalf of the Jewish people and the Zionist movement. He found many Christians to be insensitive toward the Jewish plight. This convinced him that Palestine had to become a Jewish national home, because there was no other refuge. He began a mailing campaign to 9,500 prospective members, personally following up on 8,500. By September 1943 the membership rolls of the Christian Council on Palestine had swelled to more than 1,000 who supported a Jewish national homeland in Palestine.

He also spoke to Christian and Jewish groups in places as diverse as Toronto, Denver, Detroit, Cleveland, Chicago, and Omaha. As executive secretary of the Council he gave the Balfour Day address on November 2, 1943, in Cleveland. Voss asserted in part:

> The Arabs today have vast territories—more than a million square miles —a great part of them habitable and capable of development. The Jews have none. Out of the last war the Arab gained freedom and independence for Iraq, Saudi Arabia and later Transjordan, and this in part was due to the insistence of the United States which urged justice for the Arabs, even as it urged justice for the Jews. The Arabs are destined to make new great gains at the conclusion of this conflict, and in no small part they may thank the Jewish soldiers and workers of Palestine, who laid down their lives to help repel Rommel when his tanks were thundering across Egypt. For the Arabs to permit a Jewish State in Palestine, "a tiny notch" in the vast Arab expanse, involves no sacrifice to the Arabs; on the contrary, it provides them with a progressive and democratic neighbor eager to create a joint future in which the hopes of both peoples

may be realized. For the Jews to give up Palestine would be to invite a new calamity for a people whose great misfortune is its homelessness.

Because the organizational headquarters for the Christian Council on Palestine was in New York City, Carl Hermann Voss had heavy administrative and speaking responsibilities there. Soon he had to face anti-Zionist Christians on local and national radio programs and debates.

In 1946 the American Palestine Committee (founded in 1931) combined with Voss's Christian Council on Palestine to form the American Christian Palestine Committee (ACPC). Through Voss's efforts famed theologians Reinhold Neibuhr and Paul Tillich became active members as did a brilliant archaeologist from John Hopkins University, William Foxwell Albright. Professor Tillich was a refugee from Nazi Germany, and he argued that the ACPC should not become too optimistic or complacent. He believed the academic world would increase its antagonism and hostility toward a Jewish state in Palestine. He also warned that the nations of the world would be tempted to bow to political expediency, just as they had bowed to the Nazis in the 1930s. In January 1946, Reinhold Niebuhr of Union Theological Seminary in New York testified before the Anglo-American Committee of Inquiry on Palestine in Washington, D.C. His powerful argument for a Jewish state in Palestine helped to sway the panel members.

It is significant that the president of Union Seminary, Henry Sloan Coffin, was scheduled before the Anglo-American Committee, but withdrew. Coffin was an unswerving anti-Zionist. The ACPC was reminded once again of the fragile nature of the diplomatic effort to bring a Jewish state into being. As anti-Zionist scholars and administrations of the Ivy League and other universities began pressuring the few pro-Zionist professors to back down on their stand on a Jewish homeland, Carl Hermann Voss had to answer questions and combat the latest propaganda ploys. The task was formidable. The Committee for Peace and Justice in the Holy Land, for example, was composed of such well-known pro-Arab supporters as former oil company executive Kermit Roosevelt; Barnard College's dean Virginia Gildersleeve; Yale University's archaeologist Millar Burrows; Harvard University's philosopher William Ernest Hocking; and Harry Emerson Fosdick of Riverside Church in New York.

Because of the Holocaust, many of the anti-Jewish criticisms lacked compassion. Furthermore, in light of the findings of the United Nations Special Committee on Palestine and the U.N. resolution permitting the partition of Palestine, the arguments against a Jewish state from twenty newly born Arab states were unfair. Carl Hermann Voss worked tirelessly to battle State Department animosity toward a Jewish state, met with United Nations representatives, went on international fact-finding tours, and kept close links with congressional committees.

To Voss's great joy the state of Israel was born on May 14, 1948. Under his direction, the ACPC drafted a long statement in June that began: "The American Christian Palestine Committee rejoices that the State of Israel has attained sovereign status and that it received prompt diplomatic recognition by the Government of the United States and many other nations." Calling for early admission of Israel to the United Nations, asking for financial help and security for the fledgling Jewish state, and deploring the "social malady" of anti-Semitism, the ACPC statement concluded with words from Israel's declaration of independence: "With trust in Almighty God, we set our hands to this Declaration."

The ACPC was a unique organization. The cause of a Jewish homeland and justice for the Jewish people had gathered together one of the most unlikely groupings of Christians to be in the same membership. Mostly Protestant in its constituency, the ACPC now encompassed more than 20,000 Christian leaders under its standard. Its small but capable staff sponsored seminars, distributed literature, organized a speakers' bureau, and organized study tours to Arab lands and Israel. Conservative and liberal Christians joined together in the ACPC to politic for the Jewish state. A few Catholic laymen (such as Senator Robert Wagner of New York), Mormons (such as Senator William King of Utah), and prominent international figures (such as Henry Cabot Lodge of Massachusetts) also were members.

In 1951 Carl Hermann Voss traveled to Palestinian Arab refugee camps outside Beirut (Lebanon) and Amman (Jordan). The Palestinian refugees made clear to him that the Arab High Command ordered them out of Palestine during the 1948 war. They said they were told by Arab military officials that the Jews in Palestine would be annihilated within a few weeks and that the Arab Liberation Army did not want to worry about any fellow Arabs getting in the way of such a devastating Arab jihad.

Those Palestinian refugees were bitter at their Arab compatriots who had left them homeless. Little did Voss realize that four decades later he would be reading about the intense hatred harbored toward the Jewish people by the grandchildren and great-grandchildren of those refugees. Millstones of anti-Semitism had been hung by Arab parents on the necks of their children. Accounts of Arab negligence and Arab miscalculation during the 1948 war had been forgotten, having been replaced with stories of Jewish "atrocities."

PROPHETIC PUBLICISTS

The premillennial Christian prophetic movement's positive attitudes and support for the Jewish people and their restoration to the Holy Land is amply documented throughout the twentieth century. After Israel became a state in 1948, the same support was evident and attitudes toward the Middle East situation can be illustrated. For example, *Our Hope* magazine welcomed the new nation with the ten-paragraph excerpt "Israel Becomes a Nation Again."

Although premillennial Bible teacher Arno C. Gaebelein had died in 1945, his son, Frank E. Gaebelein, and his friend E. Schuyler English carried on the premillennial teaching of the periodical. *Our Hope* (July 1948) declared: "The State of Israel, one of the world's oldest sovereignties, became the world's newest sovereignty at midnight on May 15, 1948."

Alerting its readers to the retreat of British High Commissioner Sir Alan Gordon Cunningham, the selection of new premier David Ben-Gurion, the "recognition" by U. S. President Harry S. Truman, and the impending attack by five Arab nations, *Our Hope* exclaimed that "Britain has mystified the world by having disarmed the Jews and armed the Trans-Jordan Arabs." The editors reminded their readers that "there are many Bible references to this restoration." E. Schuyler English concluded in the "Current Events in the Light of the Bible" section: "Observe that in God's sight it is their own land."

The evangelical *Christian Herald*, having a circulation approaching 400,000 in 1948, claimed to be interdenominational and nondenominational. Its editor was Daniel A. Poling, a member of the (Dutch) Reformed Church of America and honorary member of the Ohio Conference of the Evangelical United Brethren Church (his father's church, in which his own ministry had begun). A self-proclaimed "gentle fundamentalist," premillennialist Poling was senior minister of the Baptist Temple in Philadelphia and national co-chairman of the American Christian Palestine Committee.

Answering unequivocally a reader's question in the October 1947 issue, Daniel Poling declared: "I am a Christian Zionist who believes that Palestine should become, as promised, the Jewish state." He never wavered from that position.

In the June 1948 issue, the *Christian Herald* ridiculed the United States for not backing the United Nations plan, and concluded: "What then? Do we just hand Palestine over to the Arabs?" Later, in 1949, the periodical gloried in Israel's victory, asserting that "Israel has made the Arab—and the U.N.—look foolish. Egypt seems to have lost all stomach for the fight." Of England, the *Christian Herald* questioned: "How can she deal with the Jew when she supported the Arabs?"

Throughout the 1940s and 1950s Gabriel Courier interpreted the news for the periodical, including news from the Middle East. During the 1950s he emphasized that the Arab world was in flux and was by no means unified. Violence threatened the Jewish state and world peace at every juncture. In April 1958, in "Furtive Crescent," Courier wrote of Egypt and Syria's merger to form the United Arab Republic, "with Nasser, of course, as President." The Christian news analyst believed that Nasser could not be satisfied with "one bite" and alerted his readers to the fact that Egypt already had ordered the name *Israel* erased from all school maps and replaced by the name *Arab Palestine.*

Such evangelical analysis of the Middle East maze was important. A 1958 survey conducted by Opinion Research Corporation showed that most Protestant clergymen in the United States considered themselves to be either "conservative" (39 percent), "fundamentalist" (35 percent), or "neo-orthodox" (12 percent). Their influence on parishioners during the 1950s should not be underestimated. Fundamentalist-evangelical Billy Graham was an avowed premillennialist, and he gained world stature in the twentieth century comparable to Dwight L. Moody's stature in the nineteenth.

In 1950, Wilbur M. Smith wrote the Moody Correspondence School course "World Crises and the Prophetic Scriptures." On the dedication page he inscribed: "GRATEFULLY DEDICATED to that noble group of interpreters of the oracles of God, C. I. SCOFIELD, R. A. TORREY, JAMES M. GRAY, A. C. GAEBELEIN who, not slow to believe all that the prophets have said, so clearly foresaw the day in which we are now living, and faithfully proclaimed the Blessed Hope." Lesson 7 was "The Reestablishment of Israel in Her Own Land"; Lesson 8 was entitled "At the Center of the Earth—Jerusalem." To Wilbur Smith, God had not only promised the Jewish people Palestine and worked the miracle of their restored state but also would restore Jerusalem to Jewish control.

Later, in a 1960 series for *Moody Monthly,* "Jerusalem in Prophecy," Wilbur Smith declared that the Balfour Declaration could have meant a great deal to the Jewish people, but Britain never carried out her promises. He viewed the 1948 war quite differently from many Ivy League commentators and liberal Christians of the time. Smith explained that this "war for freedom" by the Jews in Palestine "in an almost miraculous way put to flight the Arabs, for whom the most part were occupying the land, and established the State of Israel—one of the most amazing events of modern history."

Writing in *Moody Monthly* (October 1960), Smith made a statement whose fulfillment he would live to see. He wrote: "If some morning we should open our newspapers and read that Israel has taken the old city of Jerusalem, and is able to hold it, we shall know that the words of our Lord have been fulfilled—and when this takes place, we are at the end of the age of the Gentiles."

CHRISTIAN REACTION TO THE 1967 SIX-DAY WAR

Little wonder then that 1967 found evangelical periodicals ablaze with eschatological fervor. The Six-Day War and Israel's victory had thrilled Christian supporters of Israel. The October 1967 issue of *Moody Monthly* featured a cover picture of the Wailing Wall. This special issue on the Bible and prophecy was headlined "The Amazing Rise of Israel!" John F. Walvoord, president of Dallas Theological Seminary, began his article of the same title with these words: "The recent dramatic victory of Israel over the Arab states electrified the entire world. The stunning impact of this war of only sixty hours on the political scene was not only a great setback for Russian designs in the Middle East, but crushed Arab hopes of destroying Israel. For students of the Bible the most significant aspect of the war lies in the fact that Israel, after 1900 years of exclusion from the capital city, Jerusalem, now possesses this holy place so rich in both history and prophecy."

Noting that Israel had been attacked by Arab nations at its inception, Walvoord related to his readers the great gains Israel had made in agriculture and in reclaiming the Holy Land. Other articles on Israel as the depository of divine revelation and Israel in prophecy followed. *Eternity* magazine (which had absorbed *Our Hope*) carried the headline "Israel Is Here to Stay" on its July 1967 cover and featured an article by Raymond Cox, "Eyewitness: Israel." The article had been written a few months before the "current violence," but the editors explained that they found it "more timely than ever." In light of the Arabs' stock-piling armaments for an attack on Israel, Cox noted that "many wonder whether Israel can survive a united assault." He, however, believed that "this is more a prophetic question than a military question . . . Israel will survive."

The following issue of *Eternity* was dedicated totally to evangelical-Jewish relations, and the Arab-Israeli war and Bible prophecy. The theme was "Loving one's neighbor as oneself." The editors had planned this special issue more than a year before in cooperation with the American Jewish Committee. And yet, the events of the Six-Day War had to be analyzed. The major article in this issue that concerned itself with the Six-Day War was written by William Sanford LaSor, professor of Old Testament at Fuller Theological Seminary.

Professor LaSor began his article by emphasizing that he was "not willing to concede that the State of Israel is to be identified as the Israel described in Holy Scripture," but he was "willing to admit that it seems quite likely that the regathering of the Jews to Palestine, the establishment of the State of Israel, and the almost incredible military successes of Israeli armies against what appeared to be overwhelming odds, are somehow to be related to God's promises."

Admitting that "it is probably true that most Evangelical Christians are more sympathetic to the Israeli than to the Arabic side of the continuing conflict," LaSor implored evangelicals not to forget "that a large number of Arabs are Christians" and "a vast number of Arabs are now wanderers on the face of the earth, and they, too, deserve a place to call home." LaSor, who interacted and lived in the Arab world and traveled widely in the Middle East, explained to his evangelical community that "only one who has lived in the Arab world and has talked intimately with Arabs knows how deep are the wounds caused by the formation of the State of Israel."

He related the extreme difficulty of using the Old Testament with its passages on Zion in a Christian service in the Arab world. "If you ask an Arab Christian what solution he has to offer to the present problem," LaSor noted with all candor, "you will get the same answer you get from a non-Christian Arab: Israel must be effaced, every Jew must be driven into the sea." From LaSor's blunt comment, one understands a crucial concept in the Middle East maze today—hatred by Christian Arabs for Jews and the Jewish state runs as deep as it does among Muslim Arabs. Periodicals and analysts who believe they are receiving an unbiased "Christian" perspective on the problems of the Middle East because they are in touch with Christian Arabs of their denomination or theological persuasion need to use extreme caution. Missionaries from the West who work among Arabs often become unwitting accomplices in spreading anti-Israel propaganda and deceit. Lest one seem to be too harsh toward such missionaries, consider that even hardened news reporters working the beat in an Arab country soon learn that their sources dry up if their reports appear to be too harsh on the Arabs or too lenient toward the Israelis.

A good example of how this process has worked historically in evangelicalism can be found in some of the 1967 issues of *Christianity Today*. Like their liberal Christian colleagues, evangelicals also could succumb to anti-Zionist rhetoric. During 1967, *Christianity Today* received most of its information on the Arab-Israeli situation from its correspondent Dwight L. Baker, chairman of the Baptist Convention in Israel. Pastor Baker was concerned that the position of missionaries in Arab nations was becoming "more dangerous" because of the Israeli victory in the Six-Day War. The views of Harry W. Genet, assistant executive secretary of the Arabic Literature Mission in Beirut, were also included in the July 7, 1967, issue, as Genet related that the "slender missionary force in the Arab world" was experiencing "the hardening Arab attitude toward foreigners."

The next issue of *Christianity Today* (July 21, 1967) contained a diatribe against Israel by James L. Kelso, former moderator of the United Presbyterian Church. So volatile and biased were his statements that the editors had to label Kelso's remarks an "interpretive appraisal of the Arab-Jewish conflict." Next to missionaries, Christian archaeologists (with notable exceptions, such as William Foxwell Albright) had been progenitors of the anti-Israel rhetoric, in both liberal and conservative circles. Kelso worked among Arabs for forty-one years and had participated in a number of archaeological expeditions in Palestine. While the world marveled that Israel had protected the holy sites by fighting hand to hand in Old Jerusalem, Kelso complained:

> How did Israel respect church property in the fighting a few weeks ago? They shot up the Episcopal cathedral just as they had done in 1948. They smashed down the Episcopal school for boys so their tanks could get through to Arab Jerusalem. The Israelis wrecked and looted the YMCA upon which the Arab refugees had bestowed so much loving handcraft. They wrecked the big Lutheran hospital, even though this hospital was used by the United Nations. The hospital had just added a new chil-

dren's center and a new research department. The Lutheran center for cripples also suffered. At Ramallah, a Christian city near Jerusalem, the Episcopal girls' school was shot up, and some of the girls were killed. So significant was this third Jewish war against Arabs that one of the finest missionaries of the Near East called it "perhaps the most serious setback that Christendom has had since the fall of Constantinople in 1453."

Kelso then went on to blame the Balfour Declaration as "the major cause of the three wars whereby the Jews have stolen so much of Palestine from the Arabs who have owned it for centuries." He expounded on the Arab refugee problem, the mothers and babies that he saw suffering in the camps "in the bitterly cold winter of 1949-1950," interjecting that "Mary and Christ received better treatment at Bethlehem than the Arab refugees did that winter."

That Kelso's interpretation of Middle Eastern history is biased and his analysis is prejudiced by years of bitterness is quite evident. That *Christianity Today* would publish such comments during Gamal Abdel Nasser's aggression and Israel's world popularity concerning the events of the Six-Day War and the aggression of so many Arab armies is enlightening. The bombardment of anti-Israel rhetoric and Arab propaganda that seems to be assailing evangelicalism in the 1990s is actually not new—it is just having more of an effect than it did in the past.

James Kelso, however, took an additional dangerous step in his article—a reasoning that has come to dominate both liberal and conservative Christian arguments against Israel. "How can a Christian applaud the murder of a brother Christian by Zionist Jews?" Kelso intoned, "The Arab church is as truly the body of Christ as the American church." Either in blatant denouncement or a secretive whisper, the anti-Israel argument took the form of anti-Jewish thought, that is, How can you support the non-Christian Jew against your Arab Christian brother? More often than not, this was blatant anti-Semitism.

A few *Christianity Today* readers responded that Kelso's statements were "contrary to the facts" and that they believed it was time Christians spoke out "on behalf of Israel." The following year, William Culbertson, then president of Moody Bible Institute, wrote an article for *Christianity Today* (June 7, 1968) that supported the Jewish restoration to the land of Israel by citing relevant biblical passages. A premillennialist, Culbertson was a former bishop of the New York and Philadelphia Synod of the Reformed Episcopal Church.

Culbertson mentioned the Arab refugee problem at the end of his article, declaring that his "heart" went out to them. But inasmuch as "Israel had incorporated hundreds of thousands of refugees" into its economic and social life, he asked: "Why have not Arab countries (especially those rich in oil) done more to help their own?" The editors of *Christianity Today* published a fifteen-point response by Kelso. Again, Kelso reminded *Christianity Today*'s readers that "10 percent of the Arab population is Christian."

Not only was there a diversity in Christian attitudes in conservative circles, but among liberal Christians attitudes also varied toward Israel and the Six-Day War. Anti-Zionist Henry P. Van Dusen, past president of Union Theological Seminary, called the Israeli victory in the Six-Day War "the most violent, ruthless (and successful!) aggression since Hitler's blitzkrieg across Western Europe." Van Dusen argued that "every square mile of Arab homeland appropriated by Israel, every additional Arab subjugated or driven into exile, will merely exacerbate the smoldering resolve for revenge." The *Christian Century* called for joint administration by Israeli and Jordanian forces, whereas the National Council of Churches favored an "international presence" to guarantee the holy sites and security. *Christianity Today* reported these opinions in its June 7, 1968, article "Perspectives on Arab-Israeli Tensions."

In May 1967, Martin Luther King, Jr., joined seven other prominent Christian clergymen, including Franklin Littell (professor of religion at Temple University), Reinhold Niebuhr, and John Sheerin (editor of the *Catholic World*), in issuing a statement urging all Americans to "support the independence, integrity and freedom of Israel in the current crisis." These clergymen declared that "men of conscience must not remain silent at this time" and warned that the Egyptian blockade of the Straits of Tiran "may lead to a major conflagration."

Shortly before he was assassinated in 1968, Dr. King made his definitive statement on Israel at a meeting before the Conservative rabbis' Rabbinical Assembly at Kiamesha Lake, New York. He spoke of Israel as a democratic force in the Middle East, as a creative factor in the life of Jewry, and as a potent force for good Jewish-Christian relations. These assertions King firmly believed and resoundingly affirmed.

Reinhold Niebuhr graced the pages of *Christianity and Crisis* (June 26, 1967) with his famous article "David and Goliath." Niebuhr had founded the journal in 1940, but by this time most members of the editorial board were anti-Israel. "No simile better fits the war between

Israel and the Arabs in lands of biblical memory," the respected theologian began, "than the legend of David and Goliath. David, of course, is little Israel, numbering less than 2.5 million souls. . . . Goliath, of course, is the Arab world under Egyptian President Abdel Nasser's leadership, numbering a population of 20 to 40 million. This Goliath never accepted Israel's existence as a nation or granted it the right of survival." Later in the article, Niebuhr declared that he approved of Jerusalem's administrative reunification, asserting that "Judaism presupposes inextricable ties with the land of Israel and the city of David, without which Judaism cannot be truly herself."

WHOSE LAND?

Famed liberal theologian Reinhold Niebuhr and world-renowned evangelist Billy Graham disagreed on many points of theology, but they seemed to agree at least on one thing: the miracle of Israel. In the fall of 1970, the Billy Graham Crusade/World Wide Pictures film *His Land* was released. It was widely shown in churches and on campuses, as well as on television and in synagogues (in a special Jewish edition without the evangelistic message at the end). The film narration (by Cliff Barrows of the Billy Graham Evangelistic Association) begins: "Do you know what impresses me about Israel? It is that, well, God really has a long memory. I mean He just doesn't forget!" Biblical verses from Jeremiah, Isaiah, Zephaniah, Ezekiel, 1 Kings, and other books abound in the film to emphasize that "Yes, God promised it [to restore the Jewish people] and He is delivering on that promise in His Land" (narration).

The film relates how the Holy Land was stripped and starved by centuries of neglect, a rocky wilderness that awaited its people. The Jewish people, after centuries of trial and struggle, had turned the desolation into thousands of acres of fertile farmland, reclaimed the dessert, and made Hebrew into a living language again. "Perhaps you have to be a Jew to really understand that work is a form of prayer when you are home," Barrows explains. The theme song reverberates:*

> And as it blooms before our eyes,
>   just like an Eden paradise,
> The world will understand,
>   this is His Land.

*Permission granted by World Wide Pictures to reprint excerpts.

In Jerusalem "the stones seem to radiate it; it just seems to hang in the air." Jerusalem "has always been a promise of God's covenant that He is not through with man." Ultimately the blessing of the whole world will come through Israel, and everyone will understand that it is God who has done it. The theme song goes on:

> This is the Israel,
>   promised of old.
> This is the miracle happening now,
>   by sages and prophets foretold.

With premillennial fundamentalism-evangelicalism permeating the greater evangelical movement and with one of the greatest evangelists of the era promoting that prophetic scenario, the majority of evangelicals had fond and positive feelings toward Israel. Yet a growing segment within evangelicalism could never share this vision and was quite antagonistic to it.

Such a view was formulated in a series of articles by Bert De Vries, which criticized the Billy Graham film. De Vries was an evangelical professor of history at Calvin College in Grand Rapids, Michigan, a graduate of both Calvin Theological Seminary and Brandeis University. Writing in the *Reformed Journal* in April and November 1971, De Vries disagreed emphatically with the film's premillennial eschatology and pro-Jewish stance. He insisted that the film's argument, "drawing a wrong conclusion from faulty premises, is false." He further asserted:

> Nevertheless, it has served to convince many Americans that the founding of Israel on Arab land was justified. And the failure of "His Land" to see through this argument turns what is supposed to be a celebration of God's faithfulness into a piece of pro-Israel political propaganda.

Reacting to Barrows's exclamation in the film "There are just no words for that first glimpse of the Sea of Galilee!" De Vries notes dryly: "These sentimental and emotional speeches bolster the mistaken claim, based on out-of-context quotations of Old Testament references to the land, that modern Palestine is God's own special piece of real estate."

By 1975, Dr. De Vries had evolved a position that some other Calvinist amillennial evangelicals, who agreed with him earlier, could no longer tolerate. De Vries declared in the January 1975 *Reformed Journal*:

Why then the vehement Israeli reaction to Arafat and the PLO? The PLO call for an end to the state of Israel does not mean the destruction of its Jews, but the destruction of its Jewishness. Arafat proposes to replace Israel with a state in which Muslim, Jew, and Christian will live together in a "democratic, humanistic, and progressive society."

A colleague at Calvin College, Ronald Wells, took issue with De Vries in an article in the March 1975 *Reformed Journal*.

Although Wells and De Vries agreed on many points of amillennial covenant theology and on the Palestinians in general, Wells maintained that "Israel is a legitimate state and it has a right to existence." Although both men had problems seeing Israel as a "special place" and both believed the Christian church had taken over all the biblical promises to the Jewish people, Wells's position is typical of those evangelicals who believe that some of their colleagues who oppose the premillennial view can go too far in their hostility toward Israel. In other words, anti-Zionism could become anti-Semitism.

The paradox of evangelical anti-Zionism saddened G. Douglas Young, an evangelical resident of Jerusalem and the founder of the Institute of Holy Land Studies. In a letter to the *Jerusalem Post* (December 24, 1969), Dr. Young related:

> As a Christian I testify to the joys, privileges and freedom in Israel for me, my institution, my students and faculty, the other Christian people, churches and institutions in this dynamically exciting part of the world, where at long last once again, Jewish energy, creativity, and "follow-through" are making the wastes a garden, the desert to blossom, the crooked places straight.
>
> I thrill to see so many of my own faith coming on pilgrimage to see and experience for themselves all that is taking place here. I could only wish that the pilgrim could find the way to stay a little longer to let the real Israel seep into his consciousness and expel the hate, the myths, the false reporting that seems to be getting through the mass media in other parts of the world, both in the secular and in the church press.

In an interview I conducted with him in Israel in 1979, Dr. Young expressed deep concern about the ugliness of the anti-Israel teaching that was being spread through evangelical liberal arts colleges and seminaries by an ever-growing, hostile force of academicians. "It is tragic that some American evangelicals can't see it," he grieved. Then he remarked about some of his skeptical liberal Protestant coreligionists in Israel: "I don't see how one can live here for so long and not see the miracle of Israel."

G. Douglas Young's frustration with the growing anti-Israel movement within evangelicalism could be echoed by liberal supporters of Israel as they listen to the sentiments of other liberals. In 1980 the National Council of Churches of Christ in the U.S.A. endorsed a pro-Arab commission report that stipulated that the Palestine Liberation Organization, with Yasser Arafat as its leader, was the accredited agency of the Palestinian people. The Camp David Accords were described as "flawed," and the report called for the establishment of a "Palestinian state" without addressing any security needs of Israel.

The Middle East agenda of the seventeen-member commission was so biased at its inception that major Jewish organizations, including the American Jewish Committee, the American Jewish Congress, and the Anti-Defamation League of B'nai Brith, refused to present testimony—the pro-PLO findings were a foregone conclusion. Continued bias and political maneuvering of these members and other NCC officials led in 1987 to the defeat of positive statements on Israel in both the 199th General Assembly of the 3.1 million-member Presbyterian Church (USA) and the 1.7 million-member United Church of Christ.

In like manner, the American Friends Service Committee (AFSC), founded by the Quakers in 1917 to enable conscientious objectors to engage in relief work, has had a history of increasing animosity toward the Jewish state. In February 1977 the AFSC held a national conference in Chevy Chase, Maryland: "The New Imperative for Israeli-Palestinian Peace: A Learning and Organizational Conference." In spite of the disarming title, speaker after speaker compared the Israelis to the Nazis and vowed to organize a nationwide pressure group to oppose "Zionist policy." Supporting unequivocally the Palestine Liberation Organization and Yasser Arafat, the AFSC entitled its 1979 symposium: "Search for Peace in the Middle East: The New Context."

Such prejudice by ecumenically oriented institutions is heartrending to American Catholics who support the Jewish state. It is phenomenal that there are priests and nuns who have been ardent supporters of Israel and its right to exist when one considers the historic view of the Vatican. The Vatican was not only opposed to the establishment of the state of Israel but has carefully refrained from giving Israel diplomatic recognition. After the Six-Day War in 1967, Pope Paul VI proposed the internationalization of all holy places in Jerusalem. Pope John Paul II stated in 1980 that in the establishment of the state of Israel "a sad condition was created for the Palestinian people who were excluded from their homeland. These are facts that anyone can see."

The National Conference of Catholic Bishops in 1975 declared that because "Jews see this tie to the land as essential to their Jewishness," Christians "should strive to understand this link between land and people which Jews have expressed in their writings and worship throughout two millennia as a longing for the homeland, holy Zion." Nevertheless, this official statement on Catholic-Jewish relations added the caution that this affirmation was not "meant to deny the legitimate rights of other parties in the region, or to adopt any political stance in the controversies over the Middle East, which lie beyond the purview of this statement."

Popular feminist and Roman Catholic theologian Rosemary Ruether wrote in the *National Catholic Reporter* (September 14, 1984) that Zionism was a "form of nationalism that most Americans regard as unacceptable and, ironically, a Fascist state if settlements continue to be established in the West Bank or annexation takes place." She concluded that if Israel is to remain a democratic state it must cease to be a Zionist state. Similar diatribes by Ruether appeared in the *Christian Century*, as well as in her recent book (coauthored with her husband), *The Wrath of Jonah.*

Father Edward Flannery deplores such attitudes among Christians—including Catholic Christians. In his essay "Israel, Jerusalem, and the Middle East," published in *Twenty Years of Jewish-Catholic Relations* (1986), he wrote:

> The Middle East (Arab-Israeli) conflict has proven a grave distraction for the Jewish-Christian dialogue and for Jewish-Christian understanding generally. Numerous Christians, unaware of any bias on their part, see the establishment of the State of Israel very simply as a serious injustice inflicted upon the Palestinian Arab population by the Israelis. Through this prism they fail to perceive much significance, historical or theological, in the new state, and direct their attention exclusively to problems of Arab refugees, a Palestinian state, and other socio-political aspects of the problem. The peril in which Israel continuously exists and the problem of its security and survival become in this way secondary considerations, if they are considered at all. The simplicity and one-sidedness of this approach, for one thing, stems in most cases from inadequate information and uncritical acceptance of Arab or anti-Zionist propaganda. The United Nations can serve as a large scale sample of this

way of approaching the Middle East problem. It is imperative, in any case, for the health and survival of the Jewish-Christian embrace that the misinformation and mythologizing that have engulfed the conflict be dispelled.

Recognizing that one must not be insensitive to the Palestinian Arabs, Father Flannery identified the root problem in the Arab-Israeli conflict as "the refusal of many of Israel's enemies to accept or respect Israel's right to live in peace and security."

To the question, Is anti-Zionism in its various degrees and forms anti-Semitic? Father Flannery calmly answered: "Not necessarily, but almost always."

4

EGYPT AND JORDAN

E gypt is the most populous Arab country, having nearly 55 million inhabitants. Its leaders have played a crucial role in the events in the Middle East in the latter half of the twentieth century, and its current president, Hosni Mubarak, continues this important legacy. Jordan has a population of more than 4 million, and its leader, King Ibn Talal Hussein, has ruled since 1953.

Tenuously working with Egypt from the inception of his monarchy and for most of his rule, King Hussein has had to maintain a delicate balance in his relationships with other Arab countries and other Arab factions. Together, Egypt and Jordan flank Israel to the south and the east, and both countries have been involved in major wars and skirmishes with Israel since the foundation of the Jewish state.

Egypt was able to break the bonds of the decrepit Ottoman Empire when the Turks became embroiled in a war with Russia in 1768. Throughout the nineteenth century, France and England struggled for control of Egypt. The British finally occupied Egypt in 1882, and in 1914 Egypt became a British protectorate.

Egypt was granted freedom by the British in 1922, becoming one of the early independent Arab kingdoms in the modern Middle East. Jordan (at this time called the Emirate of Transjordan) had been created out of the Palestine Mandate awarded to the British after the First World War. In 1923 the emirate received partial independence under British tutelage. This mandate ended May 22, 1946, and the Hashemite Kingdom of Transjordan became totally independent three days later.

The original patriarch of the Hashemite family was a disciple of Muhammad and a guardian of Mecca. The Hashemite ruler, King Abdullah ibn-Hussein, a periodically moderating influence who had been appointed by the British over Transjordan in 1922, continued to rule, and in 1950 King Abdullah's domain was renamed the Hashemite Kingdom of Jordan.

Exhibiting the pragmatism and moderation that he had displayed from time to time, King Abdullah was ready to negotiate a secret peace treaty with Israel in the early 1950s. Such secrets, however, do not remain hidden for long in the Arab world. Abdullah was assassinated in East Jerusalem on July 20, 1951.

Although his son, Talal, was proclaimed Abdullah's successor, Jordan's parliament was forced to declare him mentally incompetent within a year, and Talal's eldest son, Hussein, was appointed to rule under a regency until his eighteenth birthday. On May 2, 1953, the British-educated teenager was crowned King Hussein. For the next decade, it seemed doubtful whether or not his kingdom could survive the radical revolutionary regimes in Egypt, Syria, and Iraq (where his Hashemite cousins were overthrown in 1958).

GAMAL ABDEL NASSER

In the 1950s and 1960s, the Arab world was largely dominated by an Egyptian leader, Gamal Abdel Nasser. During World War II, Nasser had collaborated with the Nazis, along with fellow conspirator Anwar Sadat, to overthrow the British. The son of a post office employee, Nasser exhibited an energetic, charismatic leadership that surpassed his tall, muscular physique and hawk-like face. Unlike the more formal politicians of the day who spoke in classical Arabic, Nasser spoke to the people in everyday terms and expressions. They thought of him as one of their own, and, although the vast majority remained extremely poor, the Egyptian people felt a new dignity and pride. In contrast, his family life was quite formal. His wife, Tahia, and his five children addressed him as "the President."

Serving as an army officer during the war against Israel in 1948, Nasser viewed the Arab defeat as a result of inept Arab leadership rather than as a tribute to Jewish tenacity and bravery. As a teenager, he had joined other Egyptian high school students in protesting the Balfour Declaration on December 2 every year. He firmly believed that the Jewish people should not have a nation in Palestine, and as leader of the Arab world he often called for the liberation of Palestine from "Zionist imperialists." He insisted that Egypt would enter Palestine on "a carpet of blood," and the government reorganization within which he became premier on April 17, 1954, spelled doom for the Egyptian Jewish community. Although anti-Jewish riots had forced the expulsion of Jews from Egypt and the confiscation of their property in the 1940s, Nasser's rule escalated intimidation, mass arrest, imprisonment, confiscation of property, and the death of Jews.

Gamal Abdel Nasser insisted that only by Arab unity would the fight against "imperialist and colonialist forces" be won. He used his leadership capabilities as well as the resources of Egypt to rally Arab nationalist feelings throughout the Middle East and to become the champion of Pan-Arabism. His successful negotiations with Great Britain to remove its forces from the Suez Canal area seemed to prove his capable leadership and international profile. Nevertheless, there were threats against his life by the radical Muslim Brotherhood, and on October 26, 1954, eight shots were fired at him in an assassination attempt in Alexandria. Almost killed, Nasser was suspicious throughout his rule, periodically purging members of his inner circle. His paranoia spread throughout the population.

The Arab world was looking for a strong, capable leader. Nasser proved his worth by threatening the thorn in an otherwise Arab dominated Middle East—Israel. By early 1955, he was initiating guerilla raids against Israel and styling himself as the chief defender of Palestinian rights. Because Egypt controlled the Gaza Strip, such raids easily killed scores of civilians in neighboring Israeli towns, including Jewish children. Foreign diplomats would later refer to Nasser as the "Hitler on the Nile."

Unable to obtain modern weapons from Western nations, he commenced ties with the Soviet bloc, and with Moscow's blessing acquired artillery, tanks, jet fighters, bombers, destroyers, and submarines on an unprecedented scale. On October 20, 1955, Nasser signed a mutual defense treaty with Syria, and Syria began receiving Soviet arms as well. On July 27, 1956, the Egyptian president boldly nationalized the Suez Canal and with Soviet support rejected all United Nations' proposals for international supervision of the strategic waterway. As we have seen in chapter 2, this led to the 1956 conflict with Israel.

Recognizing the prestige that Nasser evoked even among the Jordanian population, King Hussein welcomed the Egyptian leader's attacks against Israel. On July 26, 1956, King Hussein telegraphed Nasser: "We look forward to the future when the Arab flag will fly over our great stolen country [Palestine]."

Jordan and Syria signed an agreement with Nasser on October 30 to put their armed forces under the joint command of an Egyptian general. By 1957, however, King Hussein of Jordan realized that Nasser's followers were plotting Hussein's overthrow. Syria attacked Jordan on April 13, 1957, and on February 1, 1958, Egypt and Syria merged into the United Arab Republic.

Jordan recognized the threat and united with Iraq the same month to form the Arab Federation. To King Hussein of Jordan's dismay, King Faisal (his grandfather's brother) was overthrown by a pro-Nasser regime in July, and the Arab Federation was dissolved August 2. Although a military coup in Syria forced the dissolution of Nasser's United Arab Republic in 1961, King Hussein of Jordan maintained a healthy distrust of Nasser's intentions in the Arab world even as he supported Nasser's ongoing conflict with Israel.

Gamal Abdel Nasser's propaganda and diplomatic ability is clearly evident in the fact that he was able to emerge from his disastrous defeat by the Israelis in the 1956 Suez conflict with his prestige and large following intact. Using the British and French incursions over Egypt as a camouflage, Nasser was able to portray himself as the champion of Arab interests against "Western colonialists."

Not only was Nasser popular with Arab revolutionaries, Communists, and socialists throughout the Middle East, but also he had captured the hearts of Israeli Arabs and the Jordanian Palestinians. The Arab world cheered as Nasser declared during a speech in Alexandria on July 26, 1959: "I announce from here, on behalf of the United Arab Republic people, that this time we will exterminate Israel." Nasser called Israel the "Arab territory of Palestine" in speeches made in the early 1960s. In a speech on August 11, 1963, he said that the Egyptian armed forces were "getting ready for the restoration of the rights of the Palestine people because the Palestine battle [in 1948] was a smear on the entire Arab nation."

By 1967, Nasser bragged of "Arab power" and the armies with which Egypt, Iraq, and Syria had surrounded Israel. Forcing the United Nations Emergency Force to pull out of its peacekeeping assignments and closing the Strait of Tiran to Israeli ships, Nasser expressed confidence that other Arab nations, including Algeria and Kuwait, would send troops to fight against Israel. In a speech to Arab Trade Unionists on May 26, 1967, Nasser said confidently: "I have recently been with the armed forces. All the armed forces are ready for a battle face to face between the Arabs and Israel."

As we have seen, the following 1967 Six-Day War was a disastrous defeat for all Arab armies involved. The Israeli air attack was devastating from the first onslaught, and the Egyptian High Command believed exaggerated reports from the field on the number of Israeli planes shot down. False reports on Egyptian incursions into Israel were fabricated from the front, and Nasser actually believed all was well. No one dared to give him the full details about the scale of the air disaster once it became known. Nasser was one of the last to realize that defeat was imminent.

To save face, the Egyptian air force declared that Britain and the United States had joined in the air attack against the Egyptian forces. Several Arab countries were so angry that they broke off diplomatic relations with Britain and the United States. The false reports only intensified Nasser's embarrassment. A haggard and broken president immediately offered his resignation on June 9 (it was rejected by massive public demonstrations) and later suggested to those assembled at Cairo University (July 23, 1967) that "perhaps Allah wanted to test us to judge whether we deserve what we have achieved, whether we are able to protect our achievements, and whether we have the courage to be patient and stand firm against affliction." Accepting Allah's "test" as their destiny, Gamal Abdel Nasser was fully confident that Allah was with them and that Allah would endow them with victory "if we be determined to be the victor."

In 1969 he would once again call for an all-out war with Israel, and he would once again cement ties with the Soviet Union. According to those close to him, however, Nasser was never the same after the Six-Day War. Behind the strong words was a defeated and death-welcoming leader of the Arab world. On September 28, 1970, Nasser died suddenly of a heart attack at the age of fifty-two. He was succeeded by his compatriot of the Nazi era, Anwar Sadat.

KING HUSSEIN OF JORDAN

The aftermath of the Six-Day War was disastrous for King Hussein and Jordan. The Israelis had begged Hussein not to enter the alliance against Israel. For a time the Jordanian king wavered; but Algeria, Iraq, Kuwait, and Saudi Arabia were putting troops at Egypt's command. The PLO was stationed in the Gaza Strip, and Syria was focused on the Golan Heights. Assuming Israel's powerlessness against an Arab onslaught and fearful that his own people would overthrow him if he did not comply, King Hussein announced that he was authorizing Iraqi troops to enter Jordan and take up positions along Israel's border. His decision to enter the 1967 war against Israel was a fateful one. Jordan lost East Jerusalem and the entire West Bank. Jordan's economy suffered, and Palestinian commandos threatened to undermine the power of the king.

Ironically, Hussein had had an ongoing quarrel with Nasser for more than a decade. Jordan caught an Egyptian military attaché plotting against its officials on June 10, 1957, and forced Nasser to recall him. King Hussein requested British help because of the pro-Nasser Iraqi coup, and on July 17, 1958, 2,000 British paratroopers landed in Jordan. In November 1958 King Hussein's private plane was dangerously buzzed by United Arab Republic MiG fighters while flying over Syrian territory. Hussein believed the leaders of the UAR were out to murder him, although Nasser denied such accusations. (Indeed, in 1960 Jordan's prime minister and ten other Jordanians were killed by a bomb placed in the prime minister's office.) King Hussein was supposed to have been in that office at the time of the explosion, and he bitterly blamed Nasser. Most of the Arab world knew that Nasser's agents were involved and that he wanted to eliminate the Hashemite king of Jordan as he consolidated his power in the Arab world. Nasser was capable of such actions, and within six months the president of Tunisia accused Nasser of sending Egyptian secret agents to assassinate him. In addition, Nasser's intrigues in Yemen put him in direct conflict with Saudi Arabia.

Putting down successive rebellions against his government and several assassination attempts, King Hussein was well aware that Gamal Abdel Nasser was not to be trusted. Nevertheless, King Hussein felt forced to cooperate with Nasser in his organization of the Palestine Liberation Organization in 1964.

Nasser had determined that focusing in on the Palestinian Arab cause could bring the Arab states under his leadership. Calling a meeting in Cairo in January, Nasser was able to gather important Arab heads of state as well as terrorist leaders. He proposed the establishment of the Palestine Liberation Organization *(Munazzamat al-Tahrir al-Filastiniyya),* and set up Ahmad Shuqairy as its president (see chapter 7). The assembled Arab leaders approved his proposal and voted funds to support the fledgling PLO.

Hussein was leery of such an organization. Though he supported anti-Israel measures, he realized that most Palestinians lived in Jordan and that they could be a threat to his government if they received political credibility. Nasser promised King Hussein that the freedom of the PLO would be "limited." When the founding conference of the Palestine National Council was held in Jordanian East Jerusalem in May and June 1964, King Hussein felt obliged to give it his blessing. Yet he emphasized that the PLO would not be allowed to operate in Jordan and that Jordan would speak for the Palestinian Arabs.

On June 1 the PLO declared that its goal was "to obtain the objective of liquidating Israel" and that it would establish a "Palestine Liberation Army." Over the Jordanian leader's objections, Ahmad Shuqairy was invited to "represent Palestine" at the Arab League summit in September, but King Hussein was placated by the fact that the Palestine National Covenant specifically denied PLO sovereignty over the West Bank of Jordan, which had been annexed by the Hashemites, over Gaza (which Egypt administered), and over the al-Hamma region, which had been annexed by Syria. The PLO was only to "liberate" the land governed by the state of Israel.

The Six-Day War in 1967, of course, wrested East Jerusalem and the West Bank from Jordan, and the Palestinians presented an increasing threat to the stability of King Hussein's rule. Palestinian commando raids on Israel from Jordan's border resulted in military reprisals from the Jewish state, and guerrilla organizations began to ignore Jordanian law and authority. Yasser Arafat's Fatah organization and other guerrillas began to control Jordanian refugee camps and Palestinian villages. They acted as a sub-state within Jordan. Sporadic fighting broke out between the Jordanian army and the Palestinian terrorists. Subsequent negotiations and settlements soon dissolved, and, finally, civil war broke out in Jordan.

Vacillating as he had done in the past, King Hussein had allowed the guerrilla forces to grow far too strong. When he was finally forced to act on September 6, 1970, because the Palestinian guerrillas had attempted to assassinate him, Hussein's forces killed approximately two thousand guerrillas and thousands of other civilian Palestinians in the ten-day civil war. The Syrians took the opportunity to attack Jordan as well, and King Hussein's air and tank forces badly defeated the Syrians. With the help of $30 million in American military aid, the Jordanian army searched out and defeated remaining Palestinian guerrillas. Hundreds more were killed. So devastating was the Jordanian onslaught that the Palestinian terrorist groups were forced to shift their base of operation to Lebanon and Syria, although the Black September terrorist group was formed with the specific goal to murder King Hussein.

For a time, King Hussein appeared to be ostracized from the Arab world. Arab states bitterly criticized his war with the Palestinians, and Kuwait and Libya cut off the subsidies they had been paying to Jordan since the 1967 war. His position did not improve when he sent only a token force to fight with the Syrians during the 1973 Yom Kippur War against Israel. At their October 1974 summit in Rabat, Morocco, the Arab states unanimously declared that the PLO (not Jordan) would represent the Palestinian people. King Hussein was forced once again to go along with the vote, rather than be ostracized from his beloved Arab community.

Because he walks a fine line to maintain his monarchy, King Hussein has been a weak reed in the negotiation process during the 1970s and 1980s. Though many Western nations (and even Israel) have placed their hopes on Jordan's role in the solution of the Palestinian problem, often with encouraging statements from the king himself, his vacillation and lack of courage are legend. Often labeled a moderate, King Hussein and his Jordanian government have made brash statements against Israel throughout his rule. Even during the clash with Palestinian forces in 1970, the Jordanian government's Radio Amman insisted that "Israel's existence in the heart of the Arab people is an absurdity and ought to be got rid of by any means whatsoever."

On December 1, 1973, King Hussein asserted: "After we perform our duty in liberating the West Bank and Jerusalem, our national duty is to liberate all the Arab occupied territories." The message was clear. Israel's existence was not acceptable. During Sadat's peace initiative with the Israelis in the late 1970s, King Hussein joined the other Arab nations in condemning and shunning him.

As the decade of the 1990s approached, King Hussein continued to struggle. The Palestinian-Jordanian community is now approximately 60 percent of the population, and Hussein's historic strong support among the Bedouin tribes appears to be eroding. Young people are being drawn to the radical demands of the Muslim Brotherhood, the fundamentalist Islamic movement that is armed, well organized, and a bastion of Arab fanaticism. The "intifada," which has occupied Israeli authorities, is creeping into Jordan as well, and Jordan's economy has been in trouble for years. In April 1989, riots broke out in Jordan over rising prices, and Prime Minister Zaid al-Rifai had to resign in the wake of the unrest.

Forced to hold the first general elections in twenty-two years to thwart mounting criticism of his monarchy, King Hussein was shocked in November 1989 to find that the Muslim Brotherhood had gained twenty seats in the eighty-member Jordanian parliament. Other opposition groups and radicals captured thirty-three additional seats. Some of these successful candidates campaigned on promises of a Holy War against Israel and full support of the intifada. Little wonder that King Hussein vacillated once again during the Iraqi invasion of Kuwait in 1990, finally throwing his support to Iraq's Saddam Hussein (as the larger Palestinian population had done).

Although King Hussein of Jordan retains the power to dissolve the parliament and rule under martial law, he risks massive revolt and civil war if he initiates such actions. To make matters worse, Palestinian terrorist units are infiltrating Israel from Jordan's long border. In a confidential message to the Israeli government in November 1990, King Hussein assured Israeli officials that he was not behind such incursions. The Israelis are becoming increasingly impatient, however, fearful that King Hussein is losing his grip on Jordan. During the same period an anti-Israel extremist, Abdel Latif Arabiat, was elected chairperson of the Jordanian parliament over the king's choice, former Interior Minister Suleiman Arar. Reports also surfaced that Force 17, the military strike unit of the PLO, had resumed its activities inside Jordan.

ANWAR SADAT

The grief-stricken image of Anwar Sadat appeared on Egyptian televison at eight o'clock in the evening reciting from the Koran. "O soul at peace! Return unto thy Lord, content in His good pleasure!" The Egyptian people realized the message even before it was related. "I bring you the saddest news of the bravest of men, the noblest of men," Sadat related slowly. "President Gamal Abdel Nasser has died after a brief illness which modern medicine has failed to cure." To Anwar Sadat, President Nasser was a casualty of the 1967 Six-Day War. "Gamal moved and talked after the war, but you could see death in his pale face and hands," Sadat told his wife, Jehan. "He did not die on September 28, 1970. He died the morning of June 5, 1967."

Anwar Sadat (1918-1981) was a survivor of the many purges initiated by Nasser during periods of paranoia. Although Sadat and Nasser had met in the latter 1930s, it was only in 1951 that Nasser contacted Sadat in the hope that Sadat's contacts with the royal palace might provide information to help the revolution. Only later was he brought into the Free Officers movement that would spearhead Nasser's revolution in Egypt.

Like Nasser during the Second World War, Anwar Sadat was a Nazi sympathizer and was imprisoned by the British in 1942 for working with Nazi spies against the British in Egypt. Sadat praised Adolf Hitler as a "hero" who should be revered and emulated by the Arab world. In his rampant anti-Semitism, Anwar Sadat believed that "a Jew would do anything if the price was right" and feared any contact that soldiers would have in enlisting the help of Jews.

Although Nasser had Sadat read the radio proclamation announcing the success of the revolution in 1952, Anwar Sadat was not one of Nasser's top leaders in the early years of the revolution. The other members of Nasser's Revolutionary Command Council appeared to be suspicious of Sadat's loyalty and to question his ability. To the contrary, Nasser believed him to be quite harmless and found positions for him in his organization. His quiet loyalty to Nasser paid off, however, and in 1957 Anwar Sadat was appointed Secretary-General of the National Union (Nasser's political organization).

Other honors would follow. In 1959 Nasser asked Sadat to campaign for the position of speaker of the national assembly. His immediate election to this post meant more exposure and travel. He held this position until 1969, and concurrently served as Nasser's vice-president from 1964 to 1967. In December 1969, Nasser swore in Sadat as vice-president once again. Nasser had to attend the Arab summit conference in Rabat, where it was rumored that the CIA was involved with the Moroccan interior minister to assassinate the Egyptian president. Just in case of Nasser's death, Sadat appeared to be a "safe" interim choice to handle ceremonial occasions while the National Union and the army looked after the nation. When Nasser returned, Sadat remained his dutiful vice-president. Nasser's sudden heart attack thrust Sadat into the presidential role.

On October 17, 1970, Anwar Sadat was sworn in as president of the United Arab Republic following an election in which he received 90 percent of the Egyptian vote. The powerful political and military leaders of Egypt (the "centers of power") felt that Sadat was a weak and dutiful bureaucrat who posed no threat to their power. He was able to campaign on the platform that he was Nasser's own choice, and the Egypt that he inherited was largely Nasser's creation. Nasser's charted path appeared to be secure. "My program is Nasser's," Sadat pledged before the Egyptian parliament.

Ironically, Anwar Sadat was much stronger than most Egyptians had imagined. He replaced Nasser's aides and advisers and swiftly relieved the "centers of power" of their positions during the evening of May 14, 1971. To the amazement of most, he also decided on July 8, 1972, to expel the large number of Soviet military experts and advisers in Egypt—an alliance upon which Nasser had depended. The U.S.S.R. was stunned. The slow process of "de-Nasserization" of Egypt had begun, and President Sadat was coordinating its every turn.

Sadat's attack on Israel during Yom Kippur in 1973 gave him instant prestige throughout the Arab world. While Israel had some idea that war could take place, the October 6 Egyptian assault on the Israeli Bar-Lev line on the eastern bank of the Suez Canal surprised a well-trained Israeli army. Egypt and the Arab world would celebrate Anwar Sadat's initial success in crossing the line and establishing bridgeheads on the east bank of the canal.

More than 2,500 Israelis were killed in the Yom Kippur War, a heavy loss for a small nation. Even though the Israeli counterattack resulted in Israeli forces holding territory in Egypt itself and culminated in the deaths of 15,000 Egyptian soldiers and 3,500 Syrian troops, the myth of Israeli invincibility had been shattered. "The risk was great and the sacrifices were big. However, the results achieved in the first six hours of the battle in our war were huge," Sadat told the people's assembly in Cairo on October 16, 1973. "The arrogant enemy [Israel] lost its equilibrium at this moment. The wounded nation [Egypt after 1967 Six-Day War] restored its honor."

Anwar Sadat's subsequent cultivation of an alliance with the United States and the West, however, would raise many questions among Arab leaders. His decision in September 1975 to sign an interim agreement with Israel caused further alarm, and his visit to Jerusalem in November 1977 sealed his fate. There was little doubt that he was destined to die by an Arab assassin's bullet. His foreign minister resigned, and other leaders of Arab nations called him a traitor.

Sadat's acceptance of the Camp David Accords in an initial framework on September 17, 1978, and in signing the Egyptian-Israeli peace treaty on March 26, 1979, isolated Sadat's Egypt from the rest of the Arab world. But it also provided the opportunity for Egypt to regain the Sinai and avert war during the decade of the 1980s. When Abba Eban, Israel's UN ambassador, asked Sadat why he went to Jerusalem and, unlike other Arab leaders, recognized the existence of the state of Israel in spite of personal cost, Sadat replied: "It was the only way to get my land [the Sinai] back."

Approximately 10 percent of the population of Egypt, Coptic Christians were increasingly being attacked by fanatical Muslim groups during Sadat's presidency. The Coptic leaders cried out to the world about Muslim persecution of minority groups. In June 1981, the clashes between Coptic Christians and Muslims were severe and had totally polarized both communities. Sadat bore the brunt of the blame from both groups. Increasingly attacked by right-wing Muslim groups in Egypt and upset at the criticism by Coptic Christian religious leaders, Sadat's government arrested more than 1,500 religious leaders, journalists, and political opponents on September 3-4, 1981.

Although Sadat had imprisoned such individuals before, this was the severest crackdown since he was made president in 1970. On September 5, Sadat denounced the Muslim Brotherhood before a special session of the Egyptian parliament, and he outlawed fundamentalist Muslim clothing and activities on university campuses. In addition, the outspoken Coptic Christian leader Pope Shenouda was banished to a monastery in the western desert.

Again ironically, it was during the October 6, 1981, anniversary celebration of Anwar Sadat's 1973 Yom Kippur War "victory" that Arabs in military uniform machine-gunned him to death in the reviewing stand. Traditionally, pride in this day had caused all animosities to be put aside in a celebration of Egyptian achievement. In contrast, Islamic fundamentalist Kaled el-Islambouli, a 1978 honor graduate of the Egyptian School of Artillery and a first lieutenant, pumped round after round into the body of his president and commander-in-chief. Seven Egyptian officials were murdered, and twenty-eight were wounded. A one-time Sadat confidant, Mohamed Heikal, had become a critic of Sadat's regime. In 1981 Heikal was jailed with other critics. Mohamed Heikal would write in *Autumn of Fury: The Assassination of Sadat* (1983): "For the first time the people of Egypt had killed their Pharaoh."

Anwar Sadat was buried with full military honors, and his funeral was attended by more than eighty international leaders, including Israeli prime minister Menachim Begin and former U.S. presidents Richard Nixon, Gerald Ford, and Jimmy Carter.

President Ronald Reagan and Vice-President George Bush were asked to stay in Washington because of feared terrorist attack. Anwar

Sadat's vice-president, Hosni Mubarak, was elected president of Egypt on October 13, 1981.

HOSNI MUBARAK

Hosni Mubarak had been on the reviewing stand with Sadat and other Egyptian officials on that fateful day in October. Miraculously, only his hand had been grazed by a bullet. Suddenly this former commander of the Egyptian Air Force during the Yom Kippur War became heir of the myriad of problems that engulfed the nation of Egypt. President Mubarak has walked a tight-rope ever since.

Soon after he became president, Mubarak commissioned a special committee of experts to discover the condition of the Egyptian economy. Not only was Egypt's alarming debt and dependence on foreign imports underscored, but also the social implications of an economy out of control. A growing rift had been created by the privileged elite of rich and the multitudes of Egyptian poor. To ease tensions that were at the breaking point during Sadat's last year, Mubarak released many dissidents from prison, and the trial of those involved in Sadat's death was televised. Mubarak also promised Egypt's commitment to the Camp David Accords and other international treaties but immediately attempted to return Egypt into the Arab fold.

The final stage of Israel's withdrawal from the Sinai according to the terms of the Israeli-Egypt peace treaty was accomplished on schedule on April 25, 1982 (although there were voices of protest because of the death of Sadat and because of President Mubarak's well-publicized efforts to assuage offended leaders throughout the Arab world). Mubarak wired Israeli Prime Minister Menachim Begin that he appreciated the prompt implementation of the treaty. When Israel Defense Forces crossed the Lebanon border in June 1982 in "Operation Peace for Galilee" (see chapter 9), however, Mubarak soundly condemned the action. Mubarak also used the opportunity of later events in Lebanon to recall Egypt's newly appointed ambassador to Israel.

Israeli leaders felt betrayed by this action and watched horrified as anti-Semitic cartoons and rhetoric appeared in the Egyptian press. Nevertheless, the Egyptian embassy continued to operate (run by the charge d'affaires) and Israel's ambassador to Egypt stubbornly continued his duties in Cairo. This frosty atmosphere brought further talks concerning the future of the West Bank and the Gaza Strip to a standstill. And yet, Egypt's monetary allocations from the United States for its signature on the peace treaty, its strong ties to the West, and the return of the Sinai oilfields by Israel seem to have been key factors in preventing Mubarak from further distancing himself from Israel.

Prime Minister Shamir of Israel and others insisted that Mubarak's meetings with Yasser Arafat in April 1983 were a violation of the Camp David Accords. They found it ludicrous that Mubarak would honor a known terrorist and give credence to Arafat, who expressed his joy at the death of Anwar Sadat. In contrast, the United States hoped that an Egypt-Jordan-PLO alliance might help solve the Palestinian problem.

King Hussein of Jordan, however, made clear on April 10, 1983, that his country would not participate in such negotiations. Although the Jordanian king had had several talks with Arafat in the previous year, he (like other Arab leaders) had severed relations with Egypt and had condemned Sadat for traveling to Israel. Nevertheless, the Arab world seemed pleased with the "cold peace" that had developed between Egypt and Israel. They gloated that Egypt appeared to reciprocate little in the new relationship with her northern neighbor.

In 1984 an Israeli diplomat was murdered in Cairo and, months later, an Egyptian security guard opened fire on seven Israeli tourists in the Sinai. The three Jewish adults and four children were killed for no apparent reason. Eyewitnesses reported that five of the Israelis could have been saved, but Egyptian forces refused medical care. The victims bled to death. Mubarak treated the incident with indifference, waiting more than a week to send condolences. The murderer was later sentenced to life imprisonment in Egypt.

Mubarak met with Israeli officials in 1985 and 1986 in Cairo but refused to visit Israel. In 1987, Austrian president Kurt Waldheim, under attack for being a Nazi war criminal, was welcomed in Cairo by Mubarak. Israelis and Jews throughout the world were not amused.

In November, an Arab summit in Amman, Jordan, indicated that Arab states could renew diplomatic relations with Egypt, and Egypt ended the year by assailing Israel's "repression" in quelling the intifada in the West Bank and Gaza. By the end of 1988, the president of Egypt criticized Prime Minister Shamir of Israel as being "stubborn," and insisted that "Camp David is passé as far as the occupied territories are concerned." Hosni Mubarak called for direct talks in an international peace conference.

Then, in a move that surprised the world, Mubarak asserted in December 1988 that he would go to Israel "if the visit would lead to a solution of the Palestinian problem." Prime Minister Shamir immediately invited the Egyptian president to Israel (even as Anwar Sadat had been invited eleven years earlier by Menachim Begin) with the hope that such a visit could produce "positive results."

President Mubarak did not believe that the results would be productive enough to jeopardize his renewed relations with other Arab states, and he changed his proposal. Mubarak declared that he was ready to visit Israel only if Israel was ready to start a dialogue with the PLO. Mubarak knew that Shamir, who had earlier condemned the terrorist organization and had responded with a proposal for the Camp David formula for Palestinian autonomy, would not accept. In April 1989, Mubarak rejected Shamir's offer to get together for an informal meeting in Washington, D.C., where they both happened to have separate meetings scheduled with President George Bush. Hosni Mubarak remembered well the day Anwar Sadat was assassinated. He was unwilling to take the risk of following in Sadat's footsteps (even on the tenth anniversary of the Camp David Accords). Egyptian society was in a turmoil that continues to this day. When President Mubarak spurned going to Israel at the end of 1988, more than 7 percent of Egypt's work force was under the age of twelve. The frightening specter of approximately one million child laborers unprotected by social security arrangements from exploitation and injury burdened the social fabric of the nation. Some of the children working in factories were four and five years old. To complicate matters, approximately three million adults were out of work, and Egypt's foreign debt stood at $44 billion (in spite of $2.3 billion a year in American aid). The following year Egypt's foreign debt would increase to $50 billion. Population growth stood at nearly 3 percent a year. "We increase by about one million and a half every year," Mubarak told reporters in July 1989. "It threatens to choke all our efforts in all fields and quashes all hope of growth, production and development."

Mubarak walked a tightrope as radical Muslims stepped up their opposition to his ties with the West. Even nonviolent Muslims who proposed that the "secular government" of Egypt be replaced by an "Islamic government" wreaked havoc in the nation.

Amnesty International reported that in 1988 Egyptian officials had tortured hundreds of political dissenters and deprived them of their civil rights. The organization was hopeful of improvement because incarcerated individuals deprived of due process fell from thousands to around nine hundred. At the end of April 1989, however, the Egyptian government arrested 1,500 Muslims in a crackdown on Islamic radicals and fundamentalists. "These extremist groups are fueling religious strife in the country, and they must be met with force," Interior Minister Zaki Badr told Cairo police. "We will meet violence with violence." By December 1989 he was doing just that. Islamic militants fought the police in Cairo with guns, knives, chains, and gasoline bombs.

The Organization of Arab Petroleum Exporting Countries (OAPEC) agreed on May 13, 1989, to readmit Egypt to its membership. Egypt had exported approximately 450,000 barrels a day during the 1980s. Ironically, the meeting was held in Kuwait, and Iraq proposed Egypt's readmission to OAPEC because of Egypt's helping Saddam Hussein in his war against the Iranian Ayatollah Khomeini. The nine-member approval signaled Egypt's return to the Arab fold after a decade of ostracism. At the end of the month at an Arab League summit in Casablanca, Morocco, Egypt attended its first Arab meeting in more than ten years.

Although only Syria, Libya, and Lebanon had not revived diplomatic relations with Egypt by this date, the Arab world had been determined that Hosni Mubarak's Egypt would go through a reestablishment process. The threat from Khomeini's Iran hastened that process, and Mubarak's willing response to help the Arab world in this conflict hastened Egypt's readmittance. For the Casablanca meeting, Hafez Assad of Syria withdrew objections to Mubarak's attending by drawing a contrast between Mubarak and Sadat. Libya's Muammar Qaddafi lobbied to prevent such attendance, but in June began a reconciliation with Egypt. As the decade of the 1990s approached, Mubarak's Egypt had regained much of her former status in the Arab world.

Hosni Mubarak's initiative against Saddam Hussein in the 1991 Gulf War has permanently established Egypt's leadership in the Arab world once again. Saddam Hussein had treated Egyptian workers in Iraq poorly, so no significant segment of the Egyptian population demonstrated against Mubarak's entry into the Gulf War. Jordan's King Hussein, however, was not able to maintain his pretense of "neutrality" in the conflict, and his pro-Iraqi sympathies have cut him off from powerful Arab supporters, including Saudi Arabia.

The Bush administration was angered at King Hussein because he openly questioned the United States's intentions in the Gulf War.

American diplomats realize, however, that Jordan at some point have to be reinstated into the process for the success of any regional peace conference. To show American displeasure at King Hussein's support of Saddam Hussein, the United States Senate voted on March 20, 1991, to eliminate economic and military aid to Jordan. In the bill's final version signed by President Bush in April, however, the administration reserved the right to reinstate aid to Jordan if the president believed it would help the Middle East peace process. Immediately after the war, King Hussein attempted to resume cordial relations with the United States, but the White House was in no hurry to accept him back into a close relationship.

5

SYRIA AND LEBANON

Since his military coup in November 1970, President Hafez al-Assad has ruled the Syrian nation of 13 million inhabitants. Like many of the leaders before him, he has refused to accept the political reality of Lebanon with its 3.5 million inhabitants and more than four thousand square miles. "The Lebanese people can never be separated from the Arab body [namely Syria]," he has asserted in speeches and interviews for the past two decades.

As the world turned its attention to Iraq's invasion of Kuwait in 1990, Assad deftly took control of the beleaguered nation of Lebanon, accomplishing the first leg of his journey toward a "Greater Syria." Both Syria and Lebanon to the north of Israel have plagued the Jewish state with confrontation and hostile conflict since 1948.

Although Syria became a nation during the twentieth century, the concept of "Greater Syria" has been an integral part of the Arab psyche. In fact, early Arab tribes in Arabia called this undefined northern expanse "Sham," a territory that included the modern territories of Jordan, Israel, Lebanon, and Syria.

Damascus, capital of Syria, is one of the oldest continuously inhabited cities in the world, and, because of its strategic position between ancient lands, the territory has been conquered by various empires of the ancient Near East. In addition, important trade routes criss-crossed the area. General Pompey made Syria a Roman province six decades before the birth of Christ. When the Roman Empire declared itself "Christian" in the fourth century, the Syrian area was dominated by Christian Arabs. The Muslim conquest in 636 was so decisive that today seven out of eight Syrians are adherents to Islam, and 70 percent are traditional Sunni Muslims.

Soon after the death of Muhammad, Damascus was made the capital of the Umayyad Empire (661-750), a Muslim empire that stretched from India to Spain. The Ottoman Turks conquered the area in 1516. The Ottomans allowed tribal sheikhs and feudal overlords control over their local domains as long they paid taxes and recognized the Turkish sultan's authority. As the Ottoman Empire grew weaker, many of the ethnic-minority groups that lay in the outlying mountainous areas of Syria challenged Turkish control.

An especially despised group to which the Ottomans sent vicious military expeditions to defeat were the Alawites, the group into which Hafez Assad was born and a minority group in Syria today. Composing only 12 percent of the Syrian population and looked upon by the Sunni Muslims as a heretical sect, the Alawites have become a class of new wealth under the presidency of their native son. This is only one indication of the complicated patterns of religious and political communities that provide intercommunal conflict and tension in Syria and Lebanon.

THE FRENCH MANDATE

The modern state of Syria was created during the First World War when the Ottoman Turks declared on the side of Germany. In Arabia, Hussein Ibn Ali, the Hashemite protector of Mecca and Medina, bargained with the British for control of Arabian, Syrian, and Mesopotamian areas in return for an Arab revolt against the Ottomans. Sir Henry McMahon, the British High Commissioner of Cairo, excluded "portions of Syria lying to the west of Damascus [Lebanon]" because they were not purely Arab. He failed to mention Palestine in his confirmation letter to Hussein (October 24, 1915).

Hussein's second son, Faisal, immediately led the Arab revolt against the Turks, helping the British and French to win the war. Faisal then set himself up as leader of Syria in 1918. The boundaries of Syria and Lebanon were drawn up by the British and French.

This son of the Hashemite family appeared to be flexible at this time concerning the proposed formation of a Jewish state in Palestine. Unfortuately for Faisal, the French were given the mandate over Syria and Lebanon, and they kicked him out of Syria in 1920. To appease the moderate Hashemite family and to honor their commitment, the British soon made Faisal king of Iraq and carved out Transjordan for his brother Abdullah (both territories were in the British mandate).

Syrian nationalism blossomed under the French Mandate, and the French were constantly put under pressure to grant Syria independence. Riots and uprisings broke out. The French were unable to improve the poverty-stricken conditions of most of the Arabs, and groups of Syrians revolted in support of Arab independence.

The Alawites were one of the few groups to prosper under French rule, as the French used them as a military force to help suppress the struggle for independence among Syrian nationalists. The French also helped the Alawites develop their region, to create a secluded and independent state in the midst of the movement for Syrian unity. Divide and conquer was a favorite French technique.

Nevertheless, the French could not stem the tide of Syrian nationalism and during the Second World War allowed the Syrians to elect a president in 1943. When the French withdrew from Syria in April 1945, this president, Shukri al-Kuwatly, assumed full control of the country under a republican form of government, and the modern nation of Syria had finally achieved independence.

Syria's loss in its 1948 attack on the new state of Israel, however, led to a military coup that overthrew Kuwatly's government (the first of several coups), and it was not until 1955 that Kuwatly was returned to power. It was President Kuwatly who agreed to form the United Arab Republic with Gamal Abdel Nasser in Cairo early in 1958. A Syrian army revolt in 1961 severed this Syrian-Egyptian agreement.

Several Syrian nationalist political parties had been organized by the Arabs to achieve independence, social reform, and economic improvement during the French Mandate. One of these was the Ba'ath (Arab Resurrection) Party founded in 1940 (it merged with the Arab Socialist Party in 1953 to become the Arab Socialist Resurrection Party). It was the Ba'ath Party that took control of Syria in March 1963, when a pro-Nasser military faction seized control. It had planned to develop a union with its sister party in Iraq, but the Ba'ath Party in Iraq was overthrown in November 1963, not to return until 1968.

Today the Ba'ath Party is the power center of Hafez Assad's rule, and the life of the current Syrian president is integrally linked with this organzation.

HAFEZ AL-ASSAD

Hafez Assad (formerly Abu Sulayman al-Wahsh) was born in October 1930, the oldest son in a farm family of eight children. His grandfather fought against the Ottoman Turks, and his father opposed the French and their mandate over Syria. The family name changed from Wahsh to Assad when he was a teenager.

In Arabic *Wahsh* literally means "wild beast," but it also had the pejorative connotation of a vulgar, evil, and uncivilized person. *Assad* meant "lion," a symbol of strength and dignity. Even as a teenager, Hafez Assad led students against the French, and at sixteen he joined the Ba'ath Party. Upon graduation, he entered the Military Academy at Homs and then registered in the Air Force Academy at Aleppo. He was a talented combat pilot who reportedly shot down a British bomber that had strayed into Syrian airspace during the 1956 Suez War. He also trained in Egypt in an aviation class that included Hosni Mubarak, the current president of Egypt.

Working his way up in the Ba'ath Party leadership as well as in the air force, Lieutenant-Colonel Hafez Assad was virtually in charge of the Syrian air force by the end of 1963. At the close of 1964, he was official-ly appointed Major-General and commander of the Syrian air force. In 1965 he added the portfolio of Defense Minister in his quest for the leadership of Syria.

Inspired by Nasser's philosophy and leadership style in the latter 1950s and early 1960s, Assad came to believe that Arabs must unite in a military and political network from the Nile to the Euphrates. For Assad, Syrian unity, a Greater Syria, was essential to lead such an Arab "nation."

Assad came to believe that, for the true Arab, a life or death struggle must be waged against Israel. To Assad, Israel is a usurper in an Arab-destined world, a lethal bacteria that must be expunged. Arab unity and the struggle against Israel became the major doctrines of the Ba'ath Party as well. Hafez Assad found that rhetoric that denigrated the Jewish people and the state of Israel was a powerful unifier among Arabs, and the last two decades of his rule have been consumed by the desire to lead the Arab world in a military victory over Israel.

Ironically, as with so many current leaders of the Arab world to-day, it was the massive defeat in the 1967 Six-Day War that weakened Assad's opponents and catapulted Assad to a position of power and prestige in the eyes of the Syrian people. Blaming the politicians for the military's failure to defeat Israel, Assad consolidated his power within the military and lavished favors on the Ba'ath leadership loyal to him. After a failed military coup in 1969, Assad led a successful overthrow of the Syrian government in November 1970. It appears that the death of Gamal Abdel Nasser convinced Assad that he would now be the leader of pan-Arabism and convinced his party and people that Syria (without Nasser) was vulnerable to Israeli attack. Consolidating a fractured party apparatus, Lieutenant-General Hafez Assad became the president of Syria in March 1971.

A shrewd politician, Assad improved his government's relations with the Sunni Muslim business community by easing restrictions imposed by the former government (while continuing to mouth the precepts of Ba'athist socialism). Battling the ever-present Muslim Brotherhood, which had labeled his community of Alawites heretics, Hafez Assad cultivated the image of a devout Muslim by regularly attending Friday congregational prayers and by cultivating the devotion of some Sunni religious leaders.

He also began improving relations with Saudi Arabia and other conservative Arab states, nations that the previous Syrian government had labeled "feudal." The oil-rich Arab states began pouring more than $500 million a year into Syria, which boosted the economy and garnered even deeper support from the Sunni merchants. Although he did not sign a peace treaty with Israel, Assad cultivated the image of a moderate by renewing relations with Western governments, governments former Syrian officials had labeled "imperialist." A new era of Syrian history had begun.

Even Anwar Sadat's expulsion of Soviet military advisers from Egypt in 1972 helped to build Assad's power base. To try to maintain their foothold in the Middle East and to rebuke Sadat for his impudent behavior, the Soviets decided to ship unprecedented armaments to Syria, including SAM-6 missiles, hundreds of MiG-21 jets, and hundreds of new state-of-the-art tanks. Overnight, Syria became a heavily armed nation. When Sadat proposed that the Syrian president join him in another campaign against Israel, Hafez Assad agreed to the two-pronged attack.

During the Yom Kippur War of 1973, the Egyptians and Syrians would command 750,000 soldiers, three times the number of Israeli forces. Whereas Sadat appears to have realized that war with Israel would provide the negotiation leverage to regain the entire Sinai, Assad's goal was to recapture the Golan Heights lost to Israel in the 1967 war, and to capture the bridges over the Jordan River.

The key to a successful surprise attack on Yom Kippur lay in a complex disinformation campaign. The shrewd Syrian president invited the United Nations Secretary-General Kurt Waldheim to discuss the political implementation of Security Council Resolution 242. Hafez Assad also sacrificed thirteen MiG fighters in an air battle on September 13, 1973. Provoking Israeli jets into a dogfight, he then used the guise of Israel's threat to build up his forces toward the Golan. He was also able to prepare the Syrian people psychologically for war by constantly appealing to them to martyr themselves "defending Allah's religion" and to follow their ancestors who "were victorious through their faith."

The Soviets appear to have helped him to convince the rest of the world that the Israelis were building up their forces in the Golan. The ruse worked, and Syria was able to take Israel by surprise in its attack on October 6, 1973. Some Israeli analysts, such as Brigadier Arye Shalev, had cautioned Premier Golda Meir that a war for Assad "wouldn't make sense" and that "the Syrian deployment is apparently only because of fear of Israeli attack." October 6, 1973, was Hafez Assad's forty-third birthday. It also marked his first struggle with Israel as a pan-Arab leader.

Hafez Assad would come out of the Yom Kippur War an Arab hero. Although he had lost the overall war, he had taken risks, had confronted the hated Israelis, and had inflicted pain on the Jews. Assad's Syria would come out of that 1973 war with the reputation of being the most uncompromising nationalists in the Arab world, defenders of the faith. Their hatred for the Israelis ran deep and seemed to be impenetrable. The seven thousand Jews in Syria during the early years of Assad's reign were horribly persecuted and were not allowed to leave Syria. Jewish human rights activists around the world wore "Free Syrian Jewry" buttons alongside "Free Russian Jewry" buttons. Henry Kissinger was exasperated as he tried to talk sense with Hafez Assad. The Syrian president was uncompromising. He demanded that the Israelis pull out of the Golan before he would negotiate. He demanded most of the area Syria had lost in 1967 as well as in 1973. He called upon his friends in Saudi Arabia to pressure the West with the weapon of oil. In addition, he would not furnish a list of POWs or allow the Red Cross to visit Syria until the Israelis totally vacated the Golan. This latter point was crucial in his ultimate achievement of regaining the 1973 territory as well as the town of Quneitra and two small hills captured by Israel in 1967. The Israelis put supreme value on the life of their POWs. Henry Kissinger would acknowledege that Hafez Assad was a proud, tough, and shrewd negotiator, gaining for Syria an outcome that defied the Israeli victory, superiority of forces, and territorial conquest during the Yom Kippur War.

As a result of Henry Kissinger's shuttle diplomacy, Syria and Israel accepted a separation of forces and a buffer zone between them, policed by the United Nations. They were to gradually thin out their forces. The agreement was signed on May 31, 1974, in Geneva. Israel returned 382 Arab prisoners of war to Syria, and Syria returned 56 Israeli POWs. President Richard Nixon and Syrian president Assad established full diplomatic relations on June 16, 1974, during Nixon's Middle East tour to Egypt, Syria, Saudi Arabia, Israel, and Jordan.

Initially, Hafez Assad made conciliatory statements on possible peace with Israel—statements apparently aimed at the United States rather than Israel. He realized that the United States could put pressure on Israel that could result in his gaining back the Golan through diplomacy.

At the same time, he maintained anti-Israel rhetoric for the benefit of his Arab constituency. While indicating to *Newsweek* and *Time* in English that he was supportive of an overall peace in the Middle East that would result in a peace treaty with Israel, he delivered fiery speeches in Arabic that denounced Israel as a "racist fascist state," insisting that the "ultimate goal of all Arabs is an all-Arab world" in Israel. Jews could continue to live in that world "with no fears for themselves," Assad suggested, but Zionist Israel and Israelis as such would cease to exist. He reminded his Arab audiences that the Jewish state of Israel had existed only one-sixth of the time that the Christian Crusader states had existed "on Arab land." Assad promised that the mighty Arab nations would destroy Israel just as they had overcome the Crusader states.

It is apparent that Assad had fostered such continual anti-Israel propaganda and pan-Arabic rhetoric among his people that even he could not back away from intransigent views in practice. Because of his shrewd, calculating vengefulness coupled with well-developed double-talk and ambitious intentions, it is impossible to ascertain whether or not he ever contemplated a diplomatic solution that would allow the Jewish state of Israel to exist. He tried to convince Anwar Sadat to refrain from a separate peace treaty with Israel. When Sadat proceeded to negotiate, Assad assailed him as a "traitor to Arab unity" and a slave to the "Jewish enemy." After the Camp David Accords were signed by President Sadat and Prime Minister Begin on September 17, 1978, Assad asserted that "the enemies of the Arabs could not have achieved a greater victory" and told his people that Sadat and Begin would militarily attack Syria in the near future.

INCURSION INTO LEBANON

After the Second World War, the modern state of Lebanon depended upon tolerance and compromise between its various communities to guarantee survival. This delicate balance has been destroyed by factional fighting from within and by forces from without. Today it is a united nation in name only. It is a heartache for its citizens scattered throughout the Western world and for its loyal partisans who continue to live there. Beautiful Beirut, a cosmopolitan city of international reputation in the 1960s and early 1970s, consists of ugly bombed-out buildings and makeshift apartments, a terrorist's haven.

In ancient times, much of Lebanon had been part of Phoenicia. With the spread of Christianity, it became a Christian refuge; Crusader states formed on its soil during the Medieval period. Absorbed by the Ottoman Empire in the sixteenth century, the Mediterranean republic enjoyed special privileges from its Turkish overlords.

Hatred between Lebanese Christians and Muslims escalated during the summer of 1859, when Druse clans from the Al-Shouf mountains were joined by Sunni and Shiite Muslim peasants in massacres and atrocities against Lebanese Christian communities. Thousands of Christians were killed. Muslims in Damascus decided to rid themselves of their Christians as well, not only killing thousands in their city but also slaughtering many communities south of the Damascus Road.

In 1860 and 1861, the European nations held conferences in Paris and Constantinople to create a semi-independent Lebanon from the predominantly Christian parts of the area.

When the Ottomans were defeated in the First World War, Lebanon came under the French mandate. Continuing to totally separate the land from Syrian territory, the French envisioned a Greater Lebanon, enlarging the old Christian territory to include Muslim territories. Gradually, Lebanon would become a democratic republic, granted independence on November 16, 1943. All French troops were withdrawn in 1946.

A diverse and enlarged Lebanon, however, was a divided Lebanon. Clans that had feuded for hundreds of years were supposed to merge into a delicate governmental experiment in democracy. The smaller Lebanon had had a 78 percent Christian majority. The greater Lebanon had only a 53 percent Christian majority, one that continued to dwindle under a much larger Muslim birthrate.

Yet the Christians maintained the political and economic power in the nation. The 1926 Lebanese constitution was implemented on the old 53 percent that was determined in Lebanon's last official census in 1932. The National Covenant of 1943 provided an unwritten convention that Lebanon's president would be a Maronite Christian, the prime minister was to be a Sunni Muslim, and the speaker of the National Assembly a Shia Muslim. At least one Greek Christian and one Druse were to be in the Cabinet. By 1958 Muslims and Christians in Lebanon were rioting against one another, and Lebanese President Camille Shamoun asked President Dwight D. Eisenhower to send in the Marines.

After a few weeks of their presence, peace was restored, and the Lebanese economy began to prosper once again. Beirut became the showcase of the Arab world, a tourist's paradise. A major shipping point to the Arab interior, Beirut handled more than $900 million worth of goods annually and was an important banking and foreign exchange center. Glistening new buildings stood in the commercial district, and a modern airport complemented its excellent harbor. Tripoli and Saida served as terminals for oil pipelines from Saudi Arabia and Iraq. Lebanon also had the highest literacy rate in the Arab world (86 percent).

Unfortunately, the concept of a greater Lebanon conflicted with the Syrian concept of a greater Syria. As we have seen, Assad and the Ba'ath Party opposed such a dichotomy between the two nations. Syrian leaders had encouraged discontent even in the 1950s. To make matters worse, the Palestine Liberation Organization had been mercilessly beaten by the armies of King Hussein of Jordan in 1970. Not welcome in other Arab countries, the PLO chose Lebanon, a democracy too delicately balanced and tenuously united to resist such an unwanted terrorist organization. Nearly 200,000 Palestinian refugees were in Lebanon in the early 1970s, and the PLO progressively took over their camps. Setting up a government within a government, Yasser Arafat and his

PLO handed out job permits, ran schools, imposed a terrorist brand of justice, controlled social institutions, and created a paramilitary training program for youth. From these southern bases and refugee camps, Arafat's Palestinians struck across the border with terrorist raids into Israel.

In 1975, civil war broke out in Lebanon. Each faction and religious group had its own paramilitary gangs, and the civilian government was unable to restore order. Assassinations, kidnappings, murders, and atrocities escalated. President Hafez Assad sent in a Syrian "peace-keeping force" in 1976. Syrian forces have been there ever since. Assad realized that the radical factions (such as the PLO) were a threat to his control over the country. He determined, instead, to align himself with the weakened Christian political establishment, which he believed he could manipulate. This led to a break with Yasser Arafat when Arafat would not bow to Assad's dictates, and the two men developed a deep hatred for one another during the 1980s.

In the latter 1970s, however, Assad would use the PLO to oppose the Israeli-Egyptian accords and to pressure Sadat. When Israel entered Lebanon in 1982 (see chapter 9) to wage war against the PLO and to dislodge Syrian control, the Syrian president left Yasser Arafat hanging high and dry. Assad instead worked to take control of at least a segment of the PLO. Arafat's guerrillas killed more than eighty members of Assad's Alawite sect, and an angry Assad promoted an internal Syrian rebellion within the PLO. He deported Arafat from Damascus in June 1983. That Hafez Assad was able to maintain his vehement pan-Arab rhetoric and control his own terrorist groups, while posing as a peacemaker in war-torn Lebanon, shows his skill in manipulation and deceit. Ambition, revenge, ambiguity, and duplicity compose a personality that is shaped by Assad's quest for power and belief in his personal destiny of greatness.

Hafez Assad proclaimed his hatred for both the United States and Israel during the Reagan administration. In his speeches he portrayed a "racist" Israel, equipped by the United States to take over the Arab world. Assad escalated his guerilla warfare and terrorist actions into a formidable assault against Israel.

He also used such terrorism against his Arab opponents, including the Muslim Brotherhood that threatened revolt in Syria. In the early 1980s he massacred thousands of members of this Sunni fundamentalist group. In fact, he was willing to sacrifice one of the most beautiful cities in Syria, Hama, with a population of 180,000 pious Sunni Muslims, because members of the Muslim Brotherhood in this community on the central Syrian plains 120 miles north of Damascus were conducting guerrilla activities against his government. In February 1982, Syrian tank divisions and thousands of troops rolled into Hama and massacred between 10,000 and 25,000 civilians, leveling this beautiful metropolitan area into a huge expanse of rubble. During the same period, Assad had the audacity to complain that Israel was mistreating Palestinians on the West Bank and Gaza.

Around the world, Syrian-sponsored terrorism (including the notorious Abu Nidal group) became horrifying. Assad seemed one of the most intrepid of the hardliners in the Arab world, feared by many Arab leaders while gaining the reverence of disheartened and dispossessed Arab masses. Felled by a serious heart attack in November 1983 and politically crippled by a diabetic relapse early in 1984, Hafez Assad has risen phoenix-like from what could have been the ashes of revolution, revolt, and exile. During his illness, his own brother Rifaat had moved against him in an early succession attempt. Today, Rifaat himself is in exile in Europe, and Hafez Assad is a highly valued member of the world coalition that rose against Saddam Hussein of Iraq. Assad continues his attempt to rule Syria and to control Lebanon with an iron hand.

GREATER SYRIA TODAY

While Hafez al-Assad's portrait is painted on buildings and hangs in businesses throughout Syria, his dictatorial administration in the 1980s (along with that of his longstanding enemy Saddam Hussein) has been continually singled out by Amnesty International and U.S. State Department reports for its arbitrary arrests, torture, and political executions. It may be that President Assad's greatest achievement in twenty years of harsh rule is that no one in the Middle East or with political interests in the area can ignore him. He has brought Syria to a position of power in the Middle East, a position that his successor would have difficulty in maintaining. Although Assad often appears to be in poor health, this sphinx of Damascus continues to elude death even as he eludes crippling political defeat.

For example, throughout the 1980s Syria appeared to be bogged down in Lebanon. The country had to expend 60 percent of its gross national product on the military. Israel's invasion of Beirut in 1982 humiliated Assad's army and air force and even destroyed lines of his Russian missiles. To his consternation, Israel still maintains a buffer zone in

Lebanon and continues to control the Golan Heights. And just when President Assad felt he had a puppet Christian Marionite regime positioned in Lebanon, General Michel Aoun (another Marionite Catholic leader) refused to recognize the Syrian-backed Lebanese government and waged a war of liberation. The Arab League tried in a four-day summit meeting in May 1989 to convince Syria to withdraw its 40,000 soldiers from Lebanon. Iraq left the meeting early in anger, insisting that Syria should totally withdraw.

When Syria shelled Beirut repeatedly in August 1989, Pope John Paul called it an "attempt at genocide" and declared that those who violated the moral rights of the weak would eventually face "both God, the Supreme Judge, and the judgment of history." The same month, Egypt and Jordan indirectly criticized Syria for its role in Lebanon. The United States and Russia had consultations with Syrian officials over the grave situation.

Fourteen months later in October 1990, General Aoun was toppled from power, and Assad was being courted by the nations of the world in their united embargo against Saddam Hussein of Iraq. In an act of conciliation, President Assad had indicated for more than a year that he would work for the release of American and European hostages. He also had offered some rapprochement with the Arab world over Egypt's return to the Arab League and the PLO's initiative to recognize Israel in an effort to create a Palestinian state. As the United States forces and those from other nations built up in the fall of 1990 for a final showdown with Saddam Hussein, Egyptian president Hosni Mubarak told President George Bush that Syria was considered one of the key countries in a successful effort and that Assad should not be neglected.

The first United States president to meet with Assad since President Carter in 1977, Bush set aside American unease with Assad's links to terrorism and the political risk that Assad would snub him. On November 23, 1990, Bush and Assad met in Geneva, agreeing that while they preferred a peaceful solution to war with Iraq, they both were committed to use force if necessary.

As war began, most analysts wondered what Syria would do if Israel entered the fray (especially when Iraq sent Scud missiles into Tel Aviv). Assad, however, had slyly negotiated a position of power once again. It came to light that he was given one billion dollars by Saudi Arabia, Kuwait, and other oil states to support the Gulf War. He took the money and deftly consolidated his power over Lebanon as the rest of the world was concentrating on Saddam Hussein.

Ironically, Hafez Assad would be the world's next fear if Iraq's defeat resulted in an imbalance of power in the Middle East. As one *New York Times* headline perceptively quipped (July 23, 1989) during Assad's struggle with the Arab League's position on Lebanon: "Even When He Compromises, Assad Takes a Hard Line."

6

IRAQ AND IRAN

During most of the 1980s, the world watched breathlessly as Iraq and Iran battled one another in a struggle of massive death and destruction. Two strong-willed leaders were engaged in this conflict, and millions of their citizens followed them in blind adoration. Huge portraits of these leaders hung from the walls of buildings and consumed hundreds of billboards. Out of the two leaders, however, it was the Ayatollah Khomeini of Iran who struck fear in the hearts of Westerners. The particulars concerning the life and demeanor of Saddam Hussein of Iraq were less known, overshadowed by the religious fanaticism of his eastern neighbor.

For the Ayatollah Ruhollah Khomeini (1901-1989), his triumphant return to Iran in January 1979 after fifteen years of clandestine attempts to overthrow the Shah was being tested by the Iraqi aggression. He was determined not to give up the struggle. For Saddam Hussein (born 1937), who became president of Iraq in July 1979, the chaotic political situation in Iran appeared to provide a perfect atmosphere to capture disputed territory. Invading Iran on September 22, 1980, Saddam Hussein soon would become bogged down in a vicious war that threatened the morale, economy, and political stability of Iraq. Only the death of Khomeini in 1989 solidified a tenuous cease-fire between the countries (negotiated in August 1988 by the United Nations).

Alas, Saddam Hussein never learned the lesson of brutal aggression. In August of 1990 he attacked and captured his tiny southern neighbor, Kuwait. In 1991 America and the world mobilized military forces to put an end to the Iraqi tyrant. His country pounded by bombs and targeted by air-to-surface missiles, Saddam Hussein's vast military armor soon smoldered on the roads and sands of Iraq and Kuwait—his million-man army suffered huge casualties, tens of thousands were captured, and most retreated in humiliating defeat.

At this writing, both Iraq and Iran lie devastated by the policies of their leaders. Both nations have regularly threatened Israel and periodically threatened their Arab neighbors. Iraq has a population of 19 million and sits on an area of ancient Mesopotamia that possesses the second largest oil reserves in the Arab world. Cultural and religious differences consume this largely Muslim nation; tribal Kurds rebel in the northeast, and Shi'ite revolutionaries contend with the Iraqi army in the south. Five percent of the Iraqi population considers itself Christian. Though the Shia Muslims are in the majority, the Sunni Muslims rule the nation.

IRAN

Iran has a population of approximately 56 million (about the size of Egypt). Almost entirely Shia Muslim, these descendants of the ancient Persians (only 4 percent of Iran is Arab) have been transformed into one of the most radical Islamic republics in the Middle East. Iran's change from the pro-Western monarchy of the Shah to an anti-Western Islamic republic ruled by religious authorities was the result of religious, social, and economic pressures that had been building for decades.

THE SHAH OF IRAN

Until 1935 most of the world called Iran ("Land of the Aryans") Persia (a European translation from "Fars," an ancient province in which early Iranians were known to live). Iran, however, is the ancient name the Iranians had for their territory. Situated between the Caspian Sea and the Persian Gulf, this predominantly Indo-European people had raised one of the greatest and most extensive ancient empires on earth (the Persian Empire), had conquered most of the Semitic peoples of the Middle East five hundred years before Christ, and had threatened to subjugate Greece and Europe. Defeated at the Battle of Marathon in 490 b.c. and at Thermopylae a decade later, the Persians maintained their power in the Middle East by allowing local peoples to preserve their own nationality and government, and by providing a fine imperial administration from divisions of twenty-three provinces (satrapies). A good communication and transportation system enhanced the Persian rule.

Persia survived both Alexander the Great's invasion and that of the Roman Empire. Only the Semitic armies of Islam could overcome the proud Indo-Europeans of Persia, and Persia fell to their onslaught in the seventh century. The Battle of Nehavend in 642 ended twelve centuries of political independence for Persia. Converting en masse to the religion of their Arab masters, Persians later would be viewed as "different" in the eyes of the larger Muslim community, because in 1502 the Shi'ites became the established religious hierarchy in Persia. Contrary to Sunnite Islam, this Shia sect traced its heritage through Muhammad's cousin and son-in-law, Ali. Bitterly persecuted by the Sunnites (from Sunna, the traditional practice of Muhammad), the Shi'ites also believed that a mahdi ("guided one") would come in the future and lead the world into justice. The Sunnites thought this was heretical.

As the nineteenth century dawned, the emerging world powers vied for Persia. The French under Napoleon Bonaparte wanted Persia as a route to British India. The British believed that control of Persia would enhance the protection of British interests in the Middle East and Asia. The Russians were interested in Persia as an avenue of access to the Persian Gulf and the southern harbor that Russia desperately wanted.

Under the Kajar Dynasty (1794-1925) Jews and Christians were believed to be "unclean" and, as in all Muslim countries, were deprived of social and political equality. In the 1800s Persian Jews faced endless restriction, discrimination, oppression, and persecution. The oath of a Jew was not acceptable in a court case. In many provinces, entire Jewish communities were forced to convert to Islam.

This situation improved somewhat under the rule of Shah Muzaffar-ed-Din (1896-1907), a shah who allowed a constitutional movement to bring reform to the Islamic system. Unfortuately, he died three months after a parliament was convened, and the new shah systematically disbanded his programs. On the brink of the First World War, Great Britain began to encroach into southern Persia, while Russia began to move in from the north. Some believed that Persia was about to be dissolved.

THE PAHLAVI DYNASTY

A new dynasty of rulers, however, turned political and social unrest in Persia to a hope for the future. Reza Khan Pahlavi captured Teheran in 1921, became prime minister in 1923, and established a new parliament. On October 31, 1925, this parliament deposed the last Ka-jar ruler and on December 15, 1925, crowned Reza Pahlavi the shah. The Pahlavi dynasty, a dynasty that would exist until the forces of Aya-tollah Khomeini would declare it null and void in 1979, had been found-ed. Reza Khan had taken the name Pahlavi, a name for a language used in pre-Islamic times, as his family name to emphasize the national as-pect of his rule and to de-emphasize any Islamic republic. In 1935 the name "Persia" was changed to the original "Iran."

Both Reza Shah (who died in 1944, three years after being forced out of power by the British and Russians because of his pro-Hitler sym-pathies) and his twenty-two-year-old son, who succeeded him in 1941, Muhammad Reza (1919-1980), limited the power of the Shi'ite clergy and brought about far-reaching constitutional reforms. Jews and Chris-tians were allowed to vote and to serve in the parliament. A few Jewish families fared very well. Lutfallah Hay, for example, was born into one of the most prominent Jewish families in Teheran. In 1966 and in 1970 he was elected as the Jewish community's representative in the Majlis (the Iranian parliament). The Shah honored him several times for his social and political service. Most Jews in Iran were so impoverished, however, that nearly half of the Iranian Jewish population (39,000) emi-grated to the new Jewish state between 1948-1956.

To promote Muslim solidarity, Iran voted against the U.N. parti-tion plan in 1947 and opposed the creation of a Jewish state. Neverthe-less, under Shah Muhammad Reza economic and commercial relation-ships began to develop with Israel, although immediate diplomatic relations were impossible in light of the attitude of the Arab states. In July of 1960, the Shah publicly confirmed Iran's recognition of the state of Israel. For this act of recognition, Egyptian president Gamal Abdel Nasser severed diplomatic relations with Iran for the rest of the de-cade.

After the 1967 Six-Day War, the Shah declared that a continued state of hostility between Israel and the Arab states stifled peace and stability in the Middle East. He insisted that Israel had a right to exist (a fact other Muslim nations were loathe to admit), and yet the Shah called for Israeli withdrawal from the occupied territories. During the 1973 Yom Kippur War, the Shah suspended oil shipments to Israel and sent 500,000 barrels of oil to Egypt. After the war, however, the Shah encouraged Sadat and King Hussein of Jordan to pursue peace with Israel.

Kept in power by the West (the CIA was involved in a well-documented plot in 1953 to assist the Shah) and perceived as an ally of democratic forces, Shah Muhammad Reza found new wealth in the oil reserves of Iran. A devoted friend of the United States and yet one of the five largest oil exporting nations in 1960, Iran was one of the founding members of the Organization of Petroleum Exporting Countries (with Iraq, Kuwait, Saudi Arabia, and Venezuela). Nationalizing his oil industry, the Shah continued to be active in OPEC, constantly calling for higher oil prices in an effort to finance his far-ranging development projects.

In October 1971 the Shah spent as much as $100 million on an international celebration of the 2500th anniversary of Iran's monarchy. The best French chefs served kings, presidents, sheikhs, prime ministers, and world-renowned celebrities in air-conditioned tents raised around the ancient ruins of the Persian capital of Persepolis. Costume designers and decorators from around the world had prepared the elaborate setting.

Shah Muhammad Reza Pahlavi was determined to bring his impoverished agrarian country into the modern world. He tried to foster Iranian industry and promote land reform. His wife, Empress Farah, was devoted to education and the arts. She promoted college education for girls at Damavand College outside Teheran and sent educators to work with the nomadic Bedouin tribes. Western dress and abandonment of the traditional headcoverings were being adopted by upper middle class Iranian women, and Empress Farah (like Jehan Sadat of Egypt) considered herself a liberated woman.

In addition, the Shah was gaining the ability to defend himself. From 1971 to 1977, Iran was the largest single purchaser of U.S. military equipment in the world ($15 billion), and additional billions of dollars of nonmilitary trade with the United States helped to offset the American bill for oil. The United States counted on the Shah as a buffer and listening post against the Soviet Union, and Iranians had not forgotten the Russian intrusion into the northern perimeters of their country during World War II. The Shah's many soldiers and modern, well-equipped army were the envy of the Arab Persian Gulf states.

His SAVAK secret service oganization, however, terrorized a basically conservative and traditional Islamic constituency, and the secular culture he tried to impose was resented in more than 61,000 small villages that dotted the Iranian landscape. Religious leaders that he had quelled, threatened, and exiled over the decades began to haunt him. As popular opinion mounted against him, the Western world became edgy. The United States began suggesting that he tone down his repression in the latter half of the 1970s, or the Shah had to contemplate the loss of future American military assistance. Such pressure was too late. Both the Iranian monarch and the United States government were surprised when the Islamic Revolution took hold and Shah Muhammad Reza Pahlavi was forced out of power.

Thin, pale, and breathing heavily, the last shah of Iran died from cancer on July 27, 1980. It is said that he maintained his dignity to the end. Anwar Sadat had taken in the Shah when other world leaders were reluctant to do so because of threats of terrorism from Ayatollah Khomeini. Sadat organized an elaborate funeral for his friend. Jehan Sadat walked side by side with Empress Farah. The Shah was laid to rest in the same Egyptian mosque where his father's remains originally had been interred (the Shah later had taken his father's remains back to Iran). Little over a year later, President Sadat was assassinated. The two widows embraced and sat together once again.

THE IRANIAN REVOLUTION

In the mid-1970s the Shah of Iran had seemed invincible. Oil revenues had brought wealth to the nation, and his strong internal security system seemed to be keeping opposition from leftists and from conservative Islamic factions in check. Yet by early 1979 the Shah was in exile, and Ayatollah Ruhollah Khomeini ruled Iran.

A number of factors shed light on this phenomenon, but none totally explains the rapid unfolding of events. Social tensions had increased as the Shah dramatically modernized Iran. Islamic religious leaders preached against the secularized society, while liberal intellectuals protested the excesses of the security police. A dramatic rise in inflation (as high as 50 percent) created an economic crisis in 1976-1977, and the Shah responded with SAVAK's stern persecution of shopkeepers. These merchants and artisans were accused of profiteering and were harassed, fined, even arrested for "causing" the economic crisis. At the same time, subsidies to the clergy were cut. Protests ensued.

Tens of thousands of Americans were involved in the Iranian state economy, military, and reconstruction. For all of his spunk in the past, the Shah was viewed as a puppet of the United States, and his past recognition of Israel and support of peace did not endear him to many in the Middle East, including his Iranian constituency.

Ironically, President Jimmy Carter's administration emphasized a human rights policy that encouraged the Shah to institute more democracy in his regime. In spite of the fact that Carter and the U.S. State Department continued to affirm their support for the Shah, Muhammad Reza Pahlavi's opponents believed that the United States was wavering in its support for "the puppet on the Peacock Throne." Opponents became braver. More demonstrations were waged by a combined group of leftists and rightists.

The Shah's response was inconsistent, a fact that may be attributable to the cancer that spread throughout his body. During a mass march on September 4, 1978, at the end of the holy month of Ramadan, the Shah's soldiers stood by as marchers cried, "Death to the Shah!" Four days later, however, on "Black Friday" (September 8, 1978), news reporters claimed that his troops massacred thousands of unarmed Iranian demonstrators. Accounts vary as to the accuracy of the extent of the massacre, but there is no doubt that Black Friday became a rallying point for opponents to the Shah's regime.

Although the Shah promised democratic elections to quell the unrest, few Iranians believed him. He even offered to step down as the head of government and only retain his title. Rioting and deaths continued. Shah Muhammad Reza Pahlavi had hoped that his son would follow him on the Iranian throne as he had followed his father, but on January 16, 1979, he announced that he was taking a "vacation" because he was fatigued. He flew to Egypt, never to return. After fifteen years of exile, Ayatollah Khomeini returned to Iran on February 1, 1979, and overthrew newly appointed premier Shahpur Bakhtiar's government in ten days.

For approximately 80,000 Jews in Iran (around 60,000 of them in Teheran), the fall of the Shah and the arrival of Khomeini's Islamic Republic significantly altered their status. Their economic situation had improved in the 1970s, and there were eighty Jewish professors in Iranian universities and institutions of higher learning early in 1978. At that time, 6 percent of Iran's physicians were Jewish, and 4 percent of Iran's university population was Jewish. By 1983 Khomeini's regime had confiscated a considerable portion of Jewish property and had executed twelve Jews. It is estimated that within four years of Khomeini's arrival half the Jewish population had left Iran, 20,000 going to Israel. Nearly 18,000 had settled in the United States.

AYATOLLAH RUHOLLAH KHOMEINI

As factors contributing to the Islamic Revolution are analyzed, the charismatic and indomitable personality of Ayatollah Ruhollah Khomeini cannot be emphasized too much. Although other dissidents and their writings set the stage for his return, Ayatollah Khomeini came to symbolize the revolution. Millions thronged the capital on February 1, 1979, to catch a glimpse of their triumphant spiritual leader in sandals, long robe, and black turban descending from the ramp of a chartered 747. "The holy one has come . . . the light of our lives!" the crowd chanted. Posters, billboards, and huge paintings of the Ayatollah suddenly appeared throughout Iran. Cassette tape recordings that the Ayatollah had made during his exile were soon sold in shops and by vendors on street corners.

The son of a mullah (religious leader) in Khomein, a town approximately 180 miles south of Teheran, Ruhollah never really knew his father. While Ruhollah was still an infant, his father was murdered. Early reports indicate that his father died in a dispute with a landowner over irrigation rights, but popular mythology asserted that the Shah's father had ordered the death of Ruhollah's father. Ruhollah Khomeini was reared by a strong-willed mother and an aunt. He began religious studies at an early age.

Although accounts of his early life are sketchy (some debate whether he was born in 1900, 1901, or 1902), he appears to have pursued further Islamic studies at Marvi Theological School in Teheran. In the 1920s he completed his studies in Qum, where he married his first wife, became interested in Islamic mysticism, and studied Plato's *Republic*. Becoming a respected mullah, he published *Unveiling the Mysteries* in 1941, a book that accused Reza Shah of persecuting the clergy and destroying Islamic culture. Insisting that all laws passed by Iran's parliament "must be burned," Khomeini called for an Islamic Republic formed by Allah. "It is the only government accepted by Allah on Resurrection Day," Khomeini wrote.

In the 1950s he received the title *Ayatollah* ("Reflection of Allah"), an honor bestowed by a mullah's followers. More than a thousand ayatollahs exist today throughout the Shi'ite world. By the early 1960s he was bestowed with the title of *Grand Ayatollah* (only six other Iranian spiritual leaders held such an honored position at that time). He was jailed in 1963 for his forceful opposition to Shah Muhammad Reza Pahlavi. In 1964 he was exiled for refusing to keep quiet. After traveling to

Turkey, he moved to Iraq, using his followers throughout Iran to spread his campaign against the Shah. In 1970 one of his sons, Mustafa, was killed. This fueled speculation that the Shah's SAVAK agents had murdered him.

Ayatollah Ruhollah Khomeini's influence became so widespread that when a critical article about him was promoted by the Shah's officials in January 1978, demonstations broke out throughout Iran. The Shah was shocked to find that by September even the workers in the oil fields were on strike. Martial law was imposed. Iraq was persuaded to expel the Ayatollah to France. The Ayatollah's followers manufactured more cassettes in France and distributed his tape recordings throughout Iran. When the Shah tried to quell the revolution by granting amnesty to the Ayatollah and thousands of exiles, Khomeini refused amnesty. Khomeini said that he would return to Iran only when the Shah was gone. That, of course, occurred early in 1979.

Many liberal opponents of the Shah had hoped that Khomeini would relinquish political power and allow Iran to have a democratic society. Khomeini understood, however, that Islam and democracy were incompatible. He retained his Islamic fervor and his dream of an Islamic Republic. Dismantling the Shah's hated SAVAK agents, he replaced them with his own SAVAMA, a ruthless group of operatives who forced the population of Iran to conform to Islamic law. A United Nations commission estimated in 1987 that 7,000 people were shot, hanged, stoned, or burned in accordance with Islamic law after the 1979 revolution. Women were ordered to wear veils and chadors (gowns that covered the entire length of the woman). Describing music as "opium that stupefies," Khomeini banned it from radio and television.

The U.S. State Department should have been listening to Khomeini's tapes. "If the religious leaders had been in power," the Ayatollah maintained, "they would not have allowed the Iranian nation to become the captive of the Americans and the British. . . . They would have prevented the American experts from taking advantage of us." Often describing the United States as "the Great Satan," he condoned the takeover of the U.S. embassy by militant students on November 4, 1979. The longstanding hatred of the United States and its ties to the Shah was unleashed when President Carter allowed the Shah to enter the United States for medical treatment. The Iranians illegally held fifty-two American hostages for 444 days.

The Ayatollah and his followers were delighted when Carter's military rescue mission in April 1980 failed miserably. Only on the inauguration day of Ronald Reagan (January 20, 1981) were the hostages released. Jimmy Carter suffered this humiliation in front of the whole world. The Ayatollah's strength in dealing with the United States and holding the hostages helped consolidate his power in Iran in 1979, passing his new constitution and establishing Iran as an Islamic Republic. Lifelong supreme authority was given to Ayatollah Ruhollah Khomeini, and he received one more title, that of *Velayat Faghi* ("Religious Leader").

As Khomeini's Iran increasingly became isolated in the 1980s, the Ayatollah became a focal point for the spread of Islamic fundamentalism. Khomeini's government began financing rebels and terrorists throughout the world, even instigating the overthrow of Arab countries, including the Persian Gulf states. In some cases, Iran directly financed international bombings and abduction of hostages. Declaring that "Islam wants all the world to be one family," Khomeini even stated that he considered "Lebanon to be a part of Iran because we are not separate from each other. We are as they and they are as us." Lebanon was located 1,000 miles from Teheran, and yet the Ayatollah's funded revolutionaries were active in its destruction.

Khomeini's hatred toward Israel remained steadfast. He insisted that "Israel must be destroyed" and his representatives in the United Nations reiterated his words. Statements against Jews and Judaism permeated his rhetoric during his decade of rule. To Israelis during the mid-1980s, Iran formed the third side of a terror triangle (with Syria and Libya). Iranians even named streets in honor of terrorists who killed Israelis. It is estimated that Iran's annual support of the Shi'ite Hizbullah (from *Hizb Allah,* the Party of God) terrorist organization operating out of Lebanon is approximately $100 million.

In his holy mission to institute a pure theocracy in Iran and to rid the nation of Western corruption and degeneracy, the Ayatollah silenced his opposition swiftly and without mercy. For those who incurred his wrath, no distance was safe. British author Salman Rushdie learned this fact the hard way when his book *The Satanic Verses* was deemed by Khomeini to have blasphemed the faith of Islam. In February 1989 the Ayatollah called for his death and put a bounty on his head. Even those close to Khomeini were expendable. In March 1989 he dismissed Ayatollah Hussein Ali Montazeri, a Shi'ite moderate who had been designated as his successor. Montazeri had suggested that the Iranian revolution was off course.

For Ayatollah Ruhollah Khomeini, the logic of Islam was clear and concise. He sought to pattern his life and his rule by that logic. On one of his tapes from France he described this to his followers as his triumphal entry approached:

> The people of Iran have reached a state where they have attracted the attention of the world. We have gained prestige in the world, from America to the Arabic countries. This is a miracle. I think it is a spiritual one. The hands of God are with you. If it wasn't the hand of Allah, the nation, from children to the elderly, would not have joined our campaign. Victory is near. Don't be afraid. The Prophet Muhammad spent most of his life struggling. Learn from the Prophet and be patient. He fought all his life to overcome oppression. And we have been doing it only a short time.

"What are we afraid of?" Khomeini concluded. "If we are killed we will go to heaven. And if we kill we will go to heaven. This is the logic of Islam because we are in the right." On June 4, 1989, Ayatollah Ruhollah Khomeini departed to meet his Maker.

Hundreds of thousands thronged to his corpse crying, "Sorrow, sorrow is this day," and chanting, "Khomeini the idol-smasher is with God today." "We have been orphaned, our father is dead," one group of women grieved. Even in death, however, the infamous Ayatollah managed to denounce his enemies. In his last will and testament, read over Teheran radio, he castigated the Great Satan, calling the United States and hostile Arab leaders "terrorists" and "pirates." "May God's curse be upon them," he wrote.

IRAQ AND SADDAM HUSSEIN

One of the Arab leaders Khomeini specifically named in this will as his enemy was the president of Iraq, Saddam Hussein. Engaged in hostilities since 1980, they had grown to hate one another. Although born more than a generation apart, the elderly Khomeini and the middle-aged Saddam Hussein agreed on at least two hatreds: their hatred for the West and their hatred of Jews and the Jewish state.

When Iraq was carved out of the territory of the Ottoman Empire, placed under the British Mandate, and given to Faisal of the Hashemite dynasty of Saudi Arabia's Hussein family (no relation to Saddam Hussein, but directly related to King Hussein of Jordan; see chapters 2 and 4), it included the Kurdish state of Kurdistan, part of Turkey, and an abundance of Shia Muslims to the south. It included "the land between the rivers [Tigris and Euphrates]," Mesopotamia, cradle of ancient civilizations, including those of the Sumerians, Akkadians, Assyrians, Babylonians, and Chaldeans. Mesopotamia was conquered by Muslim Arabs in 634; its name changed to "Iraq." During the reign of Caliph al-Mansur (754-775), the small suburb Baghdad became the capital of the Abbasid dynasty.

Jews had resided in the area of Iraq for thousands of years. Under Muslim regimes, their fate depended on the attitude of each ruler. They learned to live with periodic pogroms and the inequities of the Muslim system. Under the British Mandate and King Faisal's reign, however, Jews were granted freedom of religion, freedom of education, and freedom of employment. Jews also were active in government. Unfortunately, as Iraq moved toward its independence as an Arab state, anti-Semitism escalated, and those Jews deemed "Zionists" were severely persecuted.

When Iraq became independent in 1932, the government was openly hostile toward the Jewish community. It dismissed Jewish officials and harrassed Jewish shopkeepers. Pro-Hitler sympathies among the Iraqi population festered into oppression like that of the Nazis in the late 1930s. In the anti-British, pro-Nazi riots in 1941, hundreds of Jews were cruelly tortured and murdered by Iraqi mobs. Government officials and police stood by as Jewish homes were looted and synagogues desecrated.

When Israel became a state on May 14, 1948, Iraqi Jews were arrested and their homes searched. As the Iraqi army attacked the Jewish state, the crime of "Zionism" was added to the Iraqi criminal code (imprisonment for seven years or death on the testimony of two witnesses). Jews were placed under martial law and forbidden to leave Iraq. Tens of thousands left illegally. When permitted in May 1950 to leave legally, more than 100,000 Iraqi Jews fled to the fledgling state of Israel (with biblical precedents in mind, this was dubbed "Operation Ezra and Nehemiah" by the Jewish Agency and Jewish underground organizations). The Iraqi government confiscated more than $200 million in assets owned by these refugees, never to be repaid. By June 1952, only 6,000 Jews remained in Iraq.

It was into this Iraqi environment of hatred for the West and hatred for the Jews that Saddam Hussein was born in 1937. His life began in a small village, and little is known of his family. The Arabic word *saddam* means "one who confronts," and Saddam Hussein's life seemed to confirm his name. He left home early, and by the age of ten he arrived in Baghdad brandishing a gun. He lived there with his uncle, an Arab activist who had been jailed for anti-British activity. This uncle appears to have nurtured young Saddam's hatred. Later, as an important leader in the Ba'ath Party, Saddam Hussein would publish one of his uncle's pamphlets: *Three Things God Should Not Have Created: Persians, Jews, and Flies.*

Saddam Hussein joined the Ba'ath Party (the Arab Socialist Resurrection Party) in 1957. This small underground group of Arab nationalists were intent on "liberating" Arab countries as well as "Palestine" and wanted to unite the entire Middle East into an Arab nation. Barely out of his teens, Saddam was known as an aggressive, dedicated member. When leftist General Abdul Karim Kassim ousted the Hashemite monarchy that King Faisal had begun under the British Mandate (killing King Faisal II), the Ba'ath Party leadership believed the time was ripe to murder Kassim and grasp power for themselves. Young Saddam Hussein was dispatched as a junior member of the assassination squad.

Saddam Hussein had bragged that they would assassinate Kassim and that the streets would flow with a "lake of blood" (a favorite phrase). The assassination attempt failed, and Saddam was wounded. As blood flowed from his leg, he was forced to flee to Egypt. There Nasser protected him as a respected member of Iraq's Ba'ath Party and a cohort in the attempt to bring all Muslims into "the Arab Nation." Saddam registered as a student of law at Cairo University but was so active in student politics that he never completed a course. He was rowdy but appeared to have a natural gift for leadership.

When the Ba'ath Party joined military officers in finally assassinating General Kassim in 1963, Saddam Hussein was brought back to Iraq. The military, however, double-crossed the Ba'ath Party (already weakened by splits in the party) and seized power for themselves. Saddam was jailed for subversion. In prison, he read books about two of his heroes, Adolf Hitler and Joseph Stalin. Iraq broke off diplomatic relations with the United States during the Six-Day War. Iraqi troops joined in that devastating Arab defeat, and in July 1968 the Iraqi government fell to the Ba'ath Party in another coup. As happened in so many Arab countries after the 1967 War, Iraq was to restructure and change leadership.

That leadership would come from the Ba'ath Party and would give rise to the political aspirations of thirty-one-year-old Saddam Hussein. Not only was his revolutionary movement in power, but his older cousin, Major General Ahmed Hassan al-Bakr, was chosen president and prime minister of Iraq by the Revolutionary Command Council. Bakr appointed young Saddam to oversee the security apparatus of the government.

Saddam Hussein soon became known for using fear and terror to keep party members and Iraqi citizens in line. With the help of the Soviet KGB, he organized a brutal state security service and a dreaded military intelligence bureau. Assassinations were ordered abroad, as each area of Iraqi society was monitored. On January 27, 1969, in a travesty that provoked an international uproar, fourteen alleged spies were hanged—nine of them Jews. In the early years of the Ba'ath regime, 2,000 opponents were executed or "disappeared."

Under the Ba'ath Party control, Iraq opposed any political settlement with Israel in the aftermath of the Six-Day War, denouncing and threatening any Arab state that might negotiate. Iraq also declared its support for the Palestinian guerrilla fighters but lost face when it failed to let its 12,000 troops stationed in Jordan help the Palestinians when King Hussein was killing and deporting them in 1970-1971. Boundary disputes broke out between the Ba'ath regime and the Shah of Iran as early as 1969. Iran helped support the Kurdish rebels in the north of Iraq. Iraq responded by cementing ties with the Soviet Union.

Ironically, in the 1970s Saddam Hussein was viewed as a "peacemaker" even as he consolidated his power to become the strongman in Baghdad politics. He became vice-president of Iraq and was lauded for avoiding war and negotiating a treaty with the Shah of Iran in 1975. Actually, Iraq needed to work with Iran in the OPEC embargo. Oil revenues were flooding into Iraq. During the same period Saddam used his control of the internal security service to eliminate those who opposed him or stood in his way with regard to power. Saddam Hussein also built a devoted cult of followers among the young people of Iraq (a youth indoctrination campaign modeled after the Hitler Youth of Nazi Germany).

President Bakr had been in ill health in the latter half of the 1970s but believed that his cousin Saddam, his own "flesh and blood," would not betray him. Saddam Hussein, however, systematically eliminated each leader and friend close to Bakr. In July 1979, President Bakr announced that he was "resigning because of health reasons" and that he favored Saddam Hussein to succeed him. Some political analysts believe Saddam forced his resignation. At any rate, by this time Saddam Hussein was the most powerful man in Iraq.

Saddam Hussein became president of Iraq on July 16, 1979. He was forty-two years old. Ever paranoid, he immediately began to purge the Ba'ath Party leadership. He believed that five of his closest friends in the Iraqi leadership were not convinced that he should be president. For years he had ordered assassinations while pretending in public to grieve at the death of his "friends." Now he had one of his closest colleagues arrested, torturing him into agreeing to make a confession that he was planning a coup against Saddam. Calling a July 22 meeting of the Ba'ath Party Regional Congress, Saddam Hussein engineered the meeting and the confession to whip up patriotic fervor for him and to portray himself as a good, trusting leader who had been betrayed by his friends.

The tortured and broken confessor would name a leader, and the man would stand shaking in terror. Then the confessor would say that that particular leader would not betray Saddam. The emotionally drained man would collapse in relief. As the "true conspirators" were named and accused, they were led out of the hall. Saddam shed false tears at his "betrayal," finally going down among the remaining leaders to ask them to join the firing squad with him. They became accomplices. "Long live Saddam, long live the Party, God save Saddam from conspirators," the crowd shouted. This entire meeting was recorded on videotape by Saddam's order.

THE STRUGGLE

From a distance, Ayatollah Ruhollah Khomeini, the fervent Muslim religious leader who spent most of his life studying the Koran and who was enamored of the philosopher-king concept in Plato's *Republic*, seems quite different from Saddam Hussein, the little-educated, malevolent dictator who read Hitler and Stalin, who was a cold, calculated politician, and who appeared religious only when that helped to solidify his people. Yet both men centered their lives and their rallying speeches on the concept of "the struggle."

"The Prophet Muhammad spent most of his life struggling," Ayatollah Khomeini often told his followers. "Learn from the Prophet and be patient." Saddam Hussein, the "one who confronts," was consumed with the struggle, vying for absolute power in a volatile political arena and pursuing his goals with any terror or force available. In their total dedication to victory in the struggle, both men appear to have been oblivious to the suffering of others. In their self-absorption, both the religious Ayatollah Khomeini and the irreligious Saddam Hussein seem to have had little constraint of conscience, ridding themselves of colleagues and constituencies who impeded (or who they thought impeded) their progress in "the struggle."

To make matters worse, their devoted followers perpetuated and escalated their narcissism. Ayatollah Khomeini and Saddam Hussein surrounded themselves with a lavish personality cult of adulation and unquestioning obedience. Khomeini was convinced that he was actually pointing people to Allah, that he had dedicated himself to the struggle of Allah, that he had sacrificed his life to battle evil. Saddam Hussein was convinced that truth rested within his own being, that his power should be unquestioned, that he struggled against the forces of evil that sought to dethrone him and deprive Iraq of a great leader.

In spite of their innermost explanations to themselves of what their calling entailed, both men ended at the same "struggle." Both believed they would lead the Arab world to a unified conquest of the globe. Both believed in their own messianic role. Both devastated countries they claimed to love. In awe and amazement, the world continues to watch as the next chapter unfolds in Iran's legacy from Ayatollah Ruhollah Khomeini and Iraq's legacy from Saddam Hussein.

7

LIBYA AND THE PLO

The Zionist entity that has been among us since World War II must be removed the same way as other effects of World War II have been removed," Colonel Muammar al-Qaddafi asserted at a September 1, 1989, gathering celebrating his twentieth year in power. "All of Palestine is for the Palestinians," the leader of Libya proclaimed. Flanked by an array of foreign dignitaries, including Hafez al-Assad of Syria, Daniel Ortega of Nicaragua, King Hassan II of Morocco, and Chadli Benjedid of Algeria, Colonel Qaddafi declared that Israel "must be removed."

Muammar Qaddafi showed little enthusiasm for one of the other guests seated near him, Yasser Arafat of the Palestine Liberation Organization. Months earlier, Yasser Arafat had convinced the United States that he renounced terrorism and that he for the first time recognized Israel's existence. The United States began official contacts with the PLO on his word. Arafat seemed to rise once again from predicted demise.

To Qaddafi this proved that Arafat and the PLO were only "playing at terrorism," a serious pursuit that the Libyan leader had supported generously with oil revenues over the years. Colonel Quaddafi had cut off funds to the PLO earlier in 1989, and at his twentieth anniversary celebration there was no indication that either he or Syria's Hafez Assad had patched up their feud with Arafat.

Ironically, Arafat and Qaddafi had never much liked or respected one another. Yet both men had a reputation for terrorist activity, both at times had been thought to be madmen, and both had sought at various stages to reenter the mainstream of global politics by claiming that they wanted "peace" and that they were "not terrorists" but rather "liberators of the oppressed." The aftermath of the 1967 Six-Day War would thrust both Qaddafi and Yasser Arafat into positions of power in the Arab world.

Over two decades later, the aftermath of the 1991 Gulf War would change their positions once again. Arafat would declare on the side of Saddam Hussein, losing his wealthy Arab patrons even as his actions convinced the West that he was an opportunistic liar, not fit to lead the Palestinian Arabs. Qaddafi was forced to keep quiet during the Gulf War in an attempt to smooth over many of the feuds he had engendered with his Arab neighbors. Instead of his pompous sideshow of the past, Qaddafi increasingly appeared to be irrelevant. Nevertheless, both Libya and the PLO remain forces to contend with as the Middle East approaches the twenty-first century.

LIBYA

With a population of 4.3 million, Libya today has one of the highest per capita incomes in North Africa. Muammar Qaddafi has spent billions on cheap housing, medical clinics, and education for his people, who are 97 percent Sunni Muslim. Although 95 percent of Libya is desert or semidesert, a vast reserve of underground water has been discovered deep in those deserts, and Qaddafi has envisioned the Great Man-Made River project to pipe that water 600 miles to the coast, where the large majority of the population lives. Located west of Egypt, Libya has more than 1,000 miles of Mediterranean coastline, but the water supply of Tripoli and Benghazi (Libya's co-capitals) is threatened by salt from the sea. The Great Man-Made River appears to be Africa's most expensive project, since its final aim is to have thousands of irrigation canals to provide water for tens of thousands of farms and pasture for millions of sheep and cattle.

HISTORICAL BACKGROUND

In the ancient period, Libya surrounded Tripoli in the west and Cyrene in the east. Both cities have a rich history, and Jewish communities settled in those areas under the Greeks and Romans. Libya was conquered by the Arabs in the seventh century, and most of the population (excluding the Jews) converted to Islam. Under the Arabs, however, there was no central regime in power in Libya, and most of the great Arab empires were content to allow local autonomy among the various Libyan tribes. The Mamluks of Egypt (1249-1517), for example, had alliances with Libyan tribal chieftains. Both Jewish and Muslim refugees from the Spanish Inquisition in 1492 fled to the coastal areas of Libya.

The Ottoman Turks captured Egypt in 1517 and captured Tripoli in 1551. From 1551 to 1711 Ottoman pashas and soldiers governed Tripoli. In 1711 Ahmad Qaramanli, a Turkish soldier, seized power and established a dynasty that lasted until 1835. Tripoli was a port city noted as a refuge for pirates, and the British and French exerted their influence in the nineteenth century as they suppressed piracy. The Ottomans, however, centralized their authority throughout the Libyan area, defeated rebellious local chieftains, and separated the provinces of Tripolitania and Cyrenaica.

Italy considered Tripolitania part of her "imperial sphere of influence" and invaded the territory in 1911. The weakened Ottoman Empire could do little to stop the takeover, and the Turks were forced to cede both Tripolitania and Cyrenaica to Italy. The native population continued to resist. Only after the First World War was local opposition in Tripolitania defeated by the Italians. Regional Bedouin tribes of Cyrenaica, however, fought the Italians in a destructive, protracted war from 1923 to 1932. In 1934 the Italians united Cyrenaica and Tripolitania into modern Libya.

In the early decades of Italian rule, the Jews of Libya prospered and had equal rights. In 1931 the Jewish population was 21,000 (15,000 lived in Tripoli), 4 percent of the total population. As a result of the Hitler-Mussolini axis, however, anti-Jewish legislation began to appear in 1936. Jews were forced out of schools and government in many areas, and "Jewish race" was stamped on their official papers. In 1941, one-fourth of the population of Tripoli was Jewish and forty-four synagogues dotted the Jewish quarter. The Italian governor of Tripoli in March 1941 ordered all Jewish organizations to cease to function.

During World War II, Benghazi fluctuated between the Axis and Allied powers. On April 3, 1941, Arab youths went on a rampage and assaulted Jews throughout the city. At the end of 1941, the British briefly took Benghazi and were welcomed as liberators by the Jewish community. Nevertheless, in February 1942 the Nazis retook Benghazi and plundered Jewish homes and businesses. Twenty-six hundred Jews were deported across the desert to labor camps, where they worked long hours on road construction. In fourteen months, more than 560 Jews from Benghazi died of starvation or typhus. Nearly 2,000 Jews from Tripoli were deported to work camps in April 1942.

Axis forces were expelled from Libya in 1943, and the British and French administered the area. Unfortunately the Muslims continued the persecution of Libyan Jews that the Nazis of Germany and Fascists of Italy had begun. A succession of anti-Jewish pogroms occurred in a number of towns and villages. On July 4, 1945, Muslim masses killed and wounded Jews, setting fire to synagogues and looting businesses and homes. Between November 4 and 7, 1945, 100 Jews were murdered in another Arab pogrom.

Riots continued, and the British appeared unable to stem Muslim hostility. In the next few years hundreds of Jewish homes were destroyed and more members of the Jewish community were murdered. In June 1948 Muslims attacked Jews in Tripoli and Benghazi. Fourteen Jews were killed. More would have died had it not been for a Libyan Jewish defense organization that held off the mobs with hand grenades and weapons. Most of the Muslim thugs were on their way to fight against the new Jewish state.

Ironically, when the United Nations General Assembly voted on November 21, 1949, that Libya should become an independent Arab state before January 1, 1952, Israel voted for the resolution. Libyan Muslims showed no gratitude at this gesture of goodwill but planned more pogroms to force out the Jews. By the end of 1951, nearly nine-tenths of the Jewish community in Libya had emigrated to Israel.

Libya was the first nation to achieve independence under the auspices of the United Nations. It declared its independence as a constitutional and hereditary monarchy on December 24, 1951. King Idris I, a local ruler and early resistance fighter against the Italian occupation, became Libya's leader for the next seventeen years. Once King Idris I was in power, Libya joined the Arab League, immediately collaborating on the Arab boycott of Israel, attacking Israel at the United Nations, and spreading anti-Israel propaganda.

During the 1967 Six-Day War, only 4,500 Jews remained in Libya. Libyan Muslims rioted against them, looting and destroying their property, and killing and maiming Jewish members of their communities. Most Jews fled to Israel, giving up all hope of maintaining their Libyan civilization of more than two millennia. In 1970 Muammar Qaddafi confiscated all remaining Jewish property and canceled all debts owed Jews. Twenty Jews remained in all of Libya in 1974. There appear to be no Jews left in Libya today.

COLONEL MUAMMAR AL-QADDAFI

Born in a tent on a flat gray desert of rocks and bushes twenty miles south of the Mediterranean Sea, Muammar al-Qaddafi's father was a herder of camels and goats, a poor illiterate Bedouin Arab of the small Qaddadfa tribe. The exact date of Muammar Qaddafi's birth is unknown, but he appears to have been born between 1940 and 1942. He thus remembered the struggle of foreign powers for Libyan territory during the Second World War. In fact, his tribe maintained a healthy suspicion of all foreigners.

At an early age, Muammar received weekly religious instruction in the Koran by a Muslim teacher. He also entered primary school in the nearest seaside town of Sirte. The young Qaddafi was the first member of his family to read and write, but such formal education came at a price. He had to attend school during the day and sleep on the floor of a mosque at night. He was the oldest in his class, but because of his Bedouin heritage was seen as a country bumpkin by the urban oriented students. He trudged home across the desert once a week to worship with his tribe.

When his family moved to Sebha, Qaddafi attended secondary school there. He and many of his classmates became dedicated admirers of Gamal Abdel Nasser of Egypt. Muammar would memorize Nasser's radio speeches, repeating them word for word to his classmates. Every year Qaddafi and his student colleagues would go on strike on the date of the Balfour Declaration. Known as a charismatic and yet serious student, Qaddafi surrounded himself with friends who would form part of his later revolution in Libya. To this day, Nasser's themes of anti-Zionism, anti-West, and Arab unification permeate every speech that Qaddafi delivers.

Soon the teenage Qaddafi had a reputation for being a revolutionary and a troublemaker. At one time he railed against foreign military bases in Libya and led students in political demonstrations against the corrupt monarchy. At other times he led religious demonstrations against a hotel that purportedly allowed the consumption of alcohol. Tapping into the discontent that was swelling against King Idris, Qaddafi's revolutionaries were absorbing ideas from the Ba'ath Party as well as George Habash's radical Arab Nationalist Party (this would later develop into the Popular Front for the Liberation of Palestine, a radical Palestinian group). Qaddafi, however, continued to expound the ideas of Nasser, adding a disciplinarian code that forbade drinking, card playing, and women. Members of his student movement were told to study and pray regularly.

In an almost unbelievable lapse of security, Qaddafi was allowed to join the Royal Libyan Military Academy in Benghazi in 1963 and, in spite of his criminal record, was made part of an elite group that protected the king. The British Military Mission that helped train Libyan officers had a number of Westerners that regularly came into contact with Qaddafi, and most remember him as rude and cruel. Organizing his clandestine Free Officers' Movement in 1964, Qaddafi had his colleagues assemble a parallel civilian revolutionary organization, ordering them to enlist mainly those younger than themselves in an effort to make their faction a youth movement. Qaddafi became involved in the assassination of those whom he disliked or who threatened the spread of his movement. In spite of this fact, he was sent to Britain in 1966 for a four-month course in weaponry. He insisted on wearing his traditional Bedouin robes around London and displayed disgust at the immorality prevalent in the city.

In the meantime, King Idris was having problems. Money went through his government enterprise like water through a sieve, and graft and corruption abounded on all levels of his bureaucracy. In spite of a projected escalation of oil revenues, Libya was experiencing a cash shortage. Even the United States became edgy at the prospects of revolution within Libya. In a secret report in March 1960, the U.S. National Security Council admitted that there was little loyalty to King Idris among the young urban population, and, even though all political parties were banned, a number of pan-Arab nationalistic factions were active. Fearing that millions of dollars of American investments were in danger, the U.S. government counted on the British to step in to maintain a Libyan regime that would favor Western interests. After the 1967 Six-Day War and King Idris's failure to help the Arab cause (he offered little more than statements), few in Libya or outside its borders believed that the Idris monarchy would survive.

Indeed, Colonel Muammar Qaddafi was intent on the overthrow of the monarch and planned to take over on March 21, 1969. Ironically, it was a benefit concert in Benghazi for Yasser Arafat's Fatah organization, presented by one of the Arab world's most famous singers, Oum Kalthoum, that forced Qaddafi to reschedule the coup for September. Most of the civilian and military leaders of the government that he had planned to arrest were attending the concert, and Qaddafi thought he could not interrupt such an important performance for such a noble cause. At 6:30 A.M. on September 1, 1969, Qaddafi declared on Libyan radio:

> People of Libya. In response to your own will, fulfilling your most heartfelt wishes, answering your incessant demands for change and re-generation and your longing to strive towards these ends, listening to your incitement to rebel, your armed forces have undertaken the over-throw of the reactionary and corrupt regime, the stench of which has sickened and horrified us all.

"On this occasion I have pleasure in assuring all our foreign friends that they need have no fears either for their property or for their safety," he concluded minutes later. "This is purely an internal affair."

The radical Arab regimes in Egypt, Iraq, Syria, and Sudan gave the new government immediate recognition. Qaddafi still admired Nasser and depended on the Egyptian leader to tell him what to do in the new revolutionary order. In December 1969 Nasser stopped in Tripoli on his way back from an Arab summit and met personnally with Qaddafi and Sudan's prime minister, General Jaafar el-Numeiry. They agreed to coordinate more closely the political, economic, and military policies of their nations.

A new republic was proclaimed in Libya, but for all practical purposes its sole leadership was in the hands of Colonel Qaddafi. Executive power was concentrated in the Revolutionary Command Council composed of twelve of Qaddafi's closest military colleagues. Qaddafi became a national hero as he forced both the United States and Great Britain to evacuate their military bases in 1970. These Western nations were coerced to work with the new government in an effort to protect their oil interests in Libya.

Systematically, Qaddafi nationalized foreign banks, corporations, and finally oil company holdings. He gained sole control of the press and telecommunications. Qaddafi also became known as one of the most radical and extreme haters of Israel and of the Jewish people. A few days after his regime was established, he ordered the confiscation of all Jewish property and assets.

In April 1973 Qaddafi implemented the five-point reform program of what he called the "popular revolution." "Popular committees" were instituted throughout the nation to suspend existing laws and distribute new laws. There was to be a new emphasis on Islamic religion, and all political opposition was to be purged (including Communists and capitalists). The five-point program also provided a campaign against bureaucratic inefficiency. In 1977 the nation's name was changed to the "Socialist People's Libyan Arab Jamahiriya [State of the Masses]," and executive power was given to the General People's Congress. Qaddafi became secretary general of the secretariat of the new Congress and remained chief of state. His friends in the now disbanded Revolutionary Command Council became members of the secretariat of the Congress or served as advisers.

By this time, a rift had emerged between Libya and Egypt. Nasser had died in 1970, and although both countries had enacted a loose confederation with Syria that held through the 1973 Yom Kippur War, Anwar Sadat's negotiations with Israel and flirtations with the West drove a wedge between him and Qaddafi. In fact, Qaddafi had not been consulted about the impending Yom Kippur War, and when the war was over the Libyan leader chided Egypt and Syria for their "limited aims." Qaddafi insisted that only total annihilation of Israel should be the Arab objective. In 1975 Qaddafi threatened to sever relations with Egypt, calling Anwar Sadat and his wife, Jehan, a "20th century Antony and Cleopatra." Sadat declared in response that Qaddafi was "100 per cent sick and possessed by the devil." Following the visit of Sadat to Jerusalem in November 1977, Libya joined the rejection front of the Arab nations in isolating Egypt and opposing any negotiations with the Jewish state.

Denouncing United States support for Israel, Libya refused to go along with the March 18, 1974, decision of other Arab oil-producing nations to end the oil embargo. By the end of 1974 Qaddafi did end his embargo but used his massive oil revenues in May 1975 to purchase $1 billion in armaments from the Soviet Union. He claimed that he was stockpiling arms so that Arabs could wage a new war against Israel. Buying the latest technology from many nations, including West Germany, Italy, and Great Britain, Qaddafi even talked French president Francois Mitterrand into honoring commitments for armaments in the early 1980s. By this time, Qaddafi was well known as a supporter of terrorist groups around the world, and he brutally assassinated and maimed his opponents who had taken refuge in the West.

Increasingly using the Soviet Union for his own ends, Qaddafi invaded Chad and threatened the Sudan, Egypt, Morocco, and Tunisia by assisting revolutionary groups within their borders. He trained insurgents throughout Africa and in 1979 tried to save Idi Amin's regime in

Uganda. President Ronald Reagan's administration in the United States took a tough stand against the Libyan dictator (the U.S. was still trading with Libya but had banned shipments of arms after the coup in 1969). In August 1981 during naval maneuvers in the Mediterranean Sea, U.S. Navy F-14 Tomcats from the carrier *Nimitz* shot down two Libyan warplanes that challenged the aircraft carrier. Qaddafi let it be known that he was in the market for nuclear weapons. The world was horrified as it learned of his fascination with chemical weapons and their production.

His radical and abusive language as well as well-publicized tactics of brutality isolated him from even his Arab colleagues in the Middle East. He chided other Arabs for their inability to achieve unity and for their inability to destroy Israel. Many wondered whether or not he was mentally unbalanced. The Soviet Union had supplied him with weapons and technical assistance in the hope that he would be a bastion for Communist and Marxist ideology.

Qaddafi, however, was a dedicated Muslim who only used such efforts for his own ends. He felt loyalty only to himself, to Libyans who agreed with his revolution, and to his concept of a future united Islamic nation. In deference to the latter he joined with Syria to support Ayatollah Khomeini and Iran against the forces of Saddam Hussein's Iraq.

Dangerous as he was, Muammar Qaddafi appeared a fool as he suffered a number of reverses in the 1980s. In his quest to murder Abdul Hamid Bakoush, the exiled former Libyan prime minister under King Idris, Qaddafi financed a number of botched operations. The most publicized was an attempt in Cairo in November 1984. Egyptian security agents were apprised of the operation and set an elaborate plan to ensnare Colonel Qaddafi. They took a cooperative Bakoush to a graveyard in Cairo and had a cosmetics expert paint a bullet hole on his forehead. Using actual blood from a local hospital, the make-up expert had the blood drip down over Bakoush's face and onto his shirt.

A police photographer took a Polaroid picture of the face and body, and they brought one of the members of the plot to view the "corpse." Totally convinced, he phoned his Libyan contacts to assure them that the job was done. The Polaroid picture of the bloody scene reached Tripoli through a Libyan bureau in Malta, and Muammar Qaddafi and the General People's Congress fell for the hoax. On November 16 the Libyan news agency broadcast that "the sentence of execution on Bakoush, who had sold his conscience to the enemies of the Arab nation, has been carried out by a revolutionary force, thereby implementing the resolution of the basic people's congress which formed suicide squads to liquidate the enemies of the revolution internally and externally." To the utter humiliation of Muammar Qaddafi, the Egyptian interior minister appeared at a press conference the next day with a very much alive Abdul Hamid Bakoush, and revealed the intricate sting.

In March 1986 the United States attacked several Libyan ships and a missile installation on the Libyan mainland. President Reagan then ordered the bombing of Tripoli and Benghazi on April 15, 1986, in retaliation for a series of Qaddafi-sponsored terrorist missions. The Reagan administration had concluded that Qaddafi was responsible for an attack on a West Berlin discotheque in which an American serviceman was killed. The bombing served to embarrass Qaddafi, who had been singled out as the terrorist tyrant of the Middle East. On more than one occasion President Reagan had said of Qaddafi that "he's not only a barbarian but he's flaky."

In retaliation Qaddafi purchased American hostage Peter Kilburn, an abducted librarian at the University of Beirut, from Lebanese Shiite terrorists for a reported $1 million. Qaddafi then had the sixty-one-year old Kilburn, a man who had been held hostage for nearly two years, murdered as retaliation for the American air raid. Qaddafi made sure that he could not be totally traced to the murder. This prevented another U.S bombing, but it also prevented the Libyan leader from reaping a well-publicized revenge against "the Great Satan," the United States.

Qaddafi and Reagan had been on a collision course since 1981. A war of nerves and accusations ensued because of U.S. military operations in the Mediterranean and Libya's claim to international waters as its own. To make matters worse, two more high-priced Libyan fighters were shot down over international waters off the Libyan coast when they displayed "clear hostile intent." The January 4, 1989, incident occurred even as the United States had been warning Libya for more than a year about its building a chemical weapons factory. The U.S. intimated that it might use military action to destroy the plant before it mass produced poison gas.

Although Qaddafi insisted that his Rabta factory south of Tripoli was designed to manufacture pharmaceuticals, the former director of a West German chemical concern was arrested by German officials in May 1989. A plot had been uncovered that had provided Libya, Syria, and Iraq with chemical weapon technology. For West Germans who remembered the Nazi use of such gas, which had killed millions during the Holocaust, and who had laws against such manufacture and sales, it was a horrible realization that their own corporate executives were involved in a lucrative arrangement to provide radical Arab leaders with such exports.

Qaddafi was not only proved a liar and a liability in the eyes of the world but also suffered the humiliation of later witnessing the destruction of his plant by a fire of unknown origin. The Libyan leader blamed U.S. and Israeli agents for destroying his "pharmaceutical" facility.

The PLO

In his first international event in the Arab world, Muammar Qaddafi met Yasser Arafat, chairman of the Palestine Liberation Organization. Nasser had called them to the Nile Hilton in Cairo on September 22, 1970, to try to end the bloody massacre that King Hussein of Jordan was inflicting on the PLO forces that had dared to challenge his authority. Arafat, Qaddafi, and Hussein wore revolvers in their belts, but it was Qaddafi who got on the nerves of the Arab leaders.

The young Colonel Qaddafi chided the Arab leaders for not unifying, for not pulling down their walls of national restrictions, and for not marching their Arab masses to the borders of "Palestine," liberating the land from the Jewish intrusion and liquidating the Zionist enemy. Qaddafi also suggested that King Hussein be hanged by the Egyptian government on a gallows in the public square, and claimed that an Arab army should be dispatched against Jordan. When King Faisal of Saudi Arabia suggested that if such an army be sent it be sent to "fight the Jews," Qaddafi declared that what Hussein was doing was "worse than the Jews."

In a direct blow at the Palestinians, the Libyan leader insisted that only 10 percent of the forty organizations within the Palestinian resistance had dedicated their efforts toward the Zionist enemy. According to Qaddafi, 90 percent were feuding with each other or other Arab countries. Although Qaddafi sided with the PLO over King Hussein's cries that the Palestinians were trying to take over his country, Arafat was not amused with the new Libyan leader. Arafat believed he was being accused of going soft on terrorism. For years Arafat would amuse himself and his colleagues by telling jokes about Qaddafi.

Just two weeks before the Cairo conference, George Habash's deputy and terrorist mastermind of the Popular Front for the Liberation of Palestine (PFLP), Waddi Haddad, had led forces in their organization to a successful hijacking of four planes and 375 hostages. After negotiating the release of their colleagues held in European jails, they ended their four-day siege by freeing the hostages and blowing up the planes they had flown to Dawson's Field (a former British Royal Air Force base in the desert outside Amman, Jordan) in full view of international television cameras.

For Qaddafi, this was proof that terrorism could bring the Western nations to their knees. Although Arafat and the Palestine National Council had condemned armed attacks on civilians as detrimental to the Palestinian cause (a condemnation the PFLP had ignored), Arafat and other Arabs became more enthralled with the possibility of holding the West hostage even as they regularly had terrorized Israeli civilians. A turning point had occurred in modern Middle Eastern operations.

YASSER ARAFAT

For Yasser Arafat, terrorism had been part of his family heritage. Born in Cairo on August 27, 1929, to a wealthy businessman from Gaza who was a member of the radical Muslim Brotherhood, Arafat's real name was Abd al-Rahman Abd al-Rauf Arafat al-Qudwa al-Husseini. His mother's cousin was the infamous Grand Mufti of Jerusalem and Nazi collaborator Haj Amin al-Husseini.

In 1939 Arafat's family moved back to the Gaza, and a school-teacher who worked as the Grand Mufti's radio operator to send secret information from Palestine to the Nazis renamed him "Yasser." The name was in memory of Yasser al-Birah, a terrorist leader who was killed by the British while trying to smuggle German armaments into Palestine. Throughout the 1940s, Arafat belonged to Amin al-Husseini's Qassamite group, which fought against the rival Arab Nashashibi family in a blood-feud.

At twenty-two the young revolutionary enrolled in the civil engineering program at King Faud University (later renamed the University of Cairo). The name he used was "Yasser Arafat." In the early 1950s revolutionary fervor and a variety of political orientations were festering against the corrupt Egyptian monarchy of King Farouk in much the same manner as they would later fester against King Idris of Libya. Arafat began reorganizing the Palestinian Students' Union on campus and declared that their goal was to create a Palestinian state in the place of Israel. As we have seen, Nasser soon was to come to power, and Arafat and his colleagues received military training with other young Palestinians to become commandos in Nasser's terrorist campaign against the Jewish state.

In 1956 Arafat and two Palestinian friends attended a Soviet-sponsored student congress in Prague, Czechoslovakia, and then traveled to West Germany to study at the Stuttgart Technical University. Yasser Arafat then applied for a position in Kuwait, where he worked as a civil engineer for the Kuwaiti Department of Water Supply. Later Arafat formed his own construction company and employed Palestinians from many parts of the Middle East. By the early 1960s a strong group of revolutionaries had formed around him, and their group was nicknamed *al-Fatah*, which connotes conquest by means of Islamic *jihad* (holy war). Fatah's first significant act of terrorism was to plant explosives to damage Israel's National Water Carrier, which channeled water from the Sea of Galilee. Arafat worked closely at this time with the Ba'ath Party in Syria and had connections throughout Lebanon.

Fatah organizations actually went back to the Arab High Command set up by the Grand Mufti of Jerusalem. Arafat's new Fatah organization built upon the older organizational structure but actually had goals that had been part of his revolutionary growth experience in Cairo, Gaza, Kuwait, and Syria. These activists were united in their goal to "liberate" Palestine and destroy the Jewish state. They believed armed struggle was the only option and that Palestinians could in the final analysis rely only on themselves. They did, however, seek to cooperate with sympathetic Arab forces as well as sympathetic nations outside of the Middle East (including the Soviet Union). It would be the Fatah terrorists who would be used by Nasser and the Syrians to cross the borders of Israel and lead to the conflict of the Six-Day War.

Receiving Arab monetary support in the early 1960s, Fatah was hurt financially by the steps that led to the creation of the Palestine Liberation Organization in 1964. Fatah was critical of the PLO but negotiated with Ahmed Shuqairy (the future PLO president) to have about a dozen delegates attend the founding conference of the PLO in May 1964. There they began to turn the PLO toward resolutions that actually represented the thinking of the Fatah organization. One of the major differences that remained, however, was that Arafat's Fatah insisted that guerrilla warfare and terrorism were the keys to defeating Israel. Fatah sought to ignite a popular uprising among Arabs in Israel and on the outskirts of Israel. Shuqairy's PLO dominated by Nasser believed in direct confrontation of massive Arab armies to overrun Israel and drive every Jew into the Mediterranean.

The aftermath of the devastating 1967 Six-Day War changed opinions within the PLO. Shuqairy was discredited, and Arafat and his Fatah organization took the reins of the Palestine Liberation Organization. So popular was Arafat's Fatah that at the Arab Summit conference in Rabat, Morocco, in 1969 it was suggested that Fatah be recognized as the PLO. Arafat and his command council, however, wanted the PLO to continue as a coalition of forces. Fatah in reality would control the organization, but they thought others were needed if they ran into trouble. In essence, Arafat believed that they needed other forces to share the blame as well as to protect the infrastructure of the Palestine Liberation Organization.

Even Gamal Abdel Nasser began to believe that guerrilla warfare could not only wear down the Jewish state but could also promote sympathy throughout the world. Israel was seen as a David and the massive Arab nations as a Goliath. Now propaganda could portray Israel as a Goliath against a weak and helpless Palestinian people who only wanted a land in which to live. Originally it was difficult to promote such feelings because Egypt controlled the Gaza, and Jordan controlled the West Bank and East Jerusalem. Now Israel controlled both. Now Israel could be accused of denying Palestinian men, women, and children a homeland.

The tactic was brilliant, and it soon worked not only in the halls of individual governments but captured the heart of the United Nations and other international forums. Missionaries from mainline denominations who worked in the Arab world spread the concept in their denominational headquarters. Academics pressed harder to ensure Palestinian rights. Archaeologists on digs in Arab lands promised to promote the Palestinian cause in their native lands. Blatant terrorism was downplayed by Arafat's PLO in the years following the Six-Day War, and that is why Qaddafi's clear statements of hatred were disdained by Arafat and company. Through the mythology it had created for itself, Arafat's PLO was woven into the fabric of Palestinian communities and families in the Middle East and even in the West. When civilian Arab opposition occurred or some Palestinians questioned Arafat's authority, they were quickly silenced. For some, that meant death at the hands of their Palestinian brethren.

Arafat became increasingly confident that the task could be accomplished by secret forays against the civilian population of Israel—forays that were categorically denied by Arafat and his leadership.

Groups that were overtly radical, such as the Popular Front for the Liberation of Palestine, made Arafat's PLO look moderate. Arafat was riding high on his public relations campaign and his international status. On September 21, 1974, Sadat's Egypt and Assad's Syria recognized the PLO as the sole representative of the Palestinian people. On November 13, 1974, Arafat addressed the U.N. General Assembly and declared that the PLO's only goal was "one democratic state where Christian, Jew and Muslim live in justice, equality and fraternity." On November 10, 1975, the U.N. General Assembly passed a resolution defining Zionism as "a form of racism and racial discrimination." On December 4, 1975, the PLO was granted the speaking privileges of a member nation of the United Nations to participate on a debate about Israeli air attacks in Lebanon.

QUESTIONS ABOUT LEADERSHIP

The Palestine Liberation Organization is structured with Yasser Arafat at the head as chairman. Directly below him is a 14-member Executive Committee and below them is the policy-making Palestine Central Council of approximately 100 members. The Palestine National Council with more than 500 members and an elected chairman feed input from the Arab nations and Palestinian organizations to the Central Council. A Palestine Liberation Army with a Chief of Staff are in the command structure under Arafat and the Executive Committee. In reality, however, a variety of Arab countries have had input into the brigades they provide or support.

The Executive Committee also commands Social Affairs and Mass Organizations Departments that control the workers' union, students' union, women's union, engineers' union, and writers' union, as well as the Red Crescent (Muslim Red Cross), information bureau, political bureau, planning bureau, and industrial bureau. A Palestinian National Fund was set up in 1964 to collect a 5-7 percent income tax on Palestinians worldwide, but this income is swamped by the huge donations provided by oil-rich Arab nations. By 1980 an annual subsidy of $500 million was allocated to the PLO, and the Fatah group skimmed two-thirds of the proceeds. Nearly $150 million of the funds allocated at the Arab summit in Baghdad in 1978 was given "to bolster the Palestinian resistance inside the Israeli-occupied territories." Few realize the immense wealth that Arafat and his colleagues have garnered in the past two decades.

In June 1982 Israeli forces launched the "Peace for Galilee" campaign into war-torn Lebanon. Beirut had served as an unofficial headquarters of the PLO since Palestinian rebels were massacred and deported by King Hussein's military in 1971. In their move on Beirut, the Israelis were attempting to destroy the political and military infrastructure of the PLO. Under pressure, Arafat was forced to strike a deal, and he and 8,000 of his troops left Beirut to be dispersed in other Arab lands. By the summer of 1983, a rebellion had broken out against Arafat from within his own Fatah command structure. Ironically, the revolt was encouraged and supported by Syrian president Hafez Assad and Libyan leader Muammar Qaddafi. In 1983 President Assad declared Arafat persona non grata and broke all ties between Syria and Arafat's faction of the PLO. For six years (until June 1989) Assad held more than 200 members of Arafat's mainline Fatah movement prisoner.

That Yasser Arafat was to remain in power and rise to prominence in world politics once again was a remarkable feat. His demise had been predicted by many Middle East analysts, but the wily leader, who rarely stays in the same spot two nights in a row, kept one jump ahead of the opposition. In spite of thousands of civilian deaths by terrorist commandos for which he had been responsible, Arafat was able to convince most of the Western world (and, ultimately, the United States government) that he was the key to Middle East peace. With the development of the Palestinian Arab Intifada uprising in Israel, Arafat gained new prestige throughout the Arab world. He claimed to be "President of Palestine" and strode the corridors of world power.

On December 15, 1988, Arafat took a bold step and declared that the PLO renounced terrorism. In language that some questioned as ambiguous, he then personally accepted Israel's right to exist. The United States government announced that because of these actions it would take him at his word and, for the first time, open a dialogue with Arafat and the Palestine Liberation Organization. Accosted by some Arab terrorist groups for his "compromise" and further alienated in the eyes of Qaddafi and Assad, Arafat continued to walk the fine line of diplomatic ambiguity.

His gamble was that he and his sympathizers in the United Nations could push through a resolution that would recognize the PLO as the representative of an independent Palestinian state. He counted on his newfound dialogue with the United States to pressure Israel to accept PLO terms. Within a year of his dialogue with the United States, on November 30, 1989, a group of Arab countries introduced a resolution that would upgrade the PLO from "observer organization" at the United Nations to an "observer state." The United States headed off the action only by threatening to cancel its contributions to the UN.

During the year that he was supposed to have been turning over a new leaf, Arafat was under the scrutiny of more balanced observers of the Middle East maze. His words in Arabic as well as in English were analyzed and his actions were monitored. The information gleaned was sobering. Arafat and the PLO had continued to silence or murder Arabs who wanted to participate in a peace process with Israel. Within two weeks of his December 15 "acceptance of Israel's existence," Elias Freij, respected mayor of Bethlehem, had suggested a one-year truce in the Intifada (the Palestinian uprising in the Gaza and West Bank) if Israel would release 2,000 Palestinian prisoners. The Israelis responded that they were willing to negotiate seriously about the proposition.

Arafat, however, responded with a January 2, 1989, death threat: "Any Palestinian who proposes an end to the Intifada exposes himself to the bullets of his own people and endangers his life. The PLO will know how to deal with him." Mayor Freij got the message. He withdrew his suggestion on January 3, declaring that the PLO should make all decisions. He then dropped out of sight for a period of time. Arafat spent quite a few weeks explaining that his statements had been "taken out of context," but U.S. State Department experts in Arabic reviewed the tape and said that Arafat's statements were threats. The United States government began to worry that Arafat might not be committed to the supposed declarations he had made toward peace. To turn the tables, Arafat accused the United States of "dragging its feet" in the pursuit of peace.

The worry was well founded. As PLO guerrilla raids continued through Israel's border with Lebanon, Egyptian president Hosni Mubarak tried to get Arafat to condemn them. Arafat refused in March 1989 to condemn the raids, lamely explaining that the internal political dynamics of the PLO coalition prevented his challenging or condemning the factions responsible. To make matters worse, statements by Arafat in Arabic to Arab countries called for the destruction of Israel in the wake of a Palestinian state. Statements for consumption in the West, in contrast, were ambiguously worded within the constructs of peace and harmony in the Middle East. By October 1989, Arafat blundered badly in Tokyo by urging Japan to reduce its trade with Israel and announcing that it would be a "fatal mistake" for the oil-dependent Japanese to spurn the wishes of the oil-producing Arab world.

Assuming he was sincere, the question soon arose about whether or not Arafat could deliver on any promises he made in the midst of diplomacy. Even when he was nominated as president of Palestine in March 1989 by the PLO Palestine Central Committee "until democratic elections could take place in an independent state," some PLO factions balked. The hostile factions gathered in Tripoli with Libyan president Muammar Qaddafi, intending to set up a rival PLO leadership.

Like Qaddafi, these factions made clear that they opposed any move by Chairman Arafat to renounce terrorism and recognize Israel's right to exist. These groups included a splinter group from the PFLP, Syrian-backed Ahmed Jabril's Popular Front for the Liberation of Palestine-General Command. This PFLP-General Command castigated Arafat and his cronies. They were joined by Fatah dissidents like Saed Musa, who led the Syrian revolt against Arafat. Although the wealthy Arab sponsors of terrorism, including Saudi Arabia and Kuwait, were able to persuade many of the factions not to split with the PLO at such a crucial juncture, the United States began to realize that even if Arafat was sincere (and that was debatable) he could be assassinated by his own people—his promises of peace dying with him. Unfortunately, the U.S. State Department often suggested that "any hope" was worth a try. When Arafat declared his support for Saddam Hussein of Iraq there were many red faces in Washington. After the 1991 Gulf War, Arafat incredibly tried to explain away his commitment to the Iraqi dictator.

Certainly a reading of the draft constitution of the Palestine Liberation Organization (1963) or The Palestine National Covenant (1964) or The Constitution of the Palestine Liberation Organization (July 17, 1968, in Cairo) would have explained why Arafat, the PLO command, and local Palestinians perched on their roofs on the West Bank cheered as Iraqi Scud missiles hit Israeli civilian targets. Each of these documents called for the annihilation of Israel and the creation of a Palestinian state within the original British Mandate borders. None of these documents has ever been rescinded.

In the aftermath of the Gulf War, Muammar el-Qaddafi was quietly rebuilding his "pharmaceutical" factory in the desert. In similar fashion, Yasser Arafat was attempting to rebuild his credibilty in the West as well as to make amends to some of the large Arab patrons he had snubbed in his support for Saddam Hussein. In some ways the goals and aspirations of both men seemed to come full cycle in the maze of the Middle East.

Arafat had sponsored terrorism while trying to convince the world that he had "seen the light" regarding responsible behavior and recognition of Israel. For one moment, however, he had let down his guard and with Qaddafi-like forthrightness attached his star to the evil dictator of the moment, Saddam Hussein. Qaddafi, in contrast, had reached a point of isolation in the Arab world as well as in the international forums. By the end of 1989 he had struggled to patch up relations with the many enemies he had made through his extravagant behavior and raucous language. The Libyan tyrant from Bedouin roots worked diligently to become more of an angel of light. His people had rallied to his side in the 1986 American bombing raids, but he had personally experienced the psychological reality of his own fallibility. He seemed to realize that he had embarked on a course of personal destruction, and he was not sure that he wanted to pursue his former path with such bellicosity.

One thing appeared certain. Muammar Qaddafi's Libya and Yasser Arafat's PLO remained forces to be monitored and reckoned with in the Middle East maze.

8

THE ARABIAN PENINSULA

The vast expanse and isolated deserts of Arabia have a heritage deeply rooted in biblical tradition and world history. Arabia's geographical position between Africa, India, and the Far East fostered commercial centers and main trade routes that crisscrossed its desolate domain. Important waterways surrounded this peninsula, and commercial ventures often calculated the risk of going around or traveling through Arabia. Military strategists of the great empires charted its significance, and the Persian Gulf area was a cauldron of simmering conflicts and tribal rivalries. Sheikhdoms dotted both the arid interior and the balmy seacoasts of the Arabian Peninsula, and few empires in the ancient world could claim to control totally its perimeters.

Arabia has a diverse religious heritage as well. In the Bible, the book of Genesis records genealogical lists that emphasize the various tribes in and family links with Arabia (cf. Genesis 10:26-29 for the sons of Joktan; Genesis 25:1-5 for the sons of Abraham; Genesis 25:13-16 for the sons of Ishmael; and Genesis 36 for the sons of Esau). Most scholars believe the Queen of Sheba came from Arabia (cf. 1 Kings 10), and Jewish oral history indicates extensive trade and relationships between the Jewish people and the inhabitants of the Arabian steppe and the ports of the Red Sea. Arabic literature tells stories about Jewish settlement in the Hejaz (the area of Mecca and Medina) as early as Moses' war against the Amalekites (cf. Exodus 17:8-16), and Arab history suggests that King David fought against the idol worshipers in Yathrib (later Medina).

Numbers of Jewish and Christian settlements dotted the Arabian landscape. As early as 721 B.C. Jewish families that fled the Assyrian onslaught settled in Arabia. After the Babylonian destruction of the first

Temple, Arab commentaries relate, 80,000 Israelite priests made their way to Jewish settlements in Arabia. Centuries later, each Roman persecution resulted in Jewish communities resettling in Arabia. Jews therefore influenced a number of Arab communities and appear to have first settled the town of Yathrib. Here they were mainly artisans and agriculturalists and, with their Christian neighbors, at first welcomed the Prophet Muhammad in his flight from a hostile polytheistic Mecca.

After a year of trying to convert the Jewish community to Islam, Muhammad began punishing Yathrib's Jews for not believing his message. Muhammad soon killed, maimed, or enslaved most of Yathrib's Jewish population and forced the surrounding Jewish tribes of Hejaz to set aside a sizable yield of their produce for Muslim use. Many Christian Arabs felt forced to convert to Islam. Yathrib was renamed Medina, and Medina became the second holiest city in Islam.

According to a will later discovered during the reign of Omar (634-644), Muhammad had declared that "two religions may not dwell together on the Arabian Peninsula." Whatever the validity of this will, it was used by Muslim overlords to expel both Jews and Christians from the Hejaz. Today Muhammad's statement still holds true. With the rise of Islam and in the wake of Muslim conquests, there is no doubt as to the religious makeup of modern Arabia. Islam has become intrinsically linked to the concept of *Arab,* and the conflicts between Arabs and Jews have a long, exasperating history.

Yet the word *Arab* preceded the religion of Islam by more than 1,500 years. The first Arab mention associates them with camels and with the desert. Assyrian records as early as 854 B.C. note that Gindibu the Arab, with 1,000 camel troops from *Aribi* territory, joined Bir-'idri of Damascus (who is the Benhadad II of the Bible) in battle against the Assyrian king Shalmanassar III in the Battle of Qarqar. Isaiah 13:20 explains that God will overthrow Babylon and remarks, "No Arab will pitch his tent there." Jeremiah 3:2 uses the phrase "like an Arab in the desert." The word *nomad* is often interchanged with *Arab,* and the famous Arab historian of the fourteenth century Ibn Khaldun uses "Arab" interchangeably with "Bedouin" (desert-dwelling nomadic peoples).

Today, multimillion dollar jets and marvelously complicated communications planes fly over the Arabian wilderness. In the wake of the 1991 Gulf War, the landscape and ancient traditions of Arabia are viewed on worldwide television, while tanks and military transports create endless clouds of dust. Oil has transformed poverty-stricken societies and desert sheikhdoms into financial giants and commercial benefactors in both East and West. Blessing or curse, Arabia has approximately two-thirds of the known oil reserves in the modern world. In this chapter we discuss Saudi Arabia, briefly relating the history of Kuwait, Bahrain, Qatar, the United Arab Emirates, Oman, and Yemen in an attempt to understand better the complexion of Arabia as the world catapults toward the twenty-first century.

SAUDI ARABIA

BACKGROUND

At least 250 billion barrels of oil lie under Saudi Arabia, a country that today takes up 840,000 square miles (90 percent of the Arabian Peninsula), commands one-quarter of the world's proved crude oil reserves, and on its western coast houses the holy cities of Mecca and Medina. The massive wealth that has accompanied such phenomenal reserves and increased petroleum production has transformed the House of Saud, the dynasty that rules this kingdom of approximately 17 million, into an economic and political giant in international affairs. Increasingly the Saudis have become a crucial link in the diplomacy of the Middle East.

Certainly this could not have been foreseen by the European nations at the beginning of the twentieth century. As was related in chapter 1, Britain negotiated with the Hashemite dynasty (the House of Hashem), which controlled a strip of territory along western Arabia that included Mecca and Medina. This territory of Hejaz seemed significant in light of the fact that Islam was integral to the Arab world. The sons of the Hashemite king Hussein were given areas of the Middle East. Faisal received the newly created state of Iraq, and Abdullah received newly created Transjordan. To this day the Hashemite Kingdom of Jordan has a great-grandson of the dynasty on the throne of Jordan, King Hussein.

This House of Hashem, however, had a strong rival from central Arabia, the House of Saud. Wresting control of the Hejaz and the holy cities from the House of Hashem, the leader of the House of Saud, Abd al-Aziz, had attacked Abdullah in newly formed Transjordan in 1922. With thousands of warriors on camels and the fanatical Wahhabi Muslims at his side, Abd al-Aziz was within an hour of Abdullah's capital city, Amman, when the British sent planes and armored vehicles to deter him. This resulted in the British drawing national borders that separated the Arabia of the House of Saud from Hashemite Transjordan.

To this day those lines exist, dividing Saudi Arabia from Jordan—separating two royal dynasties that originated in Arabia.

These early animosities bubbled to the surface during the 1991 Gulf War when King Hussein of Jordan infuriated the Saudis by supporting Iraq. In March 1991 the Saudis suggested to U.S. Secretary of State James Baker that the West Bank and Gaza Strip should be combined with Jordan to create a Palestinian state. This state would be economically linked to Israel, a union much tighter than the European Common Market.

The Saudi plan took for granted that King Hussein would soon be forced to abdicate his throne and that the Palestinians (now 60 percent of Jordan's population) would subjugate the Bedouin tribesmen that have formed the base of King Hussein's support. Jordan will suffer economically unless the Saudis and other Arab oil states reinstitute their annual subsidy.

Muslim fanatics who claimed that the Mahdi (savior) had arrived seized the Sacred Mosque of Mecca on November 20, 1979. It took several days and hundreds of deaths to regain Islam's holiest shrine. Most of the insurgents were Saudis who were joined by other Muslim fundamentalists from Egypt, Kuwait, and Yemen. Although Saudi Arabia is 85 percent Sunni Muslim, the 200,000 Shiite Muslims in the eastern oil-producing province staged a violent demonstration that also had to be quelled by force. These conservative Shia Muslims and the majority of Wahhabi Sunnis could agree on one thing: they disdained any modernization of Saudi Arabia and cried out for the simpler days of well-defined traditional standards. The influx of hundreds of thousands of foreign workers in the wake of Saudi building projects exacerbated the threat of social unrest. A decade later the Saudis beheaded by sword sixteen pro-Iranian Kuwaitis (of Shiite Saudi and Iranian origin) for bombings and terrorist activities during the annual Muslim pilgrimage to the holy city Mecca.

Saudi Arabia and its rulers are constantly aware of the tensions between traditional Islam and an oil-rich modernization program. Saudi Arabia is ruled by the House of Saud, a patriarchal community of one king and 4,000 princes. Although major decisions are brought to the attention of the larger royal family, the Saudi king rules as chief of state, prime minister, and foreign minister. There is no parliament or formal constitution, but in this patriarchal monarchy a few hundred members of the royal family are active in the affairs of state. Islamic law is to be adhered to even by the king, and an Islamic Court handles all judiciary cases. This became quite evident when a nephew in the royal family assassinated King Faisal on March 25, 1975 (the birthday of the Prophet Muhammad), and was beheaded according to the dictates of the Islamic Court three months later in the public square of the capital, Riyadh.

It was King Faisal who had turned his country from an arid feudal kingdom into a $30 billion oil producer during his reign from 1965 to 1975. King Faisal emphasized that he wanted more education and health care for his people, but not to the neglect of Saudi Arabia's Islamic traditions. It was also Faisal who had appointed his half-brother Khalid as crown prince, thus ensuring a smooth transition of power. Khalid was crowned king within minutes of Faisal's death, and he carried on the $142 billion five-year modernization plan conceived during Faisal's last year of reign. Crown Prince Fahd, another half-brother who was interior minister at the time of the assassination, became an important power behind the throne of King Khalid and upon Khalid's death succeeded him as monarch.

KING FAHD'S SAUDI DYNASTY

For the Saudi citizen in King Fahd's domain today, life is quite pleasant. Government subsidized interest-free $80,000 housing loans are available to citizens who are not independently wealthy. Each is accompanied by a plot of land. Hundreds of thousands take advantage of these loans each year. Citizens pay no personal income tax and have free schooling and free medical care. Higher eduction is also free, and King Saud University has more than 35,000 students, more than one-quarter of them women. This does not mean to imply that women do not have a difficult time in an Islamic society. Those with degrees often have to settle for second class jobs (if they are fortunate enough to be able to practice their vocation at all), and feudal Islamic rules and regulations continue to relegate women to the status of second-class citizens.

All utilities, gasoline, and even airplane tickets are government subsidized, and in this welfare state the dominating theme is that security at an early age makes a cooperative subject. Strong monetary incentives also encourage agricultural cultivation, irrigation, and land reclamation projects. New roads, new homes, new mosques, and new schools dot the Saudi landscape. Carefully planned cities are springing up like oases in the desert. The per capita annual income has fluctuated between $7000 and $11,000, depending upon government spending, and Saudi living standards are among the highest in the Middle East. Saudi officials admit that "Allah was with them" in this process, because the heaviest spending in the five-year plan was just being completed when oil prices began to drop. In April 1989, the last American to preside over the Arabian-American Oil Company (ARAMCO—founded by Americans in 1933) handed over the reins of the world's largest oil company to a Saudi executive.

The Saudis found that they were counted upon to mediate diplomatically in the Arab world. Even Western powers sought their advice and help in matters concerning the Middle East. In 1989 rival Lebanese legislators met with King Fahd in the Red Sea port of Jidda, adopting a new national charter in an effort to stem the civil war in Lebanon. The accord recognized the "special" nature of Syria-Lebanese relations but did not insist in writing that Syria withdraw its troops. Hafez Assad only gave his "private assurance" to King Fahd that he planned to withdraw. Christian Lebanese opponents called it a sellout, and Muslim control of Lebanon seemed assured.

Quietly the Saudi government distributed funds to needy Arab countries and spent hundreds of millions of dollars financing Arab "liberation" movements (such as the PLO, which received upwards of $100 million annually). Western observers were shocked to find that the Saudis had paid huge sums to terrorists in the hope of keeping radical movements far from Arabian shores. Even some weapons sold to the Saudis have made their way to the Palestine Liberation Organization. Worries increased as the Saudis spent tens of billions of dollars for armaments in the 1980s, becoming the biggest Middle East customer for U.S. and European weapons.

Unfortunately, anti-Jewish literature has been distributed throughout the Middle East by the Saudi kings mentioned above, and Saudi statements in Arabic have done little to salve the Arab-Israeli tensions. King Faisal, for example, distributed beautifully bound copies of anti-Semitic literature to his guests (including foreign journalists) in the 1970s. Faisal declared in 1974 that Saudi Arabia would "sacrifice its oil and financial resources" as well as its "sons" to destroy Israel. Saudi King Khalid asserted on Arab radio and in press interviews that "Jerusalem's occupation is a deep wound bleeding in our hearts and souls," that Muslims must "liberate holy Jerusalem from the claws of Zionism," and that a unified holy war (*jihad*) must recover Palestine.

The current ruler, King Fahd, has had a history of anti-Israel and anti-Jewish rhetoric from his harsh words as crown prince in 1979 toward Anwar Sadat's peace with Israel (and subsequent cut of Saudi financial help to Egypt) to his raucous declaration to the Saudi Press Agency in 1981: "We shall not rest until our usurped land is liberated and until the Palestinian people return with dignity and pride to their independent state, with Jerusalem as its capital." King Fahd's regime has in the past decade organized boycotts against Israel, threatening companies that want lucrative Saudi contracts with cancellation if they deal with Israel. Other countries of the Arabian peninsula have joined the Saudis in this endeavor. Every year the Saudis support a resolution in the United Nations to oust Israel. As Prince Sultan, the Saudi minister of defense, admitted on television October 19, 1985: "The truth is that anything praised by the Jews is despised, and anything that is abused by the Jews and their organizations is precious."

One can imagine King Fahd and his government's shock in 1991 as Saudi citizens had to face Scud missiles from Iraq in the same fashion as their Israeli neighbors were being bombarded. Saudi citizens had to don gas masks to protect themselves from lethal Arab chemical weapons even as Israelis were required to protect themselves. Saudi children were traumatized even as Israeli children were traumatized. Palestinians cheered the Iraqis to the detriment of both Saudi Arabia and Israel. King Hussein failed the Saudis even as he failed Israel. While Saudi hatred for Jews and for Israel may not have diminished in any significant fashion, the nations of the Arabian Peninsula admired Israel's restraint when asked not to strike back at Iraq during the Gulf War. A Kuwaiti spokesman from Saudi Arabia summed up the feeling when he declared: "Saddam Hussein has done for Israel in one week what Israel's friends could not accomplish in two years." A small diplomatic opening seemed to appear in what was a closed, rigid, conservative Muslim Arabia.

KUWAIT

BACKGROUND

Nightly from the tip of northeastern Arabia on the shores of the Persian Gulf, the devastation of Kuwait and its attempt to rebuild consumed a good portion of world news broadcasts in early 1991. Slightly smaller than New Jersey, Kuwait had approximately 2.1 million people before the Iraqi invasion on August 2, 1990, and boasted a standard of living that was one of the highest in the world. Four hundred thousand Palestinians and many thousands of other foreigners found work in this flat desert kingdom. In fact, Kuwait was an economic paradise for foreign workers, who composed 60 percent of the population and 80 percent of the work force. Although foreign workers make much less than Kuwaiti citizens, they receive higher pay than they could muster in their own countries. This Kuwaiti opulence is directly related to oil reserves bordering on 100 billion barrels and the government-owned Kuwait Oil Company.

THE AL-SABAH DYNASTY

It is ironic that modern Iraq would claim Kuwait as its possession since Iraq's borders drawn by the British after World War I already encompass pieces of other territories (Turkey, Kurdistan, etc.), and current Iraqi political power dates from the aftermath of the 1967 Six-Day War. In contrast, Kuwait's leaders have ruled the area for nearly three and a half centuries. In the early 1700s, three Arab clans settled this area, which sported a small fishing village and a torrid, dusty desert. In 1756 Sheikh Sabah Abdul Rahim founded the al-Sabah dynasty, and this royal family has ruled ever since. The word *Kuwait* is derived from the term "kut" ("small fort"). To this day, Kuwaitis emphasize that "Kuwait City is Kuwait—the heart of Kuwait."

The Ottoman Turks more or less left the Kuwaitis to themselves, and only as British interest in the area increased in the latter 1800s did the al-Sabah family find it necessary to make an 1899 treaty with Great Britain. When the First World War broke out in 1914, the British recognized Kuwait as an independent state under British protection. The British had to intervene when the Wahhabi armies from Saudi Arabia attempted to take Kuwait, and a 1922 treaty set up a neutral zone between the House of Saud and the dynasty of al-Sabah.

Relative peace ensued until Britain gave Kuwait full independence in 1961. At that time Iraq attempted to seize the country, and the British moved in military forces to deter the Baghdad regime. In 1963 Iraq recognized Kuwait as an independent country. Kuwait entered the United Nations the same year and joined the Arab League soon after it became independent in 1961.

Kuwait's constitution dates from 1962 and provides for a national assembly of fifty members. Each legislator was to be elected to a four-year term by natural-born Kuwaiti males over twenty-one. Policemen, servicemen, and women were not allowed to vote. The emir was to rule as a constitutional monarch and was to be assisted by a cabinet of ten appointed ministers and four elected ministers. A prime minister was to head this cabinet. Sheikh Abdullah al-Salem al-Sabah believed that the country's wealth should be distributed among Kuwaiti citizens and that much of the nation's tribal structure had to be overcome. By his death in 1965, Kuwait's income from petroleum totaled more than $600 million.

In the midst of massive oil wealth in 1976, however, Emir Sheikh Jaber Al-Ahmed al-Sabah suspended the national assembly and took over full legislative and judicial powers. Restoring it at his whim, he disbanded it once again in 1986. This has been a bone of contention. Those favoring parliamentarian government believed that they had moved from a constitutional monarchy to a patriarchal sheikhdom. A month and a half before Saddam Hussein's invasion, an election was called to select a new national assembly. Now that recovery is taking place, the emir has indicated that there will be women's suffrage and parliamentary elections. Kuwaiti citizens hope that this promise to abide by the 1962 constitution is not a ploy to pacify an impatient population.

It has been difficult to obtain Kuwaiti citizenship in past decades, and only Kuwaiti citizens can own land on which a house can be built (or be eligible for the coveted housing subsidies). With one of the highest literacy rates in the Arab world (more than 80 percent), Kuwaiti citizens are well informed and have developed extravagant tastes. Before the Gulf War, stores and malls featured a mixture of Western dress and Muslim coverings. With no taxes for Kuwaiti citizens and virtually free housing, medical care, utilities, and education, a society of leisure is now faced with the awesome task of rebuilding the nation.

It is a sad fact, however, that Adolf Hitler's *Mein Kampf* and the infamous anti-Jewish *Protocols of the Elders of Zion* were treasured in many Kuwaiti homes before the 1991 war. In the past, Kuwait joined both the Arab war effort against Israel and the anti-Israel boycotts. How the Kuwaiti penchant for anti-Semitism and anti-Israel rhetoric will be affected by Israel's compliance with the wishes of the Gulf war allied forces (for restraint) remains to be seen.

Although billions of dollars are available from investments around the world, Kuwait has a time-consuming task of rebuilding that will not submit to shortcuts and quick fixes. Whether the average Kuwaiti citizen is able to muster the patience to endure such an ordeal remains to be seen.

BAHRAIN

The Emirate of Bahrain includes more than thirty desert islands in the Persian Gulf, an area of approximately 250 square miles, and a population of more than 500,000. The largest island is called Bahrain, and its capital is Manama. Other important islands include Muharraq, Sitra, and Umm Nasan. Like many of the Persian Gulf states, this small sheikhdom was populated by poor camel herders and pearl fishermen, nearly unknown to most of the world. And like many areas of Arabia, Jews had settled here at an early date. When Muhammad sent a force to conquer Bahrain in A.D. 630, Arabic sources record that the Jews in the capital refused to accept Islam. Jews remained in Bahrain and were heavily involved in pearl fishing and trade. A small Jewish colony existed in the 1800s and was visited by Jewish merchants from India, Iraq, and Persia. After the 1967 Six-Day War, approximately 100 Jews lived in Manama, but even this number has dwindled.

In 1507 the Portugese fleet under Admiral Albuquerque landed at Hormuz on the Persian Gulf. A trading post was set up at Bahrain. In the early 1600s the Persian shah requested British help in dislodging the Portuguese presence, and an Anglo-Persian force expelled Portuguese and Spanish traders from Bahrain and Hormuz. A number of Arab tribes conquered Bahrain, but in 1782 the current rulers, the al-Khalifas, established their dynasty. Under a British protection treaty signed in 1820, the al-Khalifa sheikh promised to refrain from piracy, war, and slavery. Oil was discovered in this British protectorate in 1932, and Bahrain was granted its independence in 1971. It immediately joined the Arab League and the United Nations. The people of Bahrain relish their independence, however, and decided not to join in a federation with either Qatar or the United Arab Emirates.

Bahrain has been searching for alternative sources of income since its oil reserves are nearly depleted. Whereas the Gulf oil-producers have reserves in the billions, Bahrain has little more than 100 million barrels of oil reserves left. Bahrain still has close ties with Britain, and it has allowed the U.S. Navy to dock at its harbor at Jufair. During the 1973 Yom Kippur War it broke some naval agreements with the United States, asserting that the U.S. was maintaining a "hostile stand against the Arab nations." After helping the United States and the allied coalition against Saddam Hussein in the 1991 Gulf War, Bahrain has been discussed as the site of a permanent U.S. presence in the Persian Gulf. Its international airport at Muharraq is strategically located, and one may well hear more of this Islamic island emirate in the near future.

QATAR

Qatar has a population about the size of Bahrain and occupies a 4,200 square mile, thumb-shaped peninsula that juts north into the Persian Gulf. Most of the population resides in its capital, Doha, on the eastern coast. A series of hills on the western coast rises above a lucrative 4.5 billion barrel oil reserve (the Dukhan oil fields). Its traditional Islamic monarchy, the al-Thani family, has ruled by Islamic law since it wrested Qatar from Persian overlords in the nineteenth century. The sheikhdom maintained close ties with Great Britain, and the British became involved in family intrigues and coups. The emir traditionally has reserved one-fourth of the oil revenue for himself. The rest is spent on public works and welfare projects. In 1975, Qatar began a three-year $250 million industrial plan to lessen its dependence on oil revenue. The results have been moderately successful.

Like Bahrain, Qatar decided not to join in confederacy with the United Arab Emirates, declaring its independence in 1971 when the British announced that they were pulling back their forces from the Gulf area. For a while Qatar and Bahrain had debated about federating with each other but then decided on total independence. Qatar also joined the Arab League and the United Nations in 1971. Since the fall of the Shah of Iran, Qatar looks for its protection to Saudi Arabia and follows the Saudi line on most of its foreign policy.

UNITED ARAB EMIRATES

As one proceeds southeast along the east coast of Arabia, the territory of the United Arab Emirates (UAE) is reached, a 32,000 square mile patch of desert that juts north to create the Strait of Hormuz between the Persian Gulf and the Gulf of Oman. Formerly known as the Trucial States and linked to Great Britain by treaty, these heirs of former Arabian pirates and Bedouin were forced to federate after Great Britain informed them that she would be departing the Gulf area by the end of 1971. This ended a relationship that had prospered since 1820. Today, approximately 2 million inhabitants of this coalition of seven sheikhdoms share in nearly 100 billion barrels of oil reserves.

Abu Dhabi is the largest of the seven emirates (Dubai, Sharja, Ras al Khaimah, Al Fujairah, Umm al Qaiwain, and Ajman are the other emirates in the federation) and has the largest oil deposits. When Bahrain and Qatar decided not to join the union, these small sheikdoms run by autocratic leaders had to overcome some internal rivalries and obstacles to cement their federation. A supreme council made up of each of the seven emirs is the highest legislative authority. One of the emirs is president of the federation, while another serves as prime minister. During much of 1989, the United Arab Emirates and Kuwait effectively boycotted the stringent oil output quotas imposed on them by OPEC, and they produced as much oil as they pleased.

Once federated, the United Arab Emirates were embroiled in a territorial conflict with the Shah of Iran over several strategic oil-bearing islands off their coast. In 1974, Saudi Arabia negotiated an outlet to the Persian Gulf between Qatar and the United Arab Emirates in return for the disputed Buraimi Oasis. In 1979 the UAE and Oman ended a longstanding border dispute. Foreign investment and banking loomed so large in the minds of some UAE leaders that the population has had to hold demonstrations from time to time to bring the sheikhs back to their primary task of caring for their people. The two most important federation members, Dubai and Abu Dhabi, have had somewhat of a rivalry over the years.

OMAN

As one travels around the southeast coast of the Arabian Peninsula from the Strait of Hormuz through the Gulf of Oman and the Arabian Sea to the border of Yemen, an area the size of Kansas (82,030 square miles) makes up the kingdom of Oman. Oman is one of the hottest countries in the world, sometimes reaching 130 degrees F., and the interior of the country is desolate. Its coastline, however, stretches 1,200 miles, and the territory of Oman has a long history of foreign rule because of its strategic significance. A sliver of Oman stretches up to the Musandam Peninsula, along the vital Strait of Hormuz.

Until recently, Oman was known as Muscat, the name of its capital on the Gulf of Oman. The Portuguese realized the importance of this port to ships headed for the Persian Gulf, and they captured Muscat in the early 1500s. By the mid-1600s, local Arab tribes had recaptured the city. The Persians were the last foreign occupiers. A sultanate was established in 1743, the ibn Said dynasty, and sultans from that line have ruled as absolute monarchs ever since. In 1798 the British signed an agreement with the sultan, and the two countries have had close relationships.

In 1951 Oman and Great Britain signed a treaty under which the British helped the sultan suppress rebellions by local tribes in the interior. When the British were forced to give up their military presence in the area in the latter 1960s, the United States assumed a protective role. In 1979 the U.S. government authorized the sale of $15 million in armaments to Oman and developed plans to use the country in an effort to upgrade U.S. military strength in the Persian Gulf. The Carter administration obtained access to military bases in Oman and in return granted military assistance of approximately $100 million in 1980.

Oman worried about the presence of Ayatollah Khomeini's regime in Iran and during the 1980s was seen as an ally of the United States. In spite of U.S. aid, however, Oman voted for a United Nations resolution in December of 1983 that declared that strategic cooperation between the U.S. and Israel threatened the security of the Middle East and that asked every nation to stop helping Israel economically and militarily.

Oman is populated by a majority of Ibadhi Muslims, a minor sect within Islam. A country of 1.5 million, Oman has oil reserves of 4.3 billion barrels and has initiated its own modernization program.

Internal squabbles within the sultan's own family have led to palace coups in the past, and rebels from neighboring Yemen also have caused instability from time to time. The Saudis pressured Oman in the 1980s to deny the United States use of a military base on the Arabian Peninsula, but current Saudi-American cooperation has lessened the pressure on Oman from its large Arab neighbor. Oman continues to be a strategic asset in the Persian Gulf strategy of the United States.

YEMEN

Just two months before Saddam Hussein's forces swarmed into Kuwait in 1990, two small countries on the southern tip of the Arabian Peninsula were finally reunited after more than 360 years of separation. The People's Democratic Republic of Yemen (South Yemen), which had spent the past two decades as a satellite of the Communist bloc, accepted an offer to unite with the Yemen Arab Republic (North Yemen). This new Republic of Yemen now comprises a population of 12 million, an area of 207,000 square miles, and oil reserves of 4 billion barrels. The once-important port city of Aden became the capital of the republic and may well regain its stature as a refueling depot, center for commerce, oil refining facility, and tourist attraction. It had lost much of its appeal to Western nations when it was drawn into the Soviet orbit in the 1960s as part of the Marxist bent of the South Yemen government.

It is said that the Queen of Sheba once ruled these lands, strategically placed at the mouth of the Red Sea and connecting the Near East with Ethiopia, Sudan, and Egypt. Many Jews of the Roman province of Judea fled to Yemen when the Romans tried to eliminate the Jewish presence from the Holy Land and renamed Judea "Palestine." Increasing numbers of Jews and Christians settled throughout southern Arabia in subsequent centuries, but the origin and spread of Islam under the leadership of Muhammad brought horrible persecution. Christianity was eradicated from southern Arabia, while fledgling Jewish communities endured pogroms and anti-Semitic legislation.

At the beginning of the twentieth century approximately 30,000 Jews lived in Yemen. By the end of the Second World War the number had increased to 45,000. Most were artisans confined to Yemenese ghettos. They were required to wear special clothing to set them apart, had to pay special taxes, and had to obey a long list of rules and regulations. For 1,900 years, the Jews of Yemen had passed on to their children stories of their heritage in the Holy Land and had continued to believe that the Messiah would lead them back to the Holy Land on the "wings of eagles." Thousands made the journey to Palestine in the late 1800s and early 1900s. During the Second World War more began to emigrate. When the state of Israel was proclaimed, the Jews of Yemen were some of the first to emigrate en masse to the new Jewish state. Some of the "wings" that brought them there were the wings of battered commuter planes.

In the seventh century, the Arabs of Yemen embraced Islam with a passion, and today 60 percent are Sunni Muslim. Adherents of the Shi'ite sect fled persecution by the Sunnis in the 700s and 800s and established their own Rassid dynasty in the highlands of northern Yemen. When the Ottoman Empire captured the coastal areas and the port of Aden, the Rassid dynasty resisted the Turks. In 1728 the sultan of the southern province broke away from the north, causing a division that remained until 1990. Although the Ottoman Turks would claim the territory of Yemen as a Turkish province, they never were able to control it. The British took control of Aden at the beginning of the nineteenth century in an effort to protect its trade routes to India.

Under the leadership of various sultans and in the midst of continual territorial strife and, ultimately, civil war, Yemen faithfully backed the dictates of the Arab League against Israel. The northern leader in 1958 linked up with Nasser's Egypt and Syria in the short-lived United Arab Republic. Syria withdrew within a year, and Nasser became embroiled in a Yemenese civil war that erupted in 1962. Pitted against a Saudi-backed royalist faction, Nasser dispatched 60,000 of his troops into a civil war that could not be won. His intrigues in the quagmire of Yemenese civil war led many nations to understand more fully the imperialist designs of Nasser's Pan-Arabism. Neither socialist South Yemen nor militarist North Yemen was particularly partial to the Western powers. A stream of radical anti-Western and anti-Israel propaganda emerged from Communist-backed South Yemen in the 1970s and 1980s.

The importance of this new united Republic of Yemen remains to be seen. The withdrawal of Soviet aid coupled with the collapse of Communist regimes in Eastern Europe has enabled it to chart its own course in the community of nations. Yet it is significant that the two-month old Yemen refused to abandon support of Saddam Hussein in his invasion of Kuwait. Yemen also abstained from an Arab League resolution that condemned the invasion. These actions by Yemen may be ominous signs that this important area has not yet learned the lessons of its volatile past.

In the aftermath of the 1991 Gulf War, foreign ministers from Saudi Arabia, Kuwait, Bahrain, Qatar, the United Arab Emirates, and Oman met with Egyptian and Syrian foreign ministers to draw up a joint security plan. This plan would create an Arab security force in the Persian Gulf region so that an Iraqi-type invasion would never occur again. Other Arab countries were invited to join in the security force and in the development of the details of a security plan, but an Iraq ruled by Saddam Hussein was not allowed to participate. Egypt and Syria would provide the bulk of the military force. Financing was to be arranged by the nations of the Arabian Peninsula. Non-Arab allied troops were to be replaced as soon as possible, although the United States was working on having a permanent base in the Persian Gulf (perhaps in Bahrain).

Although Saddam Hussein was the one who employed chemical weapons against the Kurds and had used his massive army in an attack against its weaker neighbor, these foreign diplomats could not refrain from mentioning Israel in their remarks. Israel, they declared, should be among the nations of the Middle East that must give up its weapons of mass destruction—Israel, they insisted, must totally destroy her nuclear and chemical weapons.

9
ISRAEL AND THE 1991 PERSIAN GULF WAR

As Iraqi Scud missiles systematically began to strike civilian areas of Israel in January 1991, a grave Prime Minister Yitzhak Shamir told American television that Saddam Hussein had made a "commitment to put an end to Israel's existence." Newspersons asked whether or not Israel would retaliate if there were more attacks. "The fact is that we have not retaliated," Shamir asserted, "but it may come one day."

"Kuwait is only a part of the issue," the Israeli prime minister said, referring to the Gulf War. "Now the issue is how to get rid of Saddam Hussein, of this system of dictatorship, of terrorism, and of all these unbearable threats."

During the Gulf War nearly forty Scud missiles struck indiscriminately in Israel, destroying or damaging 7,500 homes and businesses. Because Saddam Hussein had threatened to use chemical weapons to exterminate the Israeli Jews, gas masks were distributed to the population of the Jewish state. The threat seemed legitimate and revived memories of the Holocaust and the Nazi gassing of the Jewish people that resulted in two-thirds of European Jewry's being murdered. In addition, Saddam Hussein had gassed to death thousands of Kurdish men, women, and children in 1988. Thus there were endless Israeli drills with gas masks, safety lectures to schoolchildren, and fervent emergency practices by chemical burn units. Chemical-proof bassinets were put around the newborns in hospital nurseries.

Although they had kept a low profile in the 1990-1991 dispute between Iraq and the United Nations coalition forces, led by the United States, Great Britain, and Saudi Arabia, and had carefully refrained from making official statements until Iraq's missile assault attempted to draw them into the war, the Israelis were undergoing another psychological crisis. United States supplied Patriot missiles could not stop all the Scuds. Bedlam occurred among terrified masses as houses were leveled by missiles that got through defenses or were only partially deflected. Jewish children whose homes were destroyed by the Scuds had nightmares that Saddam Hussein was coming to kill them. Some did not want to go home.

A few Israeli children suffocated because their gas masks were put on wrong during the air raid alerts. As Saddam Hussein sent more and more Scuds across Jordan to fall on Israel's civilians, anger and frustration overwhelmed some Israelis, and they cried to their government for retaliation. Yet most Israelis realized they were so hated by their Arab neighbors that their retaliation against Iraq might draw Saddam Hussein's Arab opponents to his side. Even without Israeli "provocation" or threat of retaliation, Arab supporters of Saddam Hussein demonstrated in many Arab countries (even those in the coalition).

On January 29, 1991, Yasser Arafat's PLO launched eighty short-range, Soviet-built, surface-to-surface rockets toward four northern Israeli towns. PLO spokesmen claimed that the missiles were launched "in defense of Iraq" and bragged that they were "Saddam Hussein's northern front." Israeli officials could only hope that the rest of the world would take notice of their predicament and have pity on the beseiged population. As Soviet Jews arrived in Israel, they were given gas masks along with their citizenship papers. More than 5,000 Jews from the Soviet Union arrived in Israel during the first two weeks of the Gulf War.

Early in the war Americans began learning how easily the Iraqi propaganda network could fabricate atrocity stories. On January 22, 1991, Abdul Amir al-Anbari, Iraqi ambassador to the United Nations, accused the United States of carpet-bombing Iraqi cities, targeting hospitals and civilian bomb shelters, and blatantly killing women and children. Such accusations angered U.S. military officials, who had been careful not to target civilian areas. Those officials had to contend with the Arab penchant for moving women and children into targeted areas to be used as pawns in the international propaganda war.

Iraqi propaganda also included claims that the United States was deliberately bombing Muslim holy sites, that Israeli jets had joined in attacking Iraq, and that the United States was building hundreds of churches in Saudi Arabia. Besides the Iraqi claims throughout the war that they were shooting down hundreds of coalition planes, Saddam Hussein's propaganda machine cranked out fabricated stories about the Pentagon's sending 5,000 Egyptian prostitutes "to feed the lusts of the American troops." Iraq further claimed that Saudi leaders were getting drunk with the soldiers on American bases. Palestinian Arab hatred of the United States grew even deeper as such stories spread.

The Israelis had had the same problem in their effort to target terrorist bases in Lebanon. In fact, the quagmire of Lebanon influenced the decisions made in the Gulf War. Although the threat of another Vietnam affected the mobilization and size of the American forces, it was lessons from Lebanon that most influenced George Bush to pull out of Iraq quickly and not get involved in the Kurdish struggle with Saddam Hussein. In an effort to secure her northern border from ever-increasing terrorist attacks in a disintegrating Lebanon, Israel had become embroiled in the early 1980s in much more than an occasional foray across Lebanon's borders. As so often in recent history, Israel's nemesis in the Lebanon situation was Yasser Arafat.

LESSONS FROM LEBANON

"Let them come," Yasser Arafat declared in a television interview on April 14, 1982. "We are waiting for them." With 25,000 PLO fighters in Lebanon (15,000 massed on the Israeli border), with a huge cache of Soviet arms, and with the Arab nations on his side, Arafat was confident that Israel could not hurt him. In fact, since he had agreed to a U.S. negotiated cease-fire with Israel on July 21, 1981, his PLO units had committed some 248 acts of terrorism, resulting in 26 deaths and 264 wounded. Arafat reminded the world that he had only agreed not to send terrorist squads across the Lebanese border, but that the PLO could initiate any attack against Israel from other directions and in all parts of the world. The Israeli government was not amused by his creative interpretation.

On June 3, 1982, Shlomo Argov, Israel's ambassador to Britain, was shot and killed by Arab terrorists as he left a diplomatic social function. On July 4 the Israeli air force in retaliation attacked two PLO targets in Beirut and seven in southern Lebanon. In response, Arafat proceeded to aim his artillery at twenty-three Jewish settlements in Galilee and for twenty-four hours shelled the Israeli civilian population with more than 1,000 rounds. The Israeli air force began knocking out PLO artillery and ammunition centers. In order to avoid the devastation, Arafat quickly accepted another cease-fire (put forth by the U.N. Security Council).

The Israeli government of Prime Minister Menachem Begin, however, had had enough of Arafat's dealings. Murdering the Israeli ambassador had been the final straw in a long list of PLO atrocities. On the evening of June 5, 1982, the Israeli cabinet voted to send the Israel Defense Forces (IDF) into Lebanon. The massive strength and quick deployment of this "Operation Peace for Galilee" campaign surprised Arafat, his PLO terrorists, and the Arab world. Israel accomplished its objectives within one week but would be bogged down much longer in Lebanon. Arafat and his troops would be forced out of Lebanon, to set up their organizational headquarters in Tunis.

The events in Lebanon, however, would consume Israel in the first half of the 1980s as the Israelis tried to pull out of most of Lebanon while securing borders to the north. When the Maronite Christian Phalange militia entered the former terrorist base camps of Sabra and Shatilla on September 16, 1982, they murdered 425 men, 15 women, and 20 children. Two days earlier, the Palestinians had murdered the Maronite leader President Bashir Gemayel and 25 of his followers. Because Israel had allowed the Phalangists into the camps in an effort to transfer authority, Israel was blamed for the massacre.

Unlike their Arab counterparts who continually cheer terrorists and condone the murder of Jewish civilians, the people of Israel were horrified that Israel's image could be tainted in such a way. They believed that the Israeli generals should have known that such a massacre could have occurred and, to their credit, 300,000 Israelis demonstrated against Begin's government. The Kahan Commission was appointed and after months of investigation recommended that Defense Minister Ariel Sharon and General Raphael Eitan, chief of staff of the Israeli Army, be dismissed. To its discredit, a similar commission appointed by Lebanon's government declared that there was no Lebanese responsibility for the massacre (even though Lebanese soldiers had committed the murders). Incredibly, the Lebanese also blamed the Israelis. Ironically, three years later when Shi'ite Muslims killed more than 600 Palestinian Arabs and wounded more than 2,000 in the Shatilla and Burj el-Barajneh camps, there was no outcry among Muslims (or among the rest of the world).

Yasser Arafat would reappear on the Middle East scene from his new base in Tunis. In December 1987, a Palestinian uprising, or *Intifada*, broke out in the West Bank and Gaza Strip. The Arabs once again sent out their children and women to throw stones at Israeli soldiers and to riot in the streets. It was a publicity coup that Arafat had not expected, and it catapulted him back into a position of prestige as the "president of Palestine." Much less notice was given to the thousands of Palestinians who fled to the United States and other countries to escape the violence or to those whose economic status had been severely crippled. Arab states did not come to the aid of the rioters as those in the uprising had expected, and PLO funds could not make up for the wages lost in the West Bank and Gaza.

Few realize the close economic ties that Israel had with the Palestinian Arab population in the West Bank and Gaza prior to the uprising. In fact, hundreds of thousands had worked in Israel each day. Any Palestinian Arabs who complained that the Intifada was hurting them economically were killed by their PLO cohorts, and Arab deaths by Arab hands in the Intifada began to match those deaths caused by the Israeli Defense Forces attempting to quell the riots. Stones could easily crush a Jewish soldier's skull (and did), but soon more damaging weapons were back in use, and the ages of the "children" in the Intifada grew as well.

Now that the Palestinian Arabs have cast their lot with Saddam Hussein, jobs for them in Israel have dried up considerably. The average Palestinian has been hurt once again by the violence of his brothers and sisters. Arab-Americans, however, have taken pride in the accomplishments of the Intifada, and it has served as a great embarrassment to Israel in the international media.

THE RADICALIZATION OF JORDAN

We have seen in chapter 4 how Jordan has become a Palestinian enclave with a large fundamentalist Muslim element in the newly elected parliament. King Hussein showed his true colors when Saddam Hussein invaded Kuwait, and the danger that Jordan poses to Israel is best viewed in the king's double standard. In the days preceding the Gulf War, King Hussein deployed troops on the Israeli border of the Jordan Valley. More troops were deployed on this border than at any time since the 1967 Six-Day War. The Israelis were forced to mobilize their forces as well. The king of Jordan tried to keep the West from going to war with his friend Saddam Hussein, insisting that the Iraqi leader was "as concerned" about the soldiers on both sides that were about to be killed "as any one in the world." King Hussein equivocated when asked why he was not building up troops on his Iraqi border if he truly was being "neutral."

Even as the Arabs joined in coalition with the West against Saddam Hussein, both Syria and Egypt told Jordan that they would come to her aid if she became embroiled in a war with Israel. This certainly was not assuring to the Israelis concerning the ultimate goals of their Arab neighbors. King Hussein strongly warned Israel not to fly jets over his country, even if in retaliation against Iraq. On January 11, 1991, King Hussein declared: "We are determined to prevent any violation of our air space or our land by any side to this conflict." He insisted that that meant "any flights from any direction." "If anyone tries to overfly our territory," he underscored, "we will try to stop them no matter who they are or from which direction they come." And yet, when Iraq sent scores of Scud missiles across Jordan to hit civilian targets in Israel, the Jordanian king did not lift a finger to censor Saddam Hussein.

When King Hussein said nothing about Iraq's invading his air space to strike at Israel, President Bush sent an emissary to tell the king bluntly to stay out of the war and to stay out of the way. American-Jordanian relations certainly suffered a setback during the Gulf War, but most U.S. government analysts concurred that Jordan would be needed in the proposed regional peace conference for any comprehensive settlement to take place.

On January 22, 1991, Abdul Amir al-Anbari, the Iraqi ambassador to the United Nations, explained that Iraq was attacking the land of Israel with Scud missiles so that Israel might feel the damage she had caused in past years in the Middle East. The PLO Executive Committee issued a January 29 statement that declared its allegiance to Iraq and its stand "against the aggression of the United States and its coalition." "All Arab forces seeking to put an end to American Zionist hegemony and tyranny" were urged by the PLO Committee to fight against the "criminal, iniquitous American aggression on our Iraqi people."

Leaflets distributed by Islamic fundamentalist groups called upon Palestinians to go to the roofs of their homes and cheer for the Iraqi missiles. The leadership of the Intifada declared on January 30 that "the imperialist forces of aggression led by the United States" were using Kuwait as an excuse to "destroy Iraq and its people." In Nablus, hundreds of Arabs were on their roofs shouting, "Allah is great!" as the Iraqi Scuds lighted the Israeli night sky. In Tulkarm, other Arabs added, "O beloved Saddam, hit, hit, Tel Aviv," while Israeli troops stood by and watched the demonstrations. The Jordanian population demonstrated in the same manner, and the most popular posters sold in Jordan during the Gulf War pictured King Hussein embracing Saddam Hussein.

Even before the war, Jordan had been undermining the United Nations embargo against Iraq. Jordan also has become a haven for terrorists. Palestinian terrorist groups that were expelled from Jordan by force in 1970 are returning by the thousands. King Hussein is aware of the danger to his throne and has spent an incredible amount of energy in pacifying the Palestinian population, which constitutes a majority in his nation. Radical Palestinians call for a jihad against Israel and insist that they will kill the Americans if they interfere. Jordan, in fact, faces the same division that has plagued Lebanon. And, as in Lebanon, the Palestinian terrorists do not care if they destroy Jordan in the process. King Hussein is a weak reed who could be dethroned at any time. Whether he goes or stays, however, a radicalized Jordan poses one more threat to Israel.

CHEMICAL WARFARE AND THE NAZI PAST

In the late 1980s West Germany and other European nations began to prosecute chemical companies and other subsidiaries who participated in illegal sales of production facilities for chemical weapons to Arab countries of the Middle East. In light of the horrors of the Holocaust during the Second World War, many West Germans were horrified that their government had not derailed the sales and shipments before the chemicals could be used by nations that backed terrorists. Now chemical weapons threaten the entire population of the Middle East.

An additional scandal was uncovered, however, in the recent overthrow of Communist governments in Eastern Europe. It was found, for example, that East Germany had trained Arab and Palestinian terrorists since the 1970s on a scale that surprised even the best intelligence agencies of the West. Sadly, much of this training involved the use of chemical weapons against civilians, particularly Israeli and American populations. Communist East Germany was able to rationalize the training of such Arab terrorists under the rubric of their campaign against the West. During the Gulf War when George Habash of the Popular Front for the Liberation of Palestine was confronted with the existence of East German training facilities that had trained so many of his vicious terrorist squads, he smiled and explained: "To our people, your president, Mr. Bush, is the real terrorist."

Saddam Hussein and Iraq's involvement in terrorist training began in 1972 when one of East Germany's leading scientists was invited to Baghdad to speak to the Iraqi high command on his efforts to ban chemical weapons. One of the Iraqi generals stood up after his hour-long presentation and said, "OK, Professor, that is very nice, but look, the Germans have a lot of experience to kill Jewish people by gas. Can you give to us any information or any helpful hints to use this kind of weapons against Israel?" The scientist who had spent years trying to warn the world of the dangers of chemical weapons was flabbergasted. He immediately reported the incident to the East German government. Little did he know that the East Germans had plans for the Arab nations in their battle against Israel.

The Communist government of East Germany invited members of Iraq's elite Republican Guard to view their chemical training military camp. The Iraqis were quite impressed and indicated that this was precisely the training that they needed. East Germany immediately complied, and other Eastern European nations provided haven for the terrorists as well. The information and training they received was not only used for Iraqi-sponsored terrorism against Israel and other parts of the world, but was the same procedure used against the Kurds in 1988. In 1987 the United States filed a formal protest about the reported East German involvement with Arab terrorists and chemical weapons, but the East Germans categorically denied that a chemical training facility existed. They insisted that East Germany had a "humane and civilized government" that would have no part in the support and training of terrorists. As their Communist government began to crumble, East German secret service agents attempted to destroy the documents and files that incriminated the government, but young German activists not only uncovered the files but also led reporters to the camps.

What came to light was an active East German role in Arab terrorism aimed directly at Americans and Israelis. Palestinian terrorists had been secretly operating out of East Berlin for years, and during 1990-1991 a unified Berlin police force searched for hundreds of killer commandos who were still residing in the city. No longer protected by a sympathetic regime, each terrorist who is captured brings a string of horror stories to the German news media. One hour's drive from Berlin, a former East German military camp recently was uncovered where German secret police armed and trained terrorists to strike specifically at civilian targets. More than 1,000 men a year came through this camp. East Germany also issued false passports for terrorists from Libya, Iraq, Syria, the PLO, and elsewhere. These individuals carried out some of the most brutal attacks of the 1980s.

Some of the young East German activists who have publicized this terrible activity have done so because of their consciences and because of their history. One explained that his father was a Nazi and would never answer his son's questions about what had happened in the 1940s under Adolf Hitler's regime. Today, the activists point to the training camps and declare that their East German government "did not break off the history from the Nazi history." They say they are ashamed to find that many Arab terrorist atrocities were nourished in their homeland. Attuned to the democratic winds blowing through Europe, these young activists walk their children through the training camps in the hope that they will shake the millstones of prejudice. (This is part of the battle against racist, right-wing, neo-Nazi "skinhead" movements that are spreading throughout Europe today.)

DEMOCRACY IN THE MIDST OF DESPOTS

Viewing the Israeli outcry at the massacre of Palestinians by Maronite Christian Arabs in the Sabra and Shatilla camps, former Secretary of State Henry Kissinger declared that the Israeli Kahan Commission was a "great tribute to Israeli democracy." "Very few governments in the world," Kissenger added, could make "such a public investigation of such a difficult and shameful episode." For all of their faults, the Israelis pride themselves in maintaining a democracy in the midst of a Middle Eastern world that disdains popular sovereignty and admires the brutally strong despot.

As we have uncovered the history of Israel's neighbors, we have viewed time and time again the truth of this maxim. Syria, Libya, and Iraq have been crueler than many of the East European Communist regimes; and Egypt, Jordan, and the countries of the Arabian Peninsula have displayed an inordinate propensity for barbarism. The ability of Saddam Hussein to remain a hero in the eyes of the great mass of Arabs in the Middle East underscores the fact that a totalitarian system is more in line with Muslim thinking and, indeed, Muslim law. Sadly, one is faced with a more sobering conclusion: if the Palestinian Arabs viewed Saddam Hussein as a savior and welcomed his destruction of Arab Muslim Kuwait, what must the average Palestinian hope will happen to democratic Jewish Israel?

Israel actually is the only democracy in the Middle East. In Arab countries, Jews are not allowed to vote or hold office. In the Jewish state, however, both Christian and Muslim Arabs have the right to vote, to form their own political parties, and to send their elected representatives to the Knesset (parliament). Arab and other non-Jewish delagates to the Knesset are provided translations of speeches and bills into their respective languages. Non-Jewish religions are accorded full rights, and Israel protects their holy sites, allowing adherents to administer the various areas. Muslim and Christian religious courts are recognized by Israel and are given exclusive judicial authority in matters of their members' "personal status," such as marriage and divorce.

For Israeli Jews, Israel's greatest achievement is the existence of her democracy and democratic institutions, even in the midst of external and internal siege. For five decades Israel has been in a state of war or semi-war. Yet Israeli Jews view their nation's active parliament, law and order, privileges of protest, independent judicial system, and free press as a beacon in a dictator-ridden and fear-oriented Middle East. Israelis are proud that whereas the nations surrounding them honor terrorists and murderers, Israel brings charges against those Jews who revert (for even an instant) from law and order. Israel upholds justice and compassion, honesty and fairness, human rights and love of neighbor. Some Israeli Jews have joined movements to protect the rights of Palestinian Arabs, while others donate their services to represent Palestinians in court. Unfortunately, the reverse is not true in Arab lands of the Middle East. There is no Peace Now movement in Muslim countries.

Consider the difference in Israel's governmental structure from her Arab neighbors. For a four-year period, the Knesset (Hebrew for "assembly") is the supreme authority in Israel. The Knesset can dissolve itself and call new elections before the four-year term is up only if the majority of its members "lose confidence" in the way the government is being run, that is, lose confidence in their own parliament. The 120 representatives to the Knesset (MKs: members of the Knesset) are elected for four-year terms and must be twenty-one years of age. Judges, civil servants, rabbis paid by the state, active army officers, and other officials are not permitted to run for office.

Every citizen over the age of eighteen is eligible to vote, and the country is treated as one district. Any political party, group, or individual may submit a list of candidates for the Knesset, provided the group or individual obtains the signatures of 750 citizens. Voters choose from national lists of 120 such candidates. The 120 Knesset seats are distributed according to the percentage of votes each list obtains. For example, if the Labor Party receives 40 percent of the national vote for its list of candidates, the first 48 names (40 percent of 120) on its list become members of the Knesset. If one of those members resigns or dies, the next person on the list automatically takes his or her place. As one might expect, this system encourages a large number of parties, and it is not uncommon during elections for citizens to vote on twenty lists. In addition, the Israeli's fierce independence makes it nearly impossible for one list to gain a majority in the Knesset. Therefore, coalitions have been common since the founding of the Jewish state.

In Israel, a president is elected by the Knesset, but he is mainly a ceremonial figure. The key leader is the prime minister. When a new Knesset is elected, the entire former Knesset submits its resignation to the president. He, in turn, consults the newly elected representatives of the parties to determine the member of the Knesset who will form the new government. This prime-minister-elect makes sure he or she (Israel is the only country of the Middle East to have had a female head of state) has a majority coalition and then proposes a cabinet. A vote of confidence is then taken in the Knesset. If the vote is positive, the prime-minister-elect assumes office. If such a vote is negative, the process must begin over again. Parties not represented in the government majority coalition are referred to as the "opposition" parties.

As one can see, this system is quite different from that of Israel's neighbors. Israel's pursuit of democratic ideals opens herself for criticism throughout the world when she fails to measure up to those ideals. The Jewish state is often held to a standard that would not be imagined by any other state in the region. Because the press is not censored, journalists (both domestic and foreign) feel at liberty to question and belittle governmental and military actions, a liberty that would not be possible in the Arab world and in the Muslim regimes that we have studied. It is particularly galling to the Israelis that every year the Arab coalition in the United Nations introduces an amendment to exclude "the credentials of Israel."

Israelis take pride in their rescue of Jews throughout the world and their providing a haven for refugees. When the Soviet Union made advances in 1987 to reestablish diplomatic relations with Israel, the topic of Soviet Jewry was on the top of Israel's agenda. Soviet Jews are the third largest Jewish population in the world and, until the recent thaw of glasnost, were not permitted to emigrate to Israel. Now, hundreds of thousands are getting out of the Soviet Union while the possibility exists. These refugees are a great burden on the nation, just as the Jewish refugees from Arab countries were. Such rescue, however, is part and parcel of the fabric of the Jewish state and one of its key reasons for existence.

In turn, Israel is helping the Soviet Union to reestablish herself in a more positive role in Middle East diplomacy (a role the Soviets abdicated by breaking relations with Israel in 1967). When Israel proposed a regional peace conference under the auspices of the United States and the Soviet Union in April 1991, the plan was given credence by both superpowers. For better or worse, the Soviet Union is once again on the diplomatic scene of the Middle East maze. For her part, Israel monitors the growing anti-Semitic movements within the U.S.S.R, even as she is keenly aware of the Nazi and neo-Nazi anti-Jewish literature that is permeating the Arab countries.

A greater percentage of Israel's population consists of Jews with roots in Arab lands than at any other time in her history. These Jewish families lost their possessions and funds in confiscation and persecution forays by newly founded Arab states. They are a little-known and little-understood factor in the equation of the Middle East, because they believe their rights have been trampled in a more sinister fashion than have those of the Palestinian Arab refugees. They take a hard line toward Arab governments that continue to debate whether or not Israel should be a state. As one can imagine, Israeli politics are volatile and passionate. The Gulf War has opened a crack in the door of peace, and Israelis want to capture the opportunity. They realistically believe, however, that the war only magnified the problems that exist between Israel and her neighbors. They will not sacrifice their existence for an ambiguous "truce in hostilities."

LOOKING AT THE FUTURE

When it comes to Middle East analysis, one must truly be wise as a serpent and gentle as a dove. The area is so volatile that if Israel were to cease to exist tomorrow, there would be no peace among her neighbors. The Middle East maze is illusive and deceptive, replete with mine fields for the one who delves in looking for simplistic answers. Israel is here to stay, and her Arab neighbors will have to learn that the Jewish state is a part of the future for the Middle East. Israelis are convinced they may at times have to plod along alone on the international scene, but they are ably prepared for such a struggle. They will strive to maintain and to enhance their prized democracy, even as they provide a haven for oppressed Jews around the world.

Certainly the United States has provided funds to Israel on a yearly basis, but for her part Israel has reciprocated as a loyal ally surrounded by an anti-Western, anti-democratic Muslim culture. The United States provides a number of Arab countries with funds and arms as well. The results have not been nearly as dramatic. For the time being, America's interests lie in a strong Israel. Even the cultural ties and political compatibility between the United States and Israel run broad and deep. But Israel cannot (and does not) count on the United States remaining sympathetic to her plight or responsive to her needs. A number of American administrations and a cadre of State Department officials have many times worked against Israel's interests.

Still, Israelis admire the United States and the democratic traditon for which it stands—they admire Americans while being cognizant of America's flaws. According to opinion polls, a large majority of Americans admire the Israelis as well. Because of the Gulf War and other crises, the citizens of the United States want to understand better the Middle East maze and the complicated relationships between Israel and her neighbors.

Some Americans have learned too much the hard way. For them, the passions of the Middle East have consumed their being and permanently commandeered their psyche. What happened to veteran CBS news correspondent Bob Simon and three colleagues while covering the Gulf War is a good example of this. They were looking for a story at a Kuwaiti-Iraqi border crossing when suddenly they noticed a jeep approaching from the Iraqi side. They quickly calculated they could not outrun it back to the border 200 yards away. They were walking briskly toward the Kuwaiti line when the jeep with three Iraqis closed in.

The Iraqis approached them saying, "Peace! Peace! Peace!" As soon as they caught up, however, the Iraqis grabbed the newsmen, pushed their heads down, roughly shoved them into the jeep, and covered the CBS crew with guns. This began twenty-four days of solitary confinement while the world protested the disappearance of the men. Blindfolded and beaten, they were accused of being foreign spies. Veteran correspondent Simon had worked for CBS for twenty-five years, but he was reminded by his Iraqi captors that they had killed another spy who claimed to be a correspondent. During his interrogation Simon was forced to hear the screams of his news colleagues being tortured as the Iraqis attempted to pry information out of him.

At one point a captain in the Iraqi army grabbed Simon by the face and forced his mouth open, snarling, "Yehudi, Yehudi" (which from the time of Nebuchadnezzar had meant "Jew"). The captain then spit on Simon and slapped him. Bob Simon related the deep emotions that engulfed him: "I could have killed him, I would have killed him if I could have. I would have killed him and I would have had no more remorse than I had every morning when I got up and killed the cockroaches in my room."

The experience changed Bob Simon. "I think I will cover wars again, but it will never be the same," he related. The veteran correspondent, who had covered some of the most dangerous episodes of the Vietnam War, had lost his childlike sense of invulnerability.

I hope this study has helped readers achieve some sense of the Middle East maze without having to endure the torture Simon's colleagues experienced, without having to suffer such trauma. When we hear of a shooting or a killing in the Middle East, we must remember that a human being was involved and that a long history is being reenacted. May we understand that simplistic solutions imposed on others in the Middle East may end in death and destruction in the long haul —death and destruction for which we may be able to say nothing other than, "I'm sorry. I was mistaken." We must be mindful of the history of the countries within this maze as well as their present circumstances.

The crisis of the CBS newsmen perhaps holds somewhat of a parable for the student of the modern Middle East—their ordeal began with the cry of "Peace! Peace! Peace!" from soldiers who knew that there would be no peace for the captives.

BIBLIOGRAPHY

Abdalla, Ahmed. *The Student Movement and National Politics in Egypt, 1923-1973*. London: Al Saqi Books, 1985.

Abd-Allah, Umar F. *The Islamic Struggle in Syria*. Berkeley, Calif.: Mizan, 1983.

Abdullah, Muhammad Morsy. *The United Arab Emirates: A Modern History*. New York: Barnes & Noble, 1978.

Addresses of the [Fourth] International Prophetic Conference Held December 10-15, 1901 in the Clarendon Street Baptist Church, Boston, Mass. Boston: Watchword and Truth, 1901.

Addresses on the Second Coming of the Lord Delivered at the Prophetic Conference, Allegheny, Pa. December 3-6, 1895. Pittsburgh: W.W. Waters, n.d. [Third International Prophetic Conference]

American Christian Palestine Committee. *The Arab War Effort: A Documented Account*. New York: ACPC Press, 1946.

————. *The People Speak on Palestine: American Opinion on the United States and United Nations*. New York: ACPC Press, 1948.

————. *Truth About Palestine*. New York: ACPC Press, 1946.

Adams, Richard H., Jr. *Development and Social Change in Rural Egypt*. Syracuse, N.Y.: Syracuse U., 1986.

Ahmad, Feroz. *The Young Turks: The Committee of Union and Progress in Turkish Politics 1908-1914*. Oxford: Clarendon, 1969.

Ajami, Fouad. *The Arab Predicament: Arab Political Thought and Practice Since 1967*. Cambridge: Cambridge U., 1981.

Albaharna, Husain M. *The Legal Status of the Arabian Gulf States: A Study of Their Treaty Relations and Their International Problems*. Manchester, England: Manchester U., 1968.

Al-Chalabi, Fadhil J. *OPEC and the International Oil Industry: A Changing Structure*. London: Oxford U., 1980.

187

Almana, Mohammad. *Arabia Unified: A Portrait of Ibn Saud*. London: Hutchinson Benham, 1980.

Ansari, Hamied N. *Egypt: The Stalled Society*. Albany, N.Y.: State U. of New York, 1986.

Aronson, Shlomo. *Conflict and Bargaining in the Middle East*. Baltimore: Johns Hopkins U., 1978.

Atherton, Alfred L. *Egypt and U.S. Interests*. Washington, D.C.: Foreign Policy Institute of Johns Hopkins University, 1988.

Ayoub, Mahmoud. *Redemptive Suffering in Islam*. The Hague: Mouton, 1978.

Baker, Raymond W. *Egypt's Uncertain Revolution Under Nasser and Sadat*. Cambridge, Mass.: Harvard U., 1978.

Bakhash, Shaul. *The Reign of the Ayatollahs: Iran and the Islamic Revolution*. New York: Basic Books, 1984.

Bashiriyeh, Hossein. *The State and Revolution in Iran, 1962-1982*. New York: St. Martin's, 1984.

Bavly, Dan, and Eliahu Salpeter. *Fire in Beirut: Israel's War in Lebanon with the PLO*. New York: Stein and Day, 1984.

Becker, Jillian. *The PLO: The Rise and Fall of the Palestine Liberation Organization*. New York: St. Martin's, 1984.

Beling, Willard A. *King Faisal and the Modernization of Saudi Arabia*. Boulder, Colo.: Westview, 1980.

Berque, Jacques. *Egypt: Imperialism and Revolution*. Translated by Jean Stewart. New York: Praeger, 1972.

Bianco, Mirella. *Gadafi: Voice from the Desert*. London: Longman, 1975.

Blackstone, William E. *Jesus Is Coming*. New York: Revell, 1878.

————. *Palestine for the Jews: A Copy of the Memorial Presented to President Harrison, March 5, 1891*. Oak Park, Ill.: n.p., 1891.

Blair, John M. *The Control of Oil*. New York: Vintage, 1978.

Blandford, Linda. *Superwealth: The Secret Lives of the Oil Sheikhs*. New York: William Morrow, 1977.

Blundy, David, and Andrew Lycett. *Qaddafi and the Libyan Revolution*. Boston: Little, Brown, 1987.

Bricault, Giselle C. *Major Companies of the Arab World, 1980/81*. London: Graham and Trotman, 1980.

Browne, Edward G. *The Persian Revolution of 1905-1909*. Cambridge: Cambridge U., 1910.

Bulloch, John. *The Gulf: A Portrait of Kuwait, Qatar, Bahrain and the UAE*. London: Century, 1984.

Busch, Briton Cooper. *Britain and the Persian Gulf, 1894-1914*. Berkeley, Calif.: U. of California, 1967.

Cobban, Helena. *The Palestinian Liberation Organization: People, Power and Politics*. Cambridge: Cambridge U., 1984.

Cole, Juan R.I., and Nikki R. Keddie, eds. *Shi'ism and Social Protest*. New Haven, Conn.: Yale U., 1986.

Cooley, John. *Libyan Sandstorm: The Complete Account of Qaddafi's Revolution*. London: Sidgwick and Jackson, 1982.

Cordesman, Anthony H. *The Iran-Iraq War and Western Security, 1984-1987: Strategic Implications and Policy Options*. London: Jane's Publishing, 1987.

Cottrell, Alvin J., and Michael L. Moodie. *The United States and the Persian Gulf: Past Mistakes, Present Needs*. New York: National Strategy Information Center, 1984.

Cottrell, Alvin J., gen. ed. *The Persian Gulf States: A General Survey*. Baltimore: Johns Hopkins U., 1980.

Cottrell, P.L. *British Overseas Investment in the Nineteenth Century*. London: Macmillan, 1975.

Curtis, Michael, ed. *Religion and Politics in the Middle East*. Boulder, Colo.: Westview, 1981.

Darwin, John. *Britain, Egypt, and the Middle East: Imperial Policy in the Aftermath of War, 1918-1922*. New York: St. Martin's, 1981.

Davis, John. *Libyan Politics: Revolution*. Berkeley, Calif.: U. of California, 1987.

Davis, Moshe, ed. *The Yom Kippur War: Israel and the Jewish People*. New York: Arno, 1974.

Dawn, C. Ernest. *From Ottomanism to Arabism: Essays on the Origins of Arab Nationalism*. Urbana, Ill.: U. of Illinois, 1973.

Deeb, Marius K., and Mary Jane Deeb. *Libya since the Revolution*. New York: Praeger, 1982.

Dekmejian, R. Hrair. *Islam in Revolution: Fundamentalism in the Arab World*. Syracuse, N.Y.: Syracuse U., 1985.

Devlin, J.F. *The Ba'th Party: A History from Its Origins to 1966*. Stanford, Calif.: Hoover Institution Press, 1976.

————. *Syria: Modern State in an Ancient Land*. Boulder, Colo.: Westview, 1983.

Dickson, H.R.P. *The Arab of the Desert: A Glimpse into Badawin Life in Kuwait and Saudi Arabia*. London: George Allen and Unwin, 1972.

Dimbleby, Johnathan. *The Palestinians*. London: Quartet Books, 1979.

Edmonds, C.J. *Kurds, Turks and Arabs: Politics, Travel and Research in North-Eastern Iraq, 1919-1925*. London: Oxford U., 1957.

Engler, Robert. *The Brotherhood of Oil.* New York: New American Library, 1977.

―――――. *The Politics of Oil.* Chicago: U. of Chicago, 1961.

Esposito, John L., ed. *Voices of Resurgent Islam.* New York: Oxford U., 1983.

Evans, Laurence. *United States Policy and the Partition of Turkey, 1914-1924.* Baltimore: Johns Hopkins U., 1965.

Eversley, Lord. *The Turkish Empire from 1288-1914.* New York: Howard Fertig, 1969.

Fathaly, Omar, and Monte Palmer. *Political Development and Social Change in Libya.* Toronto: D.C. Heath, 1980.

Farid, Abdel Majid, and Hussein Sirriyeh, eds. *The Decline of Arab Oil Revenues.* London: Croom Helm, 1986.

Feldblum, Esther Yolles. *The American Catholic Press and the Jewish State, 1917-1959.* New York: Ktav, 1977.

First, Ruth. *Libya: The Elusive Revolution.* London: Penguin, 1974.

Fischer, Michael M.J. *Iran: From Religious Dispute to Revolution.* Cambridge, Mass.: Harvard U., 1980.

Flannery, Edward H. "Israel, Jerusalem, and the Middle East." In *Twenty Years of Jewish-Catholic Relations*, edited by Eugene J. Fisher, A. James Rudin, and Marc H. Tanenbaum. Mawhaw, N.J.: Paulist, 1986.

Friedman, Isaiah. *Germany, Turkey, and Zionism: 1897-1918.* Oxford: Clarendon, 1977.

Friedman, Thomas L. *From Beirut to Jerusalem.* New York: Farrar Straus Giroux, 1989.

Fromkin, David. *A Peace to End All Peace: The Fall of the Ottoman Empire and the Creation of the Modern Middle East.* New York: Avon, 1989.

Gaebelein, Arno C., ed. *Christ and Glory: Addresses Delivered at the New York Prophetic Conference Carnegie Hall, November 25-28, 1918.*

Gellner, Ernest. *Muslim Society.* Cambridge: Cambridge U., 1981.

Gervasi, Frank. *The Life and Times of Menachem Begin: Rebel to Statesman.* New York: G.P. Putnam's, 1979.

Gilbert, Martin. *The Jews of Arab Lands: Their History in Maps.* Oxford: Martin Gilbert, 1976.

Gilmour, David. *Lebanon: The Fractured Country.* New York: St. Martin's, 1984.

Gilsenan, Michael. *Recognizing Islam: Religion and Society in the Modern Arab World.* New York: Pantheon, 1982.

Gordon, David C. *The Republic of Lebanon: Nation in Jeopardy.* Boulder, Colo.: Westview, 1983.

Goulden, Joseph. *The Death Merchant.* New York: Simon & Schuster, 1984.

Goodell, Grace E. *The Elementary Structures of Political Life: Rural Development in Pahlavi Iran.* New York: Oxford U., 1986.

Granott, Abraham. *The Land System in Palestine, History and Structure.* London: Eyre and Spottiswoode, 1952.

Green, Jerrold D. *Revolution in Iran: The Politics of Countermobilization.* New York: Praeger, 1982.

Grenville, J.A.S. *The Major International Treaties, 1914-1973: A History and Guide with Texts.* New York: Stein and Day, 1975.

Grose, Peter. *Israel in the Mind of America.* New York: A. Knopf, 1983.

Haber, Eitan. *Menachem Begin, the Man and the Legend.* New York: Dell, 1978.

Habib, John S. *Ibn Saud's Warriors of Islam: The Ikhwan of Najd and Their Role in the Creation of the Saudi Kingdom 1910-1930.* Leiden: E.J. Brill, 1978.

Haim, Sylvia G., ed. *Arab Nationalism: An Anthology.* Berkeley, Calif.: U. of California, 1976.

Harik, Iliya F. *Politics and Change in a Traditional Society, Lebanon 1711-1845.* Princeton, N.J.: Princeton U., 1968.

Headrick, Daniel R. *The Tools of Empire: Technology and European Imperialism in the Nineteenth Century.* New York: Oxford U., 1981.

Heikal, Mohamed. *Autumn of Fury: The Assassination of Sadat.* New York: Random House, 1983.

Helmreich, Paul C. *From Paris to Sevres: The Partition of the Ottoman Empire at the Peace Conference of 1919-1920.* Columbus, Ohio: Ohio State U., 1974.

Helms, Christine Moss. *The Cohesion of Saudi Arabia: Evolution of Political Identity.* Baltimore: Johns Hopkins U., 1981.

Herzl, Theodor. *Diary.* Edited by Raphael Patai. Translated by Harry Zohn. 5 volumes. New York: Herzl Press and Thomas Yoseloff, 1960.

————. *A Jewish State: An Attempt at a Modern Solution of the Jewish Question.* Revised by J. de Haas from the translation of Herzl's *Der Judenstaat,* by Sylvie D'Avigdor. New York: Maccabaean, 1904.

Hinnebusch, Raymond A. *Egyptian Politics Under Sadat.* Cambridge: Cambridge U., 1985.

Hirst, David, and Irene Beeson. *Sadat*. London: Farber and Farber, 1981.

Holden, David, and Richard Johns. *The House of Saud: The Rise and Rule of the Most Powerful Dynasty in the Arab World*. New York: Holt, Rinehart & Winston, 1982.

Hopwood, Derek. Syria 1945-1986: *Politics and Society*. London: Unwin Hyman, 1988.

Howarth, David. *The Desert King: Ibn Saud and His Arabia*. New York: McGraw-Hill, 1964.

Hurewitz, J.C. *Diplomacy in the Near and Middle East: A Documentary Record, 1914-1956*. 2 volumes. New York: D. Van Nostrand, 1956.

Ingrams, Doreen, ed. *Palestine Papers 1917-1922, Seeds of Conflict*. London: John Murray, 1972.

Jansen, Johannes J.G. *The Neglected Duty: The Creed of Sadat's Assassins and Islamic Resurgence in the Middle East*. New York: Macmillan, 1986.

Jansen, Michael. *The Battle of Beirut*. London: Zed, 1982.

Kark, Ruth. "Landownership and Spatial Change in Nineteenth Century Palestine: An Overview." Seminar on Historical Types of Spatial Organization in Warsaw, Poland, in April 1983.

————. "Millenarism and Agricultural Settlement in the Holy Land in the Nineteenth Century." *Journal of Historical Geography*. Volume 9 (January 1983), pp. 1-19.

Kassiha, Walid. *Revolutionary Transformation in the Arab World*. New York: St. Martin's, 1975.

Katouzian, Homa. *The Political Economy of Modern Iran: Despotism and Pseudo-Modernism, 1926-1979*. New York: New York U., 1981.

Kays, Doreen. *Frogs and Scorpions: Egypt, Sadat and the Media*. London: Frederick Muller, 1984.

Keddie, Nikki R. *Roots of Revolution: An Interpretive History of Modern Iran*. New Haven, Conn.: Yale U., 1981.

Keddie, Nikki R., ed. *Scholars, Saints and Sufis: Muslim Religious Institutions Since 1500*. Berkeley, Calif.: U. of California, 1972.

Keddie, Nikki R., and Eric Hooglund, eds. *The Iranian Revolution and the Islamic Republic*. Syracuse, N.Y.: Syracuse U., 1986.

Kelly, J.B. *Arabia, the Gulf and the West*. New York: Basic Books, 1980.

————. *Britain and the Persian Gulf, 1795-1880*. Oxford: Clarendon, 1968.

Kent, Marian. *Oil and Empire*. New York: Harper & Row, 1976.

Kerr, M. *The Arab Cold War: Gamal Abd al-Nasir and His Rivals, 1958-1970.* London: Oxford U., 1971.

Khomeini, Ruh Allah. *Islam and Revolution: Writings and Declarations of Imam Khomeini.* Translated and edited by Hamad Algar. Berkeley, Calif.: Mizan, 1981.

Khoury, P.S. *Urban Notables and Arab Nationalism: The Politics of Damascus, 1860-1920.* Cambridge: Cambridge U., 1983.

――――. *Syria and the French Mandate: The Politics of Arab Nationalism, 1920-1945.* Princeton, N.J.: Princeton U., 1987.

Khuri, Fuad. *From Village to Suburb: Order and Change in Greater Beirut.* Chicago: U. of Chicago, 1975.

――――. *Tribe and State in Bahrain: The Transformation of Social and Political Authority in an Arab State.* Chicago: U. of Chicago, 1980.

Kirkbride, Sir Alec. *An Awakening: The Arab Campaign, 1917-1918.* Tavistock, England: U. Press of Arabia, 1971.

Kissinger, Henry A. *White House Years.* Boston: Little, Brown , 1979.

Kosut, Hal. *Israel and the Arabs: The June 1967 War.* New York: Facts on File, 1968.

Lacey, Robert. *The Kingdom: Arabia and the House of Saud.* New York: Harcourt Brace Jovanovich, 1981.

Lackner, Helen. *A House Built on Sand: A Political Economy of Saudi Arabia.* London: Ithaca, 1978.

Landes, David S. *Bankers and Pashas: International Finance and Economic Imperialism in Egypt.* Boston: Harvard U., 1979.

Lapidus, Ira M. *Contemporary Islamic Movements in Historical Perspective.* Policy Papers in International Affairs, number 18. Berkeley, Calif.: U. of California Institute of International Studies, 1983.

――――. *A History of Islamic Societies.* Cambridge: Cambridge U., 1988.

Laqueur, Walter. *A History of Zionism.* New York: Holt, Rinehart & Winston, 1972.

――――. *Terrorism: A Study of National and International Political Violence.* Boston: Little, Brown, 1977.

Laqueur, Walter, and Barry Rubin, eds. *The Israel-Arab Reader: A Documentary History of the Middle East Conflict.* Revised and updated. New York: Penguin, 1987.

Ledeen, Michael, and William Lewis. *Debacle: The American Failure in Iran.* New York: Alfred A. Knopf, 1981.

Lenczowski, George. *Russia and the West in Iran, 1914-1948: A Study in Big-Power Rivalry.* Ithaca, N.Y.: Cornell U., 1949.

Lesch, Ann Mosely. *Arab Politics in Palestine, 1917-1939: The Frustration of a Nationalist Movement.* Ithaca, N.Y.: Cornell U., 1979.

Levins, Hoag. *Arab Reach: The Secret War Against Israel.* Garden City, N.Y.: Doubleday, 1983.

Lewis, Bernard. *The Arabs in History.* New York: Harper Torchbooks, 1967.

Lewis, Bernard, ed. *Islam and the Arab World.* New York: Alfred A. Knopf, 1976.

Light on Prophecy: A Coordinated, Constructive Teaching Being the Proceedings and Addresses at the Philadelphia Prophetic Conference May 28-30, 1918. New York: Christian Herald Bible House, 1918.

Lippman, Thomas W. *Egypt After Nasser: Sadat, Peace and the Mirage of Prosperity.* New York: Paragon, 1989.

Lloyd George, David. *Memoirs of the Peace Conference.* 2 vols. New Haven, Conn.: Yale U., 1939.

————. *War Memoirs.* 6 volumes. Boston: Little, Brown, 1933-1937.

Lustick, Ian. *Arabs in the Jewish State.* Austin, Tex.: U. of Texas, 1980.

MacDonald, Robert W. *The League of Arab States.* Princeton, N.J.: Princeton U., 1965.

McDowall, David. *Lebanon: A Conflict of Minorities.* London: Minority Rights Group, 1983.

Ma'oz, Moshe. *Asad: The Sphinx of Damascus.* New York: Weidenfeld & Nicolson, 1988.

————. *Syria Under Assad.* London: Croom Helm, 1986.

Marsot, Afaf Lufti al-Sayyid. *A Short History of Modern Egypt.* New York: Cambridge U., 1985.

Mejcher, Helmut. *Imperial Quest for Oil: Iraq 1910-1928.* Oxford: St. Antony's Middle East Monographs, 1976.

Middle East, The. Revised 7th edition to include the Persian Gulf Crisis. Washington, D.C.: Congressional Quarterly Press, 1991.

Mitchell, Richard P. *The Society of the Muslim Brothers.* London: Oxford U., 1969.

Momen, Moojan. *An Introduction to Shi'i Islam: The History and Doctrine of Twelver Shi'ism.* New Haven, Conn.: Yale U., 1985.

Monroe, Elizabeth. *Britain's Moment in the Middle East, 1914-1971.* Baltimore: Johns Hopkins U., 1981.

Mortimer, Edward. *Faith and Power: The Politics of Islam.* New York: Vintage, 1982.

Morris, Benny. *The Birth of the Palestinian Refugee Problem, 1947-1949.* Cambridge: Cambridge U., 1987.

Mosley, Leonard. *Power Play: Oil in the Middle East.* Baltimore: Penguin, 1974.

Munson, Henry, Jr. *Islam and Revolution in the Middle East.* New Haven, Conn.: Yale U., 1988.

Nashat, Guity, ed. *Women and Revolution in Iran.* Boulder, Colo.: Westview, 1983.

Nasir, Sari J. *The Arabs and the English.* London: Longman Group, 1976.

Neff, Donald. *Warriors for Jerusalem: The Six Days That Changed the Middle East.* New York: Simon & Schuster, 1984.

Nelson, Cynthia, ed. *The Desert and the Sown: Nomads in the Wider Society.* Berkeley, Calif.: U. of California Institute of International Studies, 1973.

Nyrop, R.F., ed. *Syria.* Washington, D.C.: American U., 1979.

Olson, R.W. *The Ba'th and Syria 1947 to 1982: The Evolution of Ideology, Party and State.* Princeton, N.J.: Kingston, 1982.

Owen, Roger. *The Middle East in World Economy 1800-1914.* London: Methuen, 1981.

Pahlavi, Mohammad Reza, the Shah of Iran. *Answer to History.* Briarcliff Manor, N.Y.: Stein & Day, 1980.

Perlmutter, Amos. *Israel: The Partitioned State—A Political History Since 1900.* New York: Scribner's, 1985.

Peters, Rudolph. *Islam and Colonialism: The Doctrine of Jihad in Modern History.* The Hague: Mouton, 1979.

Petran, Tabitha. *Syria.* London: Ernest Benn, 1972.

Philby, H. St. John. *Arabia of the Wahhabis.* New York: Arno, 1973.

————. *Saudi Arabia.* New York: Arno, 1972.

Pipes, Daniel. *In the Path of God: Islam and Political Power.* New York: Basic Books, 1983.

Prophetic Studies of the International Prophetic Conference, Chicago, November, 1886. Chicago: Revell, 1886. [The Second International Prophetic Conference]

Quandt, William B. *Camp David: Peacemaking and Politics.* Washington, D.C.: Brookings Institution, 1986.

————. *Saudi Arabia in the 1980s: Foreign Policy, Security, and Oil.* Washington, D.C.: Brookings Institution, 1981.

Rabinovich, Abraham. *The Battle for Jerusalem, June 5-7, 1967.* 20th anniversary edition. Jewish Publication Society, 1987.

Rabinovitch, Itamir. *Syria Under the Ba'th, 1963-1966: The Army-Party Symbiosis.* New York: Halsted, 1972.

Ramsaur, Ernest Edmondson, Jr. *The Young Turks: Prelude to the Revolution of 1908.* Princeton, N.J.: Princeton U., 1957.

Rausch, David A. *Zionism Within Early American Fundamentalism: A Convergence of Two Traditions, 1878-1918*. New York: Edwin Mellen, 1980.

Rausch, David A., and Carl Hermann Voss. *Protestantism*. Philadelphia: Fortress, 1987.

_____. *World Religions*. Minneapolis: Augsburg-Fortress, 1989.

Rugh, Andrea B. *Family in Contemporary Egypt*. Syracuse, N.Y.: Syracuse U., 1984.

Rustow, Dankwart A. *Middle Eastern Political Systems*. Englewood Cliffs, N.J.: Prentice-Hall, 1971.

Sachar, Howard M. *A History of Israel: From the Rise of Zionism to Our Time*. Fifth printing, with update epilogue. New York: Alfred A. Knopf, 1986.

Sadat, Anwar. *Revolt on the Nile*. New York: John Day, 1957.

_____. *In Search of Identity*. New York: Harper & Row, 1977.

Sadat, Jehan. *A Woman of Egypt*. New York: Simon & Schuster, 1987.

Safran, Nadav. *Egypt in Search of Political Community: An Analysis of the Intellectual and Political Evolution of Egypt, 1804-1952*. Cambridge, Mass.: Harvard U., 1961.

Sandeen, Ernest R. *The Roots of Fundamentalism: British and American Millenarianism, 1800-1930*. Chicago: U. of Chicago, 1970.

Sanders, Ronald. The *High Walls of Jerusalem; A History of the Balfour Declaration and the Birth of the British Mandate for Palestine*. New York: Holt, Rinehart & Winston, 1983.

_____. *Saudi Arabia: The Ceaseless Quest for Security*. Cambridge, Mass.: Harvard U., 1985.

Schechtman, Jos. *The Mufti and the Fuhrer: The Rise and Fall of Hajmin el-Husseini*. New York: Thomas Yoseloff, 1965.

Schiff, Ze'ev, and Ehud Ya'ari. *Israel's Lebanon War*. New York: Simon & Schuster, 1984.

Seale, P. *The Struggle for Syria: A Study of Post-War Arab Politics, 1945-1958*. London: I.B. Tauris, 1986.

Sinai, Anne. *Israel and the Arabs: Prelude to the Jewish State*. New York: Facts on File, 1972.

Sivan, Emmanuel. *Radical Islam: Medieval Theology and Modern Politics*. New Haven, Conn.: Yale U., 1985.

Sobel, Lester A. *Israel and the Arabs: The October 1973 War*. New York: Facts on File, 1974.

_____. *Palestinian Impasse: Arab Guerrillas and International Terror*. New York: Facts on File, 1977.

Solberg, Carl. *Oil Power*. New York: New American Library, 1976.

Stein, Leonard. *The Balfour Declaration*. New York: Simon & Schuster, 1961.

Stephens, Robert. *Nassar: A Political Biography*. New York: Simon & Schuster, 1971.

Stillman, Norman A. *The Jews of Arab Lands: A History and Source Book*. Philadelphia: Jewish Publication Society of America, 1979.

Stivers, William. *Supremacy and Oil: Iraq, Turkey, and the Anglo-American World Order, 1918-1930*. Ithaca, N.Y.: Cornell U., 1982.

Tabari, Azar, and Nahid Yeganeh, eds. *In the Shadow of Islam: The Women's Movement in Iran*. London: Zed, 1982.

Taheri, Amir. *The Spirit of Allah: Khomeini and the Islamic Revolution*. Bethesda: Adler & Adler, 1986.

Teveth, Shabtai. *Ben-Gurion: The Burning Ground, 1886-1948*. Boston: Houghton Mifflin, 1987.

The Coming and Kingdom of Christ: A Stenographic Report of the Prophetic Bible Conference Held at the Moody Bible Institute of Chicago, February 24-27, 1914. Chicago: The Bible Institute Colportage Ass'n, 1914.

Tibawi, A.L. *A Modern History of Syria, including Lebanon and Palestine*. New York: St. Martin's, 1969.

Troeller, Gary. *The Birth of Saudi Arabia: Britain and the Rise of the House of Saud*. London: Frank Cass, 1976.

Tuchman, Barbara W. *Bible and Sword: England and Palestine from the Bronze Age to Balfour*. New York: Funk & Wagnalls, 1956.

Van Dam, Nikolaos. *The Struggle for Power in Syria: Sectarianism, Regionalism and Tribalism in Politics*. London: Croom Helm, 1981.

Vatikiotis, P.J. *Nasser and His Generation*. London: Croom Helm, 1978.

Voss, Carl Hermann. "The American Christian Palestine Committee." In *Essays in American Zionism 1917-1948*, edited by Melvin I. Urofsky, Herzl Year Book, vol. 8 (1978), pp. 242-62.

Voss, Carl Hermann. *The Palestine Problem Today*. Boston: Beacon, 1953.

Voss, Carl Hermann, and David A. Rausch. "American Christians and Israel, 1948-1988," in *American Jewish Archives*, vol. 40 (April 1988), pp. 41-81.

Waddams, Frank. *The Libyan Oil Industry*. London: Croom Helm, 1980.

Waterbury, John. *The Egypt of Nasser and Sadat: The Political Economy of Two Regimes*. Princeton, N.J.: Princeton U., 1983.

Weinbaum, Marvin G. *Egypt and the Politics of U.S. Economic Aid.* Boulder, Colo.: Westview, 1986.

West, Nathaniel, ed. *Premillennial Essays of the Prophetic Conference Held in the Church of the Holy Trinity, New York City.* New York: Revell, 1879. [The First International Prophetic Conference]

Wikan, Unni. *Life Among the Poor in Cairo.* Translated by Ann Henning. New York: Tavistock, 1980.

Wright, John. *Libya: A Modern History.* London: Croom Helm, 1981.

Wright, Robin. *Sacred Rage: The Crusade of Modern Islam.* New York: Linden, 1985.

INDEX OF PERSONS

INDEX OF SUBJECTS

Moody Press, a ministry of the Moody Bible Institute, is designed for education, evangelization, and edification. If we may assist you in knowing more about Christ and the Christian life, please write us without obligation: Moody Press, c/o MLM, Chicago, Illinois 60610.